Heart of the Harbor

Sharing Our Best Kept Secrets and Recipes

*Historic Olde Towne
Portsmouth, Virginia*

MISSION STATEMENT

To generate continuing financial support to benefit the Portsmouth Museums Foundation.

Portsmouth Museums Foundation generates private sector financial support for all four Portsmouth museums.

Portsmouth Naval Shipyard Museum

Children's Museum of Virginia

Courthouse Galleries

Lightship Portsmouth

Portsmouth Museums Foundation
420 High Street
Portsmouth, Virginia 23704
www.portsmouthmuseumsfoundation.org

ACKNOWLEDGEMENTS

The Portsmouth Museums Foundation is grateful to the following for their gifts of time and talent.

COPY

Martha Frances Fortson, Executive Director Portsmouth Museums Foundation

William S. Hargroves, Portsmouth Museums Foundation Board

Nancy S. Perry, Director of Museums

PHOTOGRAPHY

Cover: Courtesy of Vista Graphics & Olde Towne Business Association

Bett Cornetta

Trish Halstead

Gayle Paul, Curator, Courthouse Galleries

Jim Walker, Photographer

Dr. Ben E. Wiggins, Jr.

CONSULTANTS

Mary Hester, 2nd Floor Design, Portsmouth, Virginia

Jack Milliner, Photography, Roanoke Rapids, North Carolina

Judy Rauch, Peninsula Fine Arts Center, Newport News, Virginia

CHEFS

Peter Coe, Taste Unlimited—Norfolk & Virginia Beach, Virginia

Karl Dornemann, Still—Portsmouth & Bardo, Norfolk, Virginia

Mike Ferral, Still—Portsmouth, Virginia

Deon Foster, The Kitchen Koop—Portsmouth, Virginia

Janie Jacobson, Chef/Author—Virginia Beach, Virginia

Sydney Meers, Stove—Portsmouth, Virginia

Louis Osteen, Louis's Charleston Grill—Charleston, South Carolina

Phillip Craig Thomason, Vintage Kitchen—Norfolk, Virginia

COOKBOOK COMMITTEE

Betty St. George, Chairman

Stephanie Moreland / Bett Cornetta, Co-chairmen

Bett Cornetta, Marketing Chairman

Trish Halstead, Photography

Sandra Sher, Design Chairman

Linda Spindel, Treasurer

Ashley Brooks

Denise Goode

Robert Harrell

Tara Saunders

Dottie Seward

Copyright © 2009

ISBN: 978-0-615-15997-3

1st Printing   5000 copies   2009

A CONSOLIDATED GRAPHICS COMPANY

800.548.2537   wimmerco.com

HEART OF THE HARBOR

TABLE OF CONTENTS

APPETIZERS & BEVERAGES 7

BREAD & BREAKFAST 43

SOUPS & STEWS 61

SALADS & DRESSINGS 79

MEAT, SEAFOOD & POULTRY 109

PASTA & RICE 159

VEGETABLES & SIDES 171

DESSERTS 189

 KID FRIENDLY RECIPES

6 NOTES

Appetizers & Beverages

COURTHOUSE GALLERIES

The old courthouse, on the northwest corner of Court and High Streets, was erected in 1846, and served as Portsmouth's court building until 1971. It was renovated and rededicated in 1984 as the city's cultural center, and now displays a changing array of visual arts. The building is on the Virginia Landmarks Register and the National Register of Historic Places.

DID YOU KNOW?

The courthouse was designed and built without a front staircase. The granite steps were added in 1872.

Photograph courtesy of Gayle Paul

APPETIZERS & BEVERAGES

NUTTY GRAPES

18 red or green seedless grapes	4 ounces pistachios, finely chopped
5 ounces herb-flavored cheese spread, softened	4 ounces hazelnuts, finely chopped

Wash grapes and pat dry. Place half the cheese spread in a small bowl. Place half of each nut topping in separate small bowls. Scoop about 1 tablespoon cheese spread onto one grape at a time. Dip in desired nut topping and roll around in palms of your hands to coat well and distribute cheese evenly, adding more nuts if needed. Refill cheese and nut bowls as needed. Chill finished grapes on a wax paper-covered plate for 30 minutes before serving.

YIELDS 18 SERVINGS

NUTTY BLUE CHEESE GRAPES

1 pound large seedless grapes	2 tablespoons heavy cream
1 (4.8-ounce) carton blue cheese, crumbled	8 ounces pecans, finely chopped
8 ounces cream cheese, softened	

Wash grapes and pat dry. Using a food processor or mixer, combine cheeses and cream, blending until smooth. Spoon one-fourth of cheese mixture and one-fourth of chopped pecans into separate bowls. Using your fingers, scoop about 1 tablespoon of cheese mixture onto one grape at a time. Dip in nuts and roll around in palm of your hands to coat well and distribute cheese evenly, adding more nuts as needed. Refill cheese and nut bowls as needed. Chill finished grapes on a wax paper-covered plate for 30 minutes before serving.

YIELDS 25-30 SERVINGS

"Deliciously different."

S'HROOM SPREAD

2 tablespoons butter	1 cup shredded sharp Cheddar cheese
1 pound sliced mushrooms	3 ounces cooked and crumbled bacon (about 12 slices)
1 large onion, chopped	

Preheat oven to 350 degrees. Melt butter in a large skillet. Add mushrooms and onions and sauté; drain excess moisture. Stir in cheese and bacon. Transfer mixture to a lightly greased 8-inch square baking dish. Bake 20 minutes. Serve with toasted baguette slices.

APPETIZERS & BEVERAGES

REUBENESQUE DIP

- 4 ounces cream cheese, softened
- 1 generous cup shredded Swiss cheese, divided
- ½ generous cup Thousand Island salad dressing, divided
- ½ cup plus 2 tablespoons chopped deli corned beef
- ½ cup sauerkraut, drained and chopped
- ¼ cup grated Parmesan cheese

Preheat oven to 375 degrees. Mix cream cheese with ½ cup Swiss cheese. Spread mixture in the bottom of a 1-quart baking dish. Spread half of dressing over cream cheese layer. Top with corned beef and sauerkraut. Drizzle remaining dressing over top and sprinkle with remaining Swiss cheese and Parmesan cheese. Bake 20-25 minutes or until dip bubbles around the edges and cheese is melted. Serve with crackers.

This dip is great served with Triscuit Deli-Style Rye crackers.

MARINATED SHRIMP

- ½ cup vinegar
- ¼ cup vegetable oil
- 1 teaspoon salt
- 2 tablespoons chopped dill pickles
- 2 tablespoons chopped fresh parsley
- 2-3 garlic cloves, minced
- 2 dashes hot pepper sauce
- 2 pounds shrimp, cooked (do not overcook), peeled and deveined

Combine all ingredients except shrimp in a large bowl. Mix in shrimp. Cover and marinate in refrigerator for 3 days before serving.

JALAPEÑO-PIMENTO SQUARES

- 5 eggs, beaten
- 6 cups shredded sharp Cheddar cheese
- ¼ cup seeded and chopped jalapeño peppers
- 2 (2-ounce) jars diced pimentos, drained
- 2 teaspoons minced onions
- ½ teaspoon minced garlic

Preheat oven to 350 degrees. Combine all ingredients in a large bowl and mix well. Spread mixture in a lightly greased 9x13-inch baking pan. Bake 30-40 minutes. Remove from oven and let stand 15 minutes before cutting into squares. Best if served warm. If refrigerated before serving, warm in microwave or cover with foil and heat at 350 degrees for 5-10 minutes.

YIELDS 36-48 SQUARES

APPETIZERS & BEVERAGES

HOT FIESTA SPINACH DIP

- 8 ounces cream cheese, softened
- 1 cup salsa, mild or hot
- 1 cup chopped onions
- 1 (10-ounce) package frozen chopped spinach, thawed and squeezed dry
- ½ cup chopped black olives
- 2½ cups shredded Pepper Jack cheese, divided
- 1 cup chopped pecans

Preheat oven to 400 degrees. Combine cream cheese and salsa in a bowl. Stir in onions, spinach, olives and 2 cups cheese. Transfer mixture to a 1½ to 2-quart shallow baking dish. Top with pecans. Bake 30 minutes or until hot and bubbly. Top with remaining cheese. Serve hot with corn chips.

YIELDS 20-25 SERVINGS

Variation: Try half Pepper Jack cheese and half Parmesan cheese.

HOT VIDALIA ONION DIP

- 1 cup mayonnaise
- 1 cup shredded Swiss cheese
- 1 large Vidalia onion
  Salt to taste
- Juice of ½ lemon
- 6 drops hot pepper sauce
  Paprika

Preheat oven to 325 degrees. Mix all ingredients except paprika and transfer to a small ovenproof serving dish. Sprinkle paprika on top. Bake 18-20 minutes or until bubbly. Brown top under the broiler for about 2 minutes, watching carefully. Serve with crackers.

YIELDS 2 CUPS

Triscuit crackers are great with this dip.

DID YOU KNOW?

Though we now use the words interchangeably, there is a difference between appetizers and hors d'oeuvres. Hors d'oeuvres are finger foods served during the cocktail hour. Appetizers are plated and served after guests are seated, as a first course and usually eaten with knife and fork.

HEART OF THE HARBOR

APPETIZERS & BEVERAGES

KAHLÚA FRUIT DIP

- 8 ounces cream cheese, softened
- 8 ounces frozen whipped topping, thawed
- ¾ cup firmly packed light brown sugar
- ½ cup Kahlúa or other coffee flavored liqueur
- 1 cup sour cream
- 3 ounces unsalted chopped peanuts, optional

Combine cream cheese with whipped topping until smooth. Mix in brown sugar and liqueur. Blend in sour cream. Spoon mixture into a bowl, cover and chill; 24 hours or more enhances flavor. Garnish with peanuts and serve with fresh fruit.

YIELDS 2 CUPS

AMARETTO FRUIT DIP

- 2 cups sour cream
- ¼ cup firmly packed light brown sugar
- 2-4 tablespoons amaretto or other almond flavored liqueur

Combine all ingredients and mix well. Cover and refrigerate 8-10 hours. Serve with fresh fruit.

YIELDS 2½ CUPS

Fruits to serve with dip: Apples, bananas, cantaloupe, grapes, honeydew, mangoes, pears, peaches, pineapple and strawberries.

SAUSAGE HORS D'OEUVRES

- 1 pound sausage, Jimmy Dean recommended
- ½ cup prepared ranch dressing
- 1 (1.9-ounce) package mini phyllo shells
- Sharp Cheddar cheese, finely grated

Preheat oven to 350 degrees. Brown sausage in a skillet; drain well. Blend in ranch dressing. Fill phyllo shells with sausage mixture and top with Cheddar cheese. Bake 10 minutes or until cheese melts.

YIELDS 15 SERVINGS

APPETIZERS & BEVERAGES

LAYERED CRAB WHEEL

- 12 ounces cream cheese
- 2 tablespoons mayonnaise
- 1 tablespoon lemon juice
- ⅛ teaspoon garlic powder
- 2 teaspoons Worcestershire sauce
- ½ medium onion, minced
- ¼ teaspoon paprika
- 8 ounces cocktail sauce, such as Cross and Blackwell
- 1-1½ pounds lump or backfin crabmeat
- 12 ounces shredded Monterey Jack cheese, optional
- Sprigs of fresh parsley for garnish

Cream together cream cheese and next 6 ingredients. Spread mixture over a 12-inch round tray, mounding up edges to resemble a pizza crust. Cover mixture with cocktail sauce. Flake crabmeat on top and sprinkle with cheese. Garnish with parsley. Chill 6-8 hours before serving.

SERVES 8

Sprinkle top with 5 chopped green onions and 1 cup sliced black olives, if desired.

"This is a family favorite — always nice around Christmas with red and green colors."

To resurrect stale crackers and chips, spread on baking sheet and bake at 300 degrees in a preheated oven 5 minutes. Cool and store in airtight container.

COUNTRY HAM ROLL

- 8 ounces cream cheese, softened
- ½ cup chopped mango chutney
- 1 cup ground Virginia country ham
- 1 cup chopped pecans
- Maraschino cherries for garnish

Blend cream cheese with chutney and ham. Shape mixture into a log. Sprinkle chopped pecans on wax paper. Roll log in pecans until well coated. Wrap in foil or plastic wrap and chill until firm. Garnish with cherries. Serve with crackers.

SERVES 8

"One time I was doing a TV show in Washington and made the ham log in 1 minute and 38 seconds. I forgot to pack parsley to garnish, so I cut off a piece of plastic greenery behind the set and garnished it. No one ever knew the difference!"

WILL MAKE YOU DANCE SALSA

5 medium tomatoes, chopped	½ onion, chopped
3 tomatillas, chopped	1-2 garlic cloves, minced
¼ cup chopped fresh cilantro or parsley	Salt to taste
1 serrano pepper, seeded and minced	Fresh lime juice to taste
2 jalapeño peppers, seeded and minced	

Mix all ingredients well and refrigerate; best if refrigerated for a day before serving. Serve with tortilla chips or as a side dish with grilled meat.

YIELDS 5 CUPS

GREEN WITH ENVY SPREAD

8 ounces cream cheese, softened	½ cup chopped pecans
1 tablespoon mayonnaise	¼ cup chopped green onions
½ cup chopped green Spanish olives	

Preheat oven to 375 degrees. Mix cream cheese, mayonnaise and olives. Shape mixture into a log and wrap in plastic wrap. Chill at least 30 minutes. Meanwhile, bake chopped pecans 8 minutes or until toasted; cool completely. Roll cheese log in green onions and pecans until covered. Serve with crackers.

SERVES 10

CURRYER THAN IVES SPREAD

8 ounces cream cheese	3 green onions, cut into pieces
1 cup cottage cheese	⅓ cup raisins
¼ cup sour cream	⅓ cup coconut
2 teaspoons curry powder	2 ounces slivered almonds
½ cup chutney of choice	

Blend cream cheese with next 3 ingredients in a food processor until smooth. Add chutney and green onions and process until chopped. Stir in raisins, coconut and almonds. Firmly pack mixture into a small mold or bowl lined with plastic wrap. Chill several hours. Invert onto a serving plate and serve with crackers.

APPETIZERS & BEVERAGES

DELICIOUS CRABMEAT DIP

16 ounces cream cheese, softened	½ teaspoon dry mustard
½ cup sour cream	Juice of ½ lemon
Garlic powder to taste	¼ cup mayonnaise
Onion salt to taste	1 pound deluxe crabmeat, drained
Cayenne pepper to taste	Shredded Cheddar cheese to taste

Preheat oven to 350 degrees. Place cream cheese in a medium bowl. Add sour cream and next 6 ingredients and mix well. Gently fold in crabmeat. Spoon mixture into a greased 8-inch square casserole dish. Top with cheese. Bake 30 minutes or until bubbly. Serve with your favorite crackers.

BAKED CHEESE AND BACON DIP

8 slices bacon, cooked and crumbled	¼ cup chopped onions
2 cups shredded sharp Cheddar cheese	8 ounces cream cheese, softened and mashed
¼ cup mayonnaise	Dash of hot pepper sauce
¼ cup sour cream	Shredded Cheddar cheese for topping

Preheat oven to 325 degrees. Combine bacon and next 6 ingredients in a large mixing bowl and mix well. Transfer mixture to a 9-inch square baking dish. Top with Cheddar cheese. Bake 15-20 minutes. Serve with scoop corn chips or tortilla chips.

SERVES 8-10

BEACH SHRIMP APPETIZERS

8 ounces shrimp, cooked, peeled and deveined	¼ scant cup capers, rinsed and drained
1 tablespoon grated sweet onion	Mayonnaise
½ cup shredded Cheddar cheese or cheese of choice	Baguette rounds

Preheat broiler. Cut shrimp into small pieces. Mix shrimp, onion, cheese and capers with enough mayonnaise to bind together. Toast both sides of baguette rounds on a baking sheet under the broiler. Pile shrimp mixture on top of rounds and return to broiler until cheese is bubbling. Serve warm.

SERVES 8-10

ANCHOVIES MARINATED IN HERBS AND PIMENTOS

- 2 (2-ounce) cans good quality flat anchovies in olive oil
- 2 tablespoons lemon juice
- 3 tablespoons olive oil
- 1 tablespoon chopped shallots
- 1 teaspoon minced garlic
- Freshly ground black pepper
- 3 tablespoons minced fresh dill
- 1 tablespoon chopped fresh parsley
- 1 teaspoon finely chopped fresh chives
- 1 (4-ounce) jar pimento strips
- 24 black olives, halved lengthwise

Drain anchovy oil into a small bowl. Add lemon juice and next 4 ingredients and beat with a fork. Blend in dill, parsley and chives. Dressing should be thick but not too dense; if needed, thin with olive oil. Arrange anchovies, pimentos and olives on a round plate, alternating as if spokes in a wheel. Pour dressing over all and marinate for at least 1 hour before serving. Serve with buttered toast points; if put on toast ahead, toast points may become soggy.

SERVES 10

IT'S A BREEZE BRIE

- 1 (4-inch) round Brie cheese
- 1 (8-ounce) can crescent rolls
- ¼ cup Dijon mustard
- ¼ cup mayonnaise
- 2 green onions, chopped, including tops
- 2 garlic cloves, minced
- 1 egg white
- 1 teaspoon water
- ¼ cup sliced almonds, toasted

Refrigerate Brie or freeze about an hour prior to assembly. Preheat oven to 350 degrees. Remove top rind of cheese, if desired. Unroll crescent roll dough and separate into 2 squares. Pinch perforations to close. Mix mustard and next 3 ingredients in a bowl. Assemble on parchment or wax paper as follows: 1 square crescent roll dough spread with mustard mixture about ¼-inch thick in middle of square, about where Brie will sit. Leave a border for sealing. Place Brie on top and spread a ¼-inch thick mustard mixture on top of Brie. Place second dough square over Brie. Trim and pinch edges together all around to form a tight seal, keeping top smooth. If desired, cut leaf shapes from trimmings and place on top. Being careful not to puncture dough, place assembled Brie in a greased 8-inch square glass baking dish. Beat egg white and water together for an egg wash and brush over top of Brie pastry. Sprinkle toasted almonds on top. Bake 20-30 minutes or until brown. Serve warm with crackers.

To toast, spread almonds in a single layer on a baking sheet. Bake in center of oven at 350 degrees 3-5 minutes or until golden, shaking or stirring several times.

APPETIZERS & BEVERAGES

ARTICHOKE APPETIZER

- 1 (0.7-ounce) package Italian dressing mix, such as Good Seasons
- 1 (0.4-ounce) package Ranch dressing mix, such as Hidden Valley Ranch
- 1 globe artichoke

Prepare each dressing mix according to package directions; set aside. Rinse artichoke under cool water and prepare for cooking (sidebar.) Place artichoke, stem down or up, in a pan of salted water 1½-2 inches deep. Place lightly crumpled foil around artichoke to support it enough so it will not fall over during cooking. Cover pan and bring water to a boil. Reduce heat just enough to maintain a rolling boil. Cook 40-50 minutes, depending on size. It is done when the meaty end of the leaves are tender. Drain on folded paper towels. When cool enough to handle, place artichoke on its side and, with a very sharp knife, cut in half lengthwise. Turn over and remove fuzzy choke. Put both halves flat-side down on a serving tray. Mix about ¼ cup of each of the dressings together, shaking or whisking to blend. Adjust tanginess to taste by adding more of one or the other. Serve sauce in a bowl with artichoke. Have an empty bowl or plate close by for discarded leaves. To prepare ahead, refrigerate uncut cooked artichoke in a zip-top bag. When ready to serve, finish preparation and warm in microwave.

SERVES 4-6

Preparing an artichoke for cooking: Place artichoke on its side on a cutting board. With a sharp heavy knife, cut stem off close to dome. On opposite end, cut ¼-inch from tip of leaves, cutting all the way through and leaving a flat surface for standing up in pan. Rub all cut edges with cut lemon to prevent browning. Remove tough leaves at stem end for one or two rows. More may be removed after cooking, if needed. Use scissors to cut about ¼ inch off tip of each leaf. Rub cut tips with lemon.

ARTICHOKE DIP

- 1 (14-ounce) can artichoke hearts, drained and chopped
- 2 (4-ounce) packages feta cheese
- 1 cup mayonnaise
- ½ cup shredded Parmesan cheese
- 1 (2-ounce) jar pimentos, drained
- 1 garlic clove, minced

Preheat oven to 350 degrees. Mix all ingredients together and spoon into a 9-inch shallow baking dish. Bake 20-25 minutes. Serve with pita chips.

APPETIZERS & BEVERAGES

APPLE AND CHICKEN PÂTÉ

2	large Fuji apples, peeled and diced	¼	cup apple brandy
1	large sweet onion, diced	1	cube chicken bouillon
4	tablespoons butter	2	tablespoons all-purpose flour
1	pound chicken livers	1	large egg

Preheat oven to 350 degrees. Sauté apples and onions in butter 10 minutes. Add livers and sauté 10 minutes longer. Transfer mixture to a food processor. In same pan, add brandy and bouillon. Cook 2 minutes over medium heat, stirring constantly. Add brandy mixture, flour and egg to food processor and process until smooth. Pour mixture into a greased 9x5-inch loaf pan and cover with foil. Place in oven in a larger pan. Add water to larger pan to 1-inch depth. Bake in water bath 1 hour or until firm. Cool 30 minutes. Invert pâté onto a serving dish and serve with crackers.

WHITE CHEDDAR WITH APPLES

⅔	cup peeled and diced green apple	2	tablespoons balsamic or apple cider vinegar
⅔	cup peeled and diced red apple	8	(½-ounce) slices sharp white Cheddar cheese (2½x1½-inch, ¼-inch thick)
½	cup firmly packed brown sugar		
⅓	cup golden raisins	¼	cup coarsely chopped walnuts for garnish

In a small saucepan combine all apples, brown sugar, raisins and vinegar. Cook over medium-low heat for 15 minutes, stirring occasionally. Remove from heat and cool. For each serving, place one slice of cheese on a plate and top with one-fourth of apple mixture. Partially overlap with another slice of cheese. Garnish with walnuts.

YIELDS 4 SERVINGS

APRICOT-CREAM CHEESE DELIGHT

- 8 ounces cream cheese, softened
- 9 ounces apricot preserves
- 4-5 strips thick cut bacon, cooked crisp and crumbled
- ¼ cup chopped chives or green onion tops

Spread cream cheese on an 11- or 12-inch serving plate. Spread preserves almost to the edge over cream cheese layer. Sprinkle bacon over preserves and top with chives. Serve with light unflavored crackers.

SERVES 8-10

SESAME-GINGER SHRIMP

- ¼ cup soy sauce
- ¼ cup sesame oil
- 3 tablespoons peeled and finely chopped fresh ginger
- 1 tablespoon minced garlic
- 1 pound (21/25-count) shrimp, peeled and deveined with tails left intact
- 1 tablespoon white sesame seeds

Combine soy sauce and next 3 ingredients for a marinade, reserving ¼ cup. Add shrimp to mixture and marinate 30 minutes. When ready to cook, preheat grill or broiler to high heat. Cook shrimp 1-2 minutes per side. Toss cooked shrimp with reserved marinade and sprinkle with sesame seeds. Serve at room temperature or chilled.

YIELDS 21-25 SHRIMP

SPICY BUFFALO CHICKEN DIP

- 4 boneless, skinless chicken breasts, boiled and shredded
- ¾ cup hot pepper sauce, such as Texas Pete wing sauce
- 8 ounces cream cheese
- 1 cup bleu cheese dressing

Preheat oven to 350 degrees. Mix all ingredients in a medium bowl. Transfer to a baking dish and bake until bubbly. Serve with scoops or crackers.

SMOKED SALMON ROLL-UPS

16 ounces cream cheese, regular or low fat	Lemon juice to taste
2 tablespoons chopped dill	8 (8-inch) flour tortillas
2 tablespoons chopped chives or green onion tops	12 ounces smoked salmon
	Fresh parsley or dill for garnish

Blend cream cheese with next 3 ingredients. Divide mixture equally over tortillas, spreading to the edges. Place salmon over cream cheese layer; do not cover completely as some "paste" is needed to hold roll-ups together. Roll each tortilla up tightly and wrap in plastic wrap. Refrigerate until ready to use. To serve, slice roll-ups into 1-inch pieces and garnish with parsley or dill.

YIELDS 30 SINGLE SERVINGS

REGGIE'S WEDGES

1 cup chopped black olives	½ teaspoon salt, optional
½ cup thinly sliced green onions	½ teaspoon curry powder
1½ cups shredded sharp Cheddar cheese	4 English muffins, split
½ cup mayonnaise	

Preheat broiler. Mix olives and next 5 ingredients. Divide mixture among muffin halves and spread. Muffins may be frozen at this point and thawed before proceeding. Broil until cheese melts. Cut each muffin half into bite-size wedges.

"This was one of my mother's favorite party recipes."

QUICK AND EASY SOUTHWESTERN DIP

8 ounces cream cheese, softened	8 ounces Pepper Jack cheese, sliced
1 (15-ounce) can chili without beans	¼ cup chopped green bell peppers or sliced jalapeño peppers
1 small onion, grated	

Preheat oven to 350 degrees. Layer all ingredients in order listed in a glass 9-inch pie pan. Bake 15-20 minutes or until thoroughly warmed. Serve with large corn chips or tortilla chips.

SERVES 8-10

APPETIZERS & BEVERAGES

SAVORY BLUE CHEESE TART

1	sheet refrigerated pie crust	3	eggs
6	ounces cream cheese, softened	1/8	teaspoon cayenne pepper
6	ounces blue cheese, crumbled	1/4	teaspoon salt
2	tablespoons unsalted butter, softened	1/8	teaspoon black pepper
1/3	cup heavy cream	1	teaspoon chopped fresh chives

Preheat oven to 375 degrees. Fit pie crust into a 9-inch fluted tart pan with a removable bottom or a 9-inch pie plate. Beat cream cheese with an electric mixer in a medium bowl until creamy. Add blue cheese and blend thoroughly. Add butter and next 5 ingredients and beat until light and smooth. Stir in chives. Pour mixture into pie crust. Bake 35-45 minutes or until center is done and tart is puffy and brown. Cool 5 minutes on a wire rack. Loosen sides, cut and serve warm with fresh sliced fruit and/or crackers.

SERVES 8

PORTOBELLO BRUSCHETTA

4-6	teaspoons olive oil	1	large Portobello mushroom cap, sliced into 1/4-inch thick slices
1/2	cup chopped green onions	1	(4-ounce) jar pesto sauce
2	garlic cloves, minced	1	baguette, sliced into 1/4-inch thick rounds, toasted
1	cup diced eggplant	4	ounces shredded mozzarella cheese
1	cup diced red bell pepper		
1	medium tomato, chopped		

Preheat oven to 350 degrees. Heat oil in a saucepan. Add green onions and next 3 ingredients and sauté until tender. Remove from heat and stir in tomatoes; set aside. Place mushroom slices in a single layer on a baking sheet and rub gently with olive oil. Bake 5-6 minutes or until tender. Place 1 teaspoon pesto on each baguette slice. Add 2 teaspoons tomato mixture over pesto and top with a mushroom slice and mozzarella cheese. Bake 5-8 minutes or until cheese is melted.

SERVES 10-12

HORS D'OEUVRES: Cocktail Party: 12 per person   Dinner Party: 6 per person.
OVER 45 GUESTS: about 8 different hors d'oeuvres. Less than 45, about 6.

TIPSY EYE OF ROUND

1 cup soy sauce	1 teaspoon ground ginger
½ cup bourbon	1 (4- to 5-pound) eye of round beef roast
1 cup granulated sugar	Party rolls
2 garlic cloves, crushed	

Combine soy sauce and next 4 ingredients. Pour mixture over beef and refrigerate 24 hours, turning several times. Preheat oven to 325 degrees. Place meat in a baking dish, reserving marinade for basting. Roast meat, basting frequently, about 2 hours or until a thermometer reaches 135 degrees for medium rare. Remove from oven, cover with foil and let stand 15 minutes. Cut into thin slices and serve on party rolls with Horseradish Sauce.

HORSERADISH SAUCE

1½ cups sour cream	½ teaspoon seasoned salt
3 tablespoons snipped fresh chives	¼ teaspoon black pepper
2-3 tablespoons drained white horseradish	1 tablespoon lemon juice

Combine all ingredients and mix well. Refrigerate at least 2 hours before serving.

YIELDS 1¾ CUPS

One medium lemon will yield about 2-3 tablespoons of juice. One medium lime will yield about 2 tablespoons of juice.

EAST COAST OYSTERS

Butter	Raw oysters
Sliced country ham	

Place 1 pat butter in each cup of a microwave-safe muffin pan. Add a small slice of ham and top with 1 raw oyster. Microwave on high 20-25 seconds. Serve in small ramekins or glass votive candle holders with small forks. If using a conventional oven, bake at 325 degrees just long enough to warm ham and melt butter. Do not allow oysters to cook.

"This is a quick, easy and wonderful appetizer that can become a kitchen event that allows guests to see the appetizer prepared. Everyone can then enjoy the oysters straight out of the pan. This has become a family favorite!"

APPETIZERS & BEVERAGES

CHEESE WAFERS EXTRAORDINAIRE

- 2 cups all-purpose flour
- ½ teaspoon salt
- ¼ teaspoon cayenne pepper
- 1 cup butter, softened
- 2 cups shredded sharp or extra-sharp Cheddar cheese
- 2 cups crispy rice cereal

Blend together flour, salt and cayenne pepper until thoroughly mixed. In a separate bowl, cream butter and cheese together. Add creamed mixture to dry ingredients along with cereal and blend gently until completely mixed. Roll mixture into a 2-inch diameter log and wrap in wax paper or plastic wrap. Refrigerate about 1 hour.

When ready to bake, preheat oven to 375 degrees. Cut log into 1/4-inch thick slices and place on a baking sheet. Bake 10 minutes or until edges begin to brown. Cool on pan a couple minutes before transferring wafers to a wire rack to cool completely. Store in an airtight container or freeze.

MAKES ABOUT 3½ DOZEN WAFERS

PITA PIZZA

- 1 pita bread round
- 1 teaspoon olive oil
- 3 tablespoons pizza sauce
- ½ cup shredded mozzarella cheese
- ¼ cup sliced crimini mushrooms or vegetables of choice
- ⅛ teaspoon garlic salt

Preheat grill or toaster oven to medium-high heat. Spread one side of pita with olive oil and then pizza sauce. Top with cheese and mushrooms. Season with garlic salt. Lightly oil or spray grill grate. Place pita pizza on grill, cover and cook 5 minutes or until cheese is melted.

YIELDS 1 SERVING

HEART OF THE HARBOR

TANGY PIMENTO CHEESE

3 ounces cream cheese, softened	⅛ teaspoon celery salt
8 ounces sharp Cheddar cheese, shredded	⅛ teaspoon paprika
1-2 (4-ounce) jars chopped pimentos	⅛ teaspoon Worcestershire sauce
¼ small onion, grated	Salt and pepper to taste
⅛ teaspoon onion salt	⅓ cup mayonnaise, or as needed

Blend together cheeses. Mix in pimentos and next 5 ingredients and season with salt and pepper. Add amount of mayonnaise needed to reach desired consistency. Adjust seasonings to taste.

YIELDS 2 CUPS

SMOKED TURKEY WITH PEANUT SAUCE

PEANUT SAUCE

½ cup chunky peanut butter	2 teaspoons granulated sugar
¼ cup soy sauce	¼ cup cider vinegar
½ cup sesame oil	½ teaspoon oriental hot oil
1 garlic clove, minced	1 cup sour cream

TURKEY

1 (3-pound) whole turkey breast, skin and bone removed	36 small rolls

Combine peanut sauce ingredients except sour cream. When thoroughly mixed, fold in sour cream. Set aside half the sauce in the refrigerator. Place remaining sauce in a zip-top bag. Flatten turkey with a mallet to about 1-inch thick. Add meat to sauce in zip-top bag and marinate overnight in refrigerator. When ready to cook, place heavy foil over half of grill and preheat grill to medium-hot. Grill turkey 15 minutes per side or until firm in the center, basting with marinade remaining in zip-top bag. Occasionally, sear turkey over open flame. Expect some burning, taking care to keep flame down. Remove and cover to keep warm. Just prior to serving, cut into slices that will fit small rolls. Serve with reserved peanut sauce.

YIELDS 36 SERVINGS

Use specialty oils such as Orchids Pure Sesame Oil and Ty Ling Hot Oil or Chili Oil.

"This recipe was always served to guests in our home on Christmas afternoon. The grilling was a ritual after opening gifts and setting the table for the neighborhood Open House. It has become such a family tradition that it was requested by our daughter to be served at her wedding reception."

POTENT MEATBALLS

4 cups catsup	1 tablespoon Worcestershire sauce
1 medium onion, finely chopped	1-1½ cups bourbon
1¼ cups firmly packed light brown sugar	1-2 (75-count) bags frozen meatballs, thawed
¼ cup mustard of choice	

Mix together all ingredients except meatballs. Warm mixture over medium heat. Add meatballs and refrigerate overnight in a covered container. Reheat over medium heat before serving.

Easy "do ahead" for a large party.

YIELDS 75 SINGLE SERVINGS

BLACK BEAN AND GOAT CHEESE QUESADILLAS

3 tablespoons olive oil, divided	½ cup water
1 small yellow onion, finely chopped	¼ cup chopped fresh cilantro
1 (15½-ounce) can black beans, rinsed and drained	Kosher salt to taste
	Freshly ground black pepper to taste
1 teaspoon ground cumin	6 (8-inch) flour tortillas
1 teaspoon chili powder	3-4 ounces fresh goat cheese, crumbled

OPTIONAL TOPPINGS
Sour cream, guacamole, salsa

In a medium skillet, heat 2 tablespoons oil over medium heat until hot but not smoking. Add onions and sauté 5 minutes or until soft. Add beans and next 3 ingredients and cook, stirring occasionally, for 5-7 minutes or until most of water is evaporated. Remove from heat. Mash beans with a fork until chunky. Stir in cilantro and season with salt and pepper. Spread mixture evenly over 3 tortillas. Scatter goat cheese over mixture and top with remaining 3 tortillas. Lightly coat a large, heavy skillet or griddle with about 1 teaspoon of remaining oil and heat over medium heat. Working with 1 quesadilla at a time, cook 2 minutes or until lightly browned, then flip over and cook on other side for about 1½ minutes. Remove from pan and repeat with remaining quesadillas and oil. Cut each quesadilla into 8 wedges and serve with toppings of choice.

YIELDS 24 SERVINGS

LIGHTSHIP PUFFED SHRIMP

- ½ pound shrimp, cooked, cleaned and chopped
- 2 ounces Pepper Jack cheese, shredded
- 2 tablespoons mayonnaise
- 1 teaspoon chili pepper, optional
- Salt to taste
- ½ (17-ounce) package frozen puff pastry, thawed (1 sheet)
- 1 egg, lightly beaten

Preheat oven to 400 degrees. Blend shrimp and next 4 ingredients; set aside. Roll pastry sheet into a 12-inch square, then cut into 3-inch squares. Spoon 2 teaspoons of mixture diagonally across center of each square. Bring opposite corners up over filling and press corners to seal. Place on a greased baking sheet and brush with egg. Bake 12-14 minutes or until puffed and golden brown.

YIELDS 16 SERVINGS

DID YOU KNOW?

Block cheese that is to be grated is usually measured in ounces because the volume will change with each style grater. Hand, rotary, rasp or box graters will all yield a different amount when measured by cup or tablespoon.

BEST PICKLED SHRIMP

- 4 pounds medium shrimp, peeled and deveined
- 2 garlic cloves, peeled
- 3 pounds large red onions, thinly sliced
- ½ cup bay leaves
- Juice of 1 large lemon
- 1 (10¾-ounce) can condensed tomato soup
- 1 (8-ounce) bottle French dressing
- 1 (14-ounce) bottle catsup
- 3 tablespoons granulated sugar
- Hot pepper sauce or cayenne pepper to taste

Cook shrimp, making sure to not overcook. Place 1 whole garlic clove in a 4-quart crockpot or earthenware pot with a lid. Layer with half each of onions, shrimp and bay leaves. Repeat layers, including the second whole garlic clove near the top. In a blender, process lemon juice and remaining 5 ingredients. Pour sauce over layers. Cover pot and refrigerate 48 hours. Transfer to a serving dish and serve with toothpicks.

SHRIMP SUPREME

- ¼ cup kosher salt
- 5 quarts water
- 4 pounds large shrimp in shells
- Fresh lemons
- 2 cups mayonnaise, Hellmann's recommended
- 1½ tablespoons prepared mustard
- 2 tablespoons dry white wine or white wine vinegar
- 1 teaspoon salt
- 1 teaspoon freshly ground black pepper
- 3-4 tablespoons catsup, or to taste
- 2 teaspoons horseradish, or to taste
- 6 tablespoons minced fresh dill
- 1 cup minced red onions
- 3 cups minced celery

Add kosher salt to water in a saucepan and bring to a boil. Add half the shrimp, reduce heat to medium and cook, uncovered, 3 minutes or until shrimp are just cooked through. Remove shrimp quickly with a slotted spoon to a bowl of cool water to stop cooking process; drain. Return water in saucepan to a boil and repeat with remaining shrimp. Cool, peel and devein shrimp. Squeeze juice from lemons over shrimp and toss. In a medium bowl, whisk together mayonnaise and next 7 ingredients. Toss desired amount of dressing with shrimp. Mix in onions and celery. Adjust seasonings and serve, or cover and refrigerate up to a day or 2 ahead.

SERVES 8-10

For tailgating, skewer shrimp with grape tomatoes.

For a delicious salad, chop celery into larger pieces and serve on a bed of greens with sliced tomatoes and avocados.

To avoid overcooked shrimp, watch very closely. Most shrimp will be done in 3 minutes or less from the time they are placed in boiling water, depending on size and whether frozen or at room temperature. Do not wait until water returns to boiling to start timing. The surest way to determine doneness is taste. Shrimp will be opaque and tender to the bite. If they are still a little translucent, they are not quite ready. Drain and cool quickly with cold water to stop cooking.

TEXAS CAVIAR

2 (15½-ounce) cans black-eyed peas, drained	1 (2¼-ounce) can sliced black olives, drained
1 (15½-ounce) can black beans, drained	1 medium-size green bell pepper, chopped
1 (15½-ounce) can white corn, drained	1 bunch green onions, chopped
1 (15½-ounce) can yellow niblet corn, drained	2-3 tomatoes, diced
2 (14½-ounce) cans chopped green chiles, drained	1 (8-ounce) bottle Italian dressing, such as Good Season's Zesty Italian

Combine all ingredients except dressing in a large bowl. Pour dressing over mixture. Refrigerate overnight. Serve with tortilla chips.

PORT O' CALL CLAM DIP

1 cup Italian bread crumbs	1 tablespoon ground green peppercorns
2 (6½-ounce) cans minced clams with juice	3 tablespoons chopped fresh parsley
½ cup margarine, melted	2 tablespoons lemon juice
2 tablespoons chopped onions	Parmesan cheese

Preheat oven to 350 degrees. Mix together all ingredients except Parmesan cheese. Transfer mixture to a greased 9x9-inch baking dish. Sprinkle with Parmesan cheese. Bake 15-20 minutes. Serve with crackers.

CURRIED CHEESE BALL

16 ounces cream cheese, softened	1 tablespoon sherry or brandy
3 tablespoons curry powder	2 green onions, chopped, divided
½ teaspoon garlic powder	5 ounces chutney
½ teaspoon salt	Ginger thins
¼ teaspoon white pepper	

Blend together cream cheese and next 4 ingredients with an electric mixer. Add sherry and continue to beat, adding more sherry if mixture is too thick. Stir in half the onions. Shape mixture into a ball and refrigerate several hours. Before serving, pour chutney over top and sprinkle with remaining green onions. Serve with ginger thins.

CRISPY PROSCIUTTO CHEESE BALLS WITH PEACHES AND HAZELNUT-MINT VINAIGRETTE

VINAIGRETTE
- 1 cup fresh mint leaves
- 1 shallot, finely chopped
- 1 tablespoon chopped garlic
- 2 tablespoons honey
- 1 tablespoon sea salt
- ½ cup extra virgin olive oil
- ¼ cup hazelnut oil
- ½ teaspoon granulated sugar
- ¼ cup red wine vinegar
- ¼ cup coarsely chopped hazelnuts, roasted

CHEESE BALLS
- 20 ounces goat cheese
- 3 tablespoons cherry jam
- 1 tablespoon water
- 4 ounces shaved prosciutto, fried crisp and crumbled
- 4 peaches, pitted and peeled, each peach cut into 4 wedges
- 1 cup watercress for garnish
- 4 fresh cherries, pitted and halved for garnish
- 8 seedless green grapes for garnish, optional

In a blender, combine mint and next 7 ingredients. Blend together until mint is nicely chopped. Pour into a container and add vinegar and hazelnuts. Set aside; vinaigrette is best if flavors infuse at room temperature for at least an hour, or store overnight in refrigerator.

To make cheese balls, roll goat cheese into 16 bite-size balls, about a tablespoon each. In a small pan or microwave-safe dish, heat cherry jam with water until slightly melted. Roll balls in jam until completely coated, then gently roll in prosciutto crumbs until well crusted.

To serve, divide vinaigrette among 4 plates, thinly coating the bottom of each plate. Place 4 peach wedges on each plate, leaving room to place a cheese ball in between each wedge. Garnish with watercress, cherries and grapes.

YIELDS 4 SERVINGS

Can be served over mixed greens as an entrée salad with extra dressing on the side.

ALMOND-RASPBERRY BRIE

1	(12-ounce) wedge Brie cheese	1½	teaspoons firmly packed brown sugar
2	tablespoons raspberry jam	3	tablespoons sliced almonds
1	tablespoon raspberry-flavored liqueur, such as Chambord		Honey for topping
			Wafer cookies or ginger thins

Remove top rind of Brie, if desired. Slice Brie in half horizontally and place bottom half on a microwave-safe serving dish. In a small bowl, combine jam and liqueur and spread over cheese, leaving a 1-inch edge around the sides. Top with remaining cheese half. Sprinkle with brown sugar and almonds. Drizzle with honey. Microwave on high for 1 minute or until just soft. Serve warm with ginger thins or wafer cookies.

SERVES 8-10

CAVIAR PIE

8	ounces cream cheese	3	tablespoons mayonnaise
1	small onion, chopped	2	(3½-ounce) jars red or black caviar
⅔	cup sour cream	1	lemon, peeled and thinly sliced
9	hard-cooked eggs, finely chopped		

Combine cream cheese, onions and sour cream and mix well. Transfer mixture to a 7-inch springform pan. In a separate bowl, mix chopped eggs with mayonnaise and spread over cream cheese layer. Drain caviar and add to form a third layer. Refrigerate several hours before serving. Garnish with sliced lemon and serve with crackers or baguettes.

If doubling recipe, use a 9-inch springform pan.

For ease in peeling boiled eggs, begin at the wide end where the air pocket between the membrane and egg is the largest. Peel under water.

APPETIZERS & BEVERAGES

BLACK OLIVE DIP

- 1½ cups sour cream
- 1½ cups mayonnaise
- 2 tablespoons grated onion
- 2 tablespoons finely chopped fresh parsley
- 2 teaspoons seasoned salt
- 1 tablespoon dill weed
- 2 (4-ounce) cans chopped black olives, drained
- 1 loaf boule or sourdough, or bread of choice

Combine all ingredients except bread in a bowl. Cover and refrigerate at least 24 hours. Cut center out of bread and fill with dip. Tear center portion of bread into bite-size pieces to use as dippers.

SERVES 12-14

ZIPPY MUSHROOMS

- ⅔ cups tarragon vinegar
- ⅓ cup vegetable oil
- 1 garlic clove, minced
- 1 tablespoon granulated sugar
- 2 tablespoons water
- 1 medium onion, sliced and separated into rings
- 2 (6-ounce) cans mushroom crowns, drained, or 2 pints fresh small mushrooms, trimmed
- Freshly ground black pepper
- Dash of hot pepper sauce

Combine vinegar and next 4 ingredients in a glass bowl. Add onions and mushrooms and cover. Season with pepper and pepper sauce. Refrigerate at least 8 hours, stirring several times. Drain and serve with toothpicks.

GOURMET CASHEWS

- 1½ pounds raw jumbo cashews
- 2 tablespoons unsalted butter, melted
- 1 tablespoon firmly packed light brown sugar
- ½ teaspoon cayenne pepper
- 2 teaspoons fine grind sea salt
- 2 tablespoons finely minced fresh rosemary

Preheat oven to 350 degrees. Spread cashews in a single layer on a baking sheet. Roast about 7 minutes. Thoroughly combine warm melted butter with remaining 4 ingredients. Toss mixture with roasted nuts to coat well. Spread cashews on baking sheet to cool and dry. Store in refrigerator or freezer.

HEART OF THE HARBOR

MOM'S LOBSTER MOLD

3 ounces cream cheese	1 cup chopped cooked lobster
½ cup condensed tomato soup	2 generous tablespoons mayonnaise
1 (¼-ounce) package unflavored gelatin	1 teaspoon horseradish
¼ cup milk	¼ cup chopped pimento, optional
½ cup chopped celery	Salt and pepper to taste

Heat cream cheese and soup in the top of a double boiler; allow to cool. Dissolve gelatin in milk and whisk into cooled soup. Combine mixture with celery and next 4 ingredients in a large bowl. Season with salt and pepper. Pour mixture into a greased 4-cup mold. Refrigerate 12 hours. Invert mold onto a serving plate. Serve with crackers.

SERVES 16

"My mother was famous for this cocktail party favorite!"

SPICY ROASTED PECANS

½ cup butter	¼ teaspoon black pepper
1 tablespoon Worcestershire sauce	1 teaspoon garlic salt
½ teaspoon hot sauce, such as Tabasco	1 pound pecan halves
1 teaspoon hot pepper sauce, such as Texas Pete	

Preheat oven to 300 degrees. Melt butter in a large saucepan. Whisk in Worcestershire sauce and next 4 ingredients. When blended, stir in pecan halves until coated. Spread pecans on a jelly roll pan. Bake 30 minutes, stirring every 10 minutes. Drain on paper towels. When thoroughly cooled, refrigerate or freeze in an airtight container or zip-top bag.

YIELDS 1 POUND PECANS

SO GOOD ALMONDS

Shelled almonds
Unsalted butter

Salt

Blanch almonds, removing from water very quickly; drain. When cool to the touch, remove skins; you should be able to pinch almond on one end and squeeze it from the skin (best done over the sink.) Heat butter in a nonstick skillet. Add almonds and sauté to desired color. Spread almonds in a single layer on paper towels. Sprinkle with salt and allow to drain. Place cooled almonds in a brown bag and shake to remove excess salt. Store in an airtight container.

CRANBERRY-NUT CHEESE SPREAD

1   (12-ounce) container whipped cream cheese
½ cup sweetened dried cranberries
½ cup chopped walnuts or pecans
¼ cup frozen orange juice concentrate

Thoroughly blend all ingredients. Cover and refrigerate at least 6 hours, or store in refrigerator up to 2 weeks. Serve with ginger thins.

YIELDS ABOUT 2 CUPS

CUCUMBER-SALMON CANAPÉS

1   seedless cucumber (wrapped in plastic)
4   ounces smoked salmon, thinly sliced
½ cup sour cream or crème fraîche
2   ounces small capers, drained and patted dry
Fresh dill sprigs

Score cucumber with a fork and slice into ¼-inch thick rounds; pat dry. Place salmon on each cucumber slice. Top each with about ½ teaspoon sour cream, 2-3 capers and a small dill sprig.

YIELDS 40 CANAPÉS

CHUCK FULL OF CHILI DIP

1½ pounds lean ground beef, cooked and drained	1 (15-ounce) can refried beans
1 (8-ounce) bottle taco sauce	1 (15-ounce) can chili without beans
2 (4-ounce) cans chopped green chiles, drained	1 (16-ounce) processed cheese loaf, cut into cubes, such as Velveeta

Preheat oven to 350 degrees. Combine all ingredients in a large bowl. Transfer mixture to a shallow 1-quart baking dish. Bake, uncovered, 45-60 minutes or until cheese is melted. Serve with scoop corn chips or tortilla chips.

PRETZEL DIP

8 ounces cream cheese, softened	1 (1-ounce) package dry ranch dressing mix, Hidden Valley recommended
4-5 green onions, chopped	
6 ounces beer of choice	1 cup shredded Cheddar cheese

Mix cream cheese, onions and beer. Add dressing mix to taste. Blend in cheese and adjust seasoning. Chill. Serve with pretzels.

YIELDS ABOUT 2 CUPS

SEASONED PRETZELS

1 cup buttery popcorn oil	1¾ pounds tiny twist pretzels, such as Rold Gold
3-4 teaspoons lemon pepper	
1 (1-ounce) package dry ranch dressing mix, Hidden Valley Original recommended	

Whisk together oil, lemon pepper and dressing mix in a very large bowl or pan. Add pretzels and toss gently to coat about every 30 minutes. Pretzels will absorb all the mixture; this may take several hours. Store in zip-top bags.

YIELDS 20-25 SERVINGS

APPETIZERS & BEVERAGES

BAKED CHEESE OLIVES

- ½ cup butter, softened
- 1 cup all-purpose flour
- 2 cups shredded Cheddar cheese
- 1 teaspoon paprika
- ½ teaspoon ground cumin
- ¼ teaspoon hot pepper sauce (your favorite)
- 40 large pimento-stuffed green olives

In a medium bowl, cream butter. Mix in flour, cheese, paprika, cumin and hot sauce. Cover bowl and refrigerate at least an hour, or up to 1 day. Dry olives on paper towels. With a ball of cheese mixture that is close in size to the olive, flatten the cheese mixture in your palm. Plop an olive in the center, work the mixture up around the olive and then very gently roll it around between your palms. Make sure the cheese mixture completely seals in the olive. Repeat with remaining olives. If baking immediately, place in freezer 15 minutes. For longer storage, place cheese-wrapped olives on a parchment-lined baking sheet and place in freezer until frozen. Once frozen, store in zip-top plastic bags in the freezer until ready to bake. Prior to baking, remove frozen olives from the freezer and allow to stand at room temperature for about 15 minutes while the oven is heating.

Preheat oven to 400 degrees. Place olives on a baking sheet and bake 15 minutes. Remove from oven and cool to slightly warm. Serve at room temperature or slightly warm.

YIELDS 40 BALLS

"One of the favorite things I like to make for parties is this appetizer. Usually I make a double batch, keep them in the freezer, and then pull out what I need and bake them. Honestly, these things are always the hit of the party. They are sooooo delicious!"

FRENCH KISS

- 1 ounce chocolate-flavored vodka
- 1 ounce vanilla-flavored vodka
- ½ ounce crème de cacao
- 1 chocolate kiss

Mix all liquor in a cocktail shaker with ice and strain into a martini glass. Drop in chocolate kiss and enjoy.

TIDAL WAVE

- 12 ounces fresh grapefruit juice
- 10 ounces cranberry juice
- 10 ounces vodka
- 10 ounces orange-flavored liqueur, such as Triple Sec or Cointreau
- Fresh orange slices for garnish

Mix all ingredients except garnish and store in refrigerator. Serve over ice in tall glasses, garnished with orange slices.

YIELDS 4 SERVINGS

VODKA SLUSH

- 2 cups granulated sugar
- 9 cups water
- 1 (12-ounce) can frozen orange or lime juice concentrate
- 1 (12-ounce) can frozen lemonade concentrate
- 3 cups vodka
- 1 (1-liter) bottle lemon-lime soda, such as Sprite
- Fresh mint, strawberries or other fresh fruit for garnish

Combine sugar and water in a saucepan and bring to a boil. Cook until sugar dissolves; cool slightly. Add juice concentrate, lemonade and vodka. Mix well, place in a covered container and freeze. When ready to serve, fill each glass half with frozen mixture and half with soda. Garnish as desired.

SERVES 25-30

APPETIZERS & BEVERAGES

DECKSIDE SUMMER TEA

1   quart boiling water
1   cup granulated sugar
6   small tea bags
1   (12-ounce) can frozen orange juice concentrate
1   (12-ounce) can frozen lemonade concentrate
2   quarts cold water

Pour boiling water over sugar and tea bags in a bowl and steep 5 minutes. Remove tea bags, squeezing excess liquid back into bowl. Blend in concentrates and cold water. Refrigerate until ready to serve.

YIELDS 3 QUARTS

SUNDOWNER

1   (12-ounce) can pink lemonade concentrate, thawed
12 ounces gin
12 ounces milk

Mix all ingredients together. Serve over ice.

YIELDS 6 SERVINGS

MOJITOS

1   bunch fresh mint leaves (about 2 cups)
1   cup granulated sugar or sugar substitute equivalent
    Juice of 4 lemons
    Juice of 4 limes
1   (1-liter) bottle light rum
    Ice cubes
1   (33.8-ounce) bottle club soda
    Fresh mint sprigs, optional
    Lime wedges, optional

In a small bowl or food processor, pulverize mint with sugar. Combine mint mixture, citrus juices and rum in a 2-quart freezer container and shake well. To serve, fill a tall glass with ice. Add to glass equal amounts of strained Mojito mixture and club soda. Garnish with a mint sprig and lime wedge. Remaining Mojito mixture can be strained and stored in the freezer until ready to serve.

YIELDS 8 SERVINGS

Light rum can be replaced with Malibu coconut rum for added flavor.

HEART OF THE HARBOR

HOT BUTTERED RUM CIDER

2 quarts apple cider	1 tablespoon whole cloves
Juice of ½ large orange	3 (3- to 5-inch) cinnamon sticks
1-2 teaspoons lemon juice	3 tablespoons butter
½ cup firmly packed brown sugar	½ cup rum or brandy
1 tablespoon whole allspice	Cinnamon sticks for garnish

Combine apple cider and next 6 ingredients in a heavy pan and bring to a boil. Reduce heat and simmer about 15-20 minutes. Discard spices. Place 1 teaspoon butter in the bottom of each mug. Add 1 tablespoon brandy, or to taste. Pour hot cider over top. Serve each with a cinnamon stick.

YIELDS 8 SERVINGS

"Warms the body on a cold winter night."

Do not chill wines in the freezer as it can ruin the aroma and flavor. Prepare ahead with buckets of ice and coolers for chilling.

CHOCOLATE MARTINI

2½ cups vodka	Ground chocolate or cocoa powder
1¼ cups chocolate liqueur	Chocolate kiss or fresh raspberry for garnish
¼ cup raspberry liqueur	
1 (6-ounce) package milk chocolate chips, melted	

Mix vodka and both liqueurs in a pitcher and chill for 1-2 hours. Working with 1 glass at a time, dip rim of a chilled martini glass in melted chocolate and immediately dust with ground chocolate. Let glasses stand until dry. Place a chocolate kiss or raspberry in the bottom of each glass. Pour chilled martini mixture into prepared glasses and serve immediately.

YIELDS 8-10 SERVINGS

To melt chocolate chips, microwave on high for 1 minute. Stir and, if needed, microwave at 15-second intervals, stirring until chips are just melted.

APPETIZERS & BEVERAGES

OLDE TOWNE COSMOPOLITAN

- 1½ ounces wild berries vodka, Finlandia recommended
- ½ ounce orange-flavored liqueur
- 2 ounces white cranberry juice
- 2 ounces pomegranate juice
- Splash of lime juice

Pour all ingredients over ice in a shaker and shake well. Serve in a martini glass.

YIELDS 1 SERVING

COFFEE PUNCH

- 2 quarts hot strong coffee
- ¾ cup granulated sugar
- 1 cup half-and-half or milk
- 1 cup chocolate syrup, warmed in microwave
- 5 scoops vanilla ice cream

Combine coffee and sugar and stir until dissolved; cool. Add half-and-half and chocolate syrup. Chill in refrigerator. Just before serving, pour mixture into a punch bowl. Scoop ice cream on top; ice cream will melt to form a creamy delicious topping.

YIELDS 10 SERVINGS

AMARETTO SLUSH

- 1 cup boiling water
- 3 regular tea bags
- 3½ cups water
- 1½ cups almond-flavored liqueur, such as amaretto
- 1 cup granulated sugar
- 1 (6-ounce) can frozen orange juice concentrate
- 1 (6-ounce) can frozen pink lemonade concentrate
- 2 (33.8-ounce) bottles ginger ale
- Maraschino cherries and orange slices for garnish

Pour boiling water over tea bags. Cover and let stand 15 minutes; discard tea bags. Pour mixture into a 2-quart freezer container. Stir in 3½ cups water and next 4 ingredients. Cover and freeze until firm. Pour equal parts slush and ginger ale into glasses. Garnish with cherries and orange slices.

YIELDS 12 (8-OUNCE) SERVINGS

BOURBON SLUSH

- 2 cups boiling water
- 4 regular tea bags
- 1½ cups granulated sugar
- 6 cups water
- 2 cups bourbon
- 1 (12-ounce) can frozen orange juice concentrate, thawed
- 8 (12-ounce) bottles lemon-lime soda, such as Sprite or 7-Up
- Orange slices for garnish

Pour boiling water over tea bags; cover and let steep 15 minutes. Discard tea bags and pour tea into a 2-quart freezer container. Stir in sugar until dissolved. Mix in water, bourbon and juice concentrate. Freeze until firm. To serve, combine equal parts slush and soda in each glass and stir. Garnish with orange slices.

YIELDS 24 (8-OUNCE) SERVINGS

BUTTERBALL

- 1 ounce coffee-flavored liqueur, such as Kahlúa
- 1 ounce butternut schnapps
- 6 ounces milk
- Ice cubes, optional

Pour liqueur into a tall glass. Add schnapps and fill glass with milk. Add ice cubes and stir.

YIELDS 1 (8-OUNCE) SERVING

CABLE CAR MARTINI

- 4-6 cracked ice cubes
- 2 parts spiced rum, such as Captain Morgan Spiced Rum
- 1 part orange-flavored liqueur, such as Cointreau
- 1 part fresh lime juice

Place ice in a cocktail shaker. Pour rum, liqueur and lime juice over ice and shake vigorously until frost forms. Strain mixture into a chilled martini glass.

YIELDS 1 SERVING

This is a variation of the classic cocktail, Sidecar. It is very pretty served in a glass rimmed with orange-tinted sugar.

APPETIZERS & BEVERAGES

CHILLED STRAWBERRY SMOOTHIE

4	pints strawberries, hulled	¾-1	cup granulated sugar
3	(6-ounce) containers plain yogurt	1	cup water
2	(6-ounce) containers vanilla yogurt	¼	teaspoon ground cardamom
1	cup orange juice	2	teaspoons vanilla, optional

Combine all ingredients in a blender and purée until well mixed. Chill and serve.

YIELDS 10 SERVINGS

"This drink is very refreshing on a summer afternoon. My children enjoy making popsicles with the leftover mix."

DID YOU KNOW?

A small dab of butter smeared on the lip of a pitcher's spout will prevent cold beverages from dripping.

BLUSHING BRIDE'S PUNCH

4	(750 ml) bottles Chablis wine	1	(6-ounce) can frozen lemonade concentrate
1	fifth light rum	2	quarts soda water
1	fifth brandy		Fresh strawberries for garnish

Pour all ingredients except garnish over an ice ring in a large punch bowl. Float fresh whole strawberries on top.

YIELDS 25 SERVINGS

An ice ring can be made by pouring cold water into a tube cake pan or ring mold and freezing. Add fruit or flowers to the water for added color.

HEART OF THE HARBOR

WHITE SANGRÍA

1 cup granulated sugar	1 (750 ml) bottle sparkling grape juice
Zest of 1 lemon or lime	¼ cup brandy
1 cup water	2 lemons, cut into thin rounds for garnish
3 liters Pinot Grigio wine	2 limes, cut into thin rounds for garnish

Combine sugar, zest and water in a saucepan and bring to a boil. Simmer 30 minutes; cool. When cool, add wine, juice and brandy and refrigerate overnight. Serve over ice and garnish with lemon and lime slices.

YIELDS 25 SERVINGS

Add fruit for color, such as strawberries, raspberries or orange rounds. This is the perfect complement for a summer Mexican or Spanish themed party.

HALF-AND-HALF

Ice cubes	½ cup iced tea
½ cup lemonade	Granulated sugar to taste

Fill a 10-ounce glass with ice cubes. Add lemonade and top with iced tea. Sweeten to taste with sugar.

YIELDS 1 SERVING

Substitute cranberry juice or orange juice for lemonade.

RED SANGRÍA

3 tablespoons granulated sugar	2 ripe peaches, peeled and cut into wedges
3 tablespoons spiced dark rum	3 ripe plums, cut into wedges
3 tablespoons orange liqueur or orange juice	1 cinnamon stick
1 navel orange, sliced	1 (750 ml) bottle red wine, such as Rioja or other Spanish red wine
1 lemon, sliced	Seltzer

Combine sugar and next 7 ingredients in a large pitcher. Cover with wine and chill several hours. To serve, spoon fruit into large glasses. Pour spiced wine over fruit and top off with a splash of seltzer.

YIELDS 4 SERVINGS

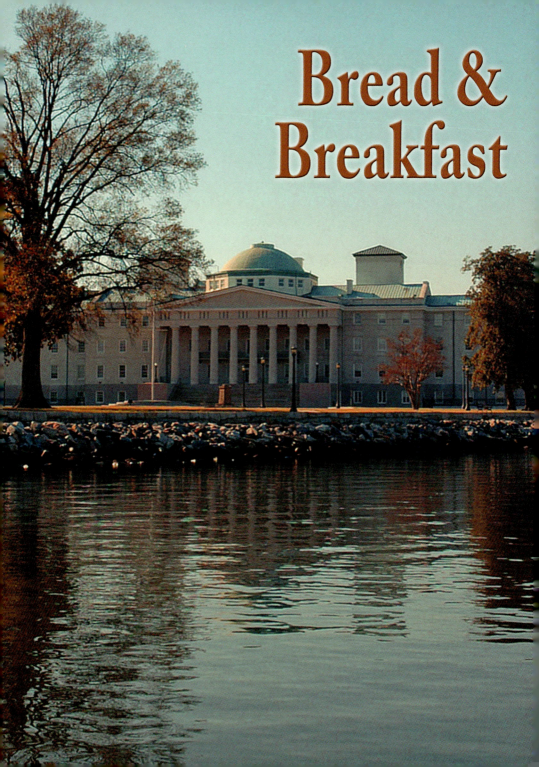

Bread & Breakfast

BREAD & BREAKFAST

UNITED STATES NAVAL HOSPITAL

Built 1827-1830, the Greek Revival-style Naval Hospital is the oldest such facility in the United States. It occupies a prominent peninsula in the harbor on the site of Revolutionary war-era Fort Nelson. The distinctive neoclassical dome was added during a 1907-1909 renovation to provide more light in the operating rooms. The building still serves an important role as part of the Naval Regional Medical Center.

DID YOU KNOW?

Some of the bricks used in constructing the Naval Hospital came from Fort Nelson, which was built to guard the harbor during the Revolutionary War.

Photograph courtesy of Dr. Ben E. Wiggins, Jr.

YUMMY TUMMY FRENCH TOAST

3 eggs	⅓ cup cornflakes, optional
¼ cup milk	12 slices bread, cut ½-inch thick
2½ tablespoons maple syrup	Butter
1½ teaspoons vanilla	Confectioners' sugar for dusting
1¼ teaspoons cinnamon	

Beat together eggs and next 4 ingredients in a medium bowl. If desired, crumble cornflakes into egg mixture and stir well. Soak each bread slice in egg mixture for 5-10 seconds on each side or until thoroughly coated. Set bread aside on a plate. Melt butter in a skillet over medium heat. Add bread and brown on both sides. Dust with confectioners' sugar and serve hot.

YIELDS 8-10 SERVINGS

"My mommy taught me how to make French toast. I added my secret ingredient, maple syrup, and make it for her every Mother's Day and sometimes on Sundays for the whole family."

TOMATO QUICHE

1 (9-inch) deep-dish pie crust	¾ cup minced green onions
3 large ripe tomatoes, sliced ½-inch thick	4 slices provolone cheese, or ½ cup shredded mozzarella
½ cup all-purpose flour	2 eggs
Salt and pepper to taste	1 cup shredded Cheddar cheese
1 (4¼-ounce) can sliced ripe black olives, drained	1 cup half-and-half
2 tablespoons olive oil, or more as needed	

Preheat oven to 400 degrees. Prick pie crust with a fork and bake 5 minutes or until lightly browned; cool. Reduce oven temperature to 375 degrees. Dredge tomato slices in flour and sprinkle with salt and pepper. Heat olive oil in a saucepan over medium-high heat. Add tomato slices and sauté quickly until brown; set aside. Scatter olive slices in baked pie crust. Sprinkle with green onions and cover all with provolone cheese. Layer sautéed tomato slices over cheese. In a separate bowl, lightly beat eggs. Blend in Cheddar cheese and half-and-half. Pour egg mixture over pie. Bake 40-45 minutes or until set. Cool 5 minutes before cutting.

YIELDS 6-8 SERVINGS

SERBIAN EGG CASSEROLE

6 eggs	1 cup milk
1 pound small curd cottage cheese	½ cup butter, melted
1 pound Monterey Jack cheese, shredded	1 (7-ounce) can chopped green chiles, drained, optional
1 cup biscuit baking mix, such as Bisquick	

Preheat oven to 350 degrees. Beat eggs in a mixing bowl. Add cheeses. Stir in biscuit mix. Add milk and melted butter and stir well. Mix in chiles. Pour mixture into a greased 8x10-inch baking dish. Bake 35-40 minutes or until center does not jiggle.

YIELDS 6-8 SERVINGS

"We absolutely love this dish and hope you do, too. It is a favorite of my vegetarian grandson."

To check eggs for freshness, put one in a pan of cold water. If it sinks, it is fresh; if it stands up, it is fine to use; if it floats, discard it.

MUSHROOM CRUST DEEP DISH

8 ounces fresh mushrooms, minced	1½ cups small curd cottage cheese
5 tablespoons butter, divided	4 eggs, beaten
¾ cup freshly crushed saltine cracker crumbs	¼ teaspoon cayenne pepper
¾ cup chopped green onions	½ teaspoon paprika
2 cups shredded Monterey Jack or Swiss cheese	

Preheat oven to 350 degrees. Sauté mushrooms in 3 tablespoons butter in a skillet over medium heat. Stir in cracker crumbs and press mixture into a greased 10-inch deep-dish pie plate. In same skillet, sauté green onions in remaining 2 tablespoons butter over medium heat until tender. Sprinkle green onions over cracker crust and top with shredded cheese. Combine cottage cheese, eggs and cayenne pepper in a bowl and blend well with a fork. Spoon mixture into crust and sprinkle with paprika. Bake 25-30 minutes or until light brown. Remove from oven and let stand 10-15 minutes before cutting.

YIELDS 6-8 SERVINGS

This is easy to substitute with your favorite savory quiche filling.

MUSEUM'S LUNCH BUNCH QUICHE

6 large eggs	Salt and pepper to taste
1⅔ cups heavy cream	1 cup packed chopped fresh baby spinach
¼ teaspoon dried red pepper flakes, or to taste	1 pound bacon, cooked and crumbled
¼ teaspoon dried marjoram, or to taste	1½ cups shredded Swiss cheese
Chopped onion to taste, optional	1 (9-inch) pie crust
	Paprika

Preheat oven to 375 degrees. Using a food processor or mixer, combine eggs and next 4 ingredients. Season with salt and pepper. Layer spinach, bacon and cheese in pie crust. Pour egg mixture over all and sprinkle paprika on top. Bake 40-45 minutes or until egg mixture is set.

YIELDS 8 SERVINGS

Substitute dried herbs for fresh at a ratio of 1 to 3. 1 teaspoon dried = 3 teaspoons fresh.

MINI BACON AND EGG PASTRIES

1 tablespoon butter	10-12 slices lean bacon, cooked crisp and crumbled
1 (15-ounce) package refrigerated pie dough	12 small eggs
All-purpose flour for rolling	Black pepper to taste
2 tablespoons whole grain mustard	1 generous cup shredded Cheddar cheese
	2 tablespoons chopped fresh parsley

Preheat oven to 350 degrees. Use butter to lightly grease 12 muffin cups. Roll dough ¼-inch thick on a lightly floured board. Cut dough into twelve 5-inch diameter circles. Use circles to line prepared muffin cups, gently pleating edges as dough is eased into cups. Place ½ teaspoon mustard in bottom of each pastry and top with a sprinkle of bacon. For each pastry, break 1 egg into a separate cup. Spoon egg yolk into pastry shell, then add enough of egg white to fill pastry about two-thirds full; do not overfill. Season with pepper. Sprinkle cheese evenly over top of each pastry. Bake 20-25 minutes or until eggs are set and cheese is golden brown. Garnish with parsley.

YIELDS 12 SERVINGS

Great for a brunch.

SLUMBER PARTY CASSEROLE

1 (16-ounce) loaf French bread, sliced 1½-inches thick	1 tablespoon vanilla
8 eggs	5-6 Granny Smith apples, peeled and sliced ⅜-inch thick
3 cups whole milk	2 teaspoons cinnamon
¾ cup granulated sugar, divided	

Fit bread slices into a 9x13-inch baking dish. Beat eggs, milk, ¼ cup sugar and vanilla until thoroughly mixed. Pour over bread. Cover with apples in an overlapping pattern. Mix cinnamon with remaining ½ cup sugar and sprinkle over apples. Cover and refrigerate overnight. When ready to bake, preheat oven to 400 degrees. Bake uncovered 30-35 minutes or until a knife inserted in the center comes out clean. Serve with warm maple syrup.

YIELDS 9-12 SERVINGS

EGG WHITE TIPS

Eggs are easier to separate when cold. Make sure no trace of yolk is in the whites. Bowls, beaters and whisks must be completely free of any grease or the whites will not foam properly. Bring whites to room temperature before beating for best volume.

STUFFED FRENCH TOAST FEAST

8 (1-inch thick) slices country bread	1 tablespoon granulated sugar
½ cup apricot preserves	1 teaspoon vanilla
½ cup ricotta cheese	1 teaspoon kosher salt
3 eggs	Finely grated zest of 1 orange
1½ cups milk	Softened butter
½ cup heavy cream	Confectioners' sugar for dusting

Cut a pocket in one side of each bread slice. Combine, until blended, apricot preserves and ricotta cheese; spoon about 4 heaping teaspoons into each pocket. Whisk together eggs and next 6 ingredients. Dip each slice into egg mixture, soaking both sides; set aside. Brush surface of a large frying pan with butter. When temperature reaches about 350 degrees, begin cooking bread. Cook about 3-4 minutes per side or until golden brown and crispy. Dust with confectioners' sugar and serve.

YIELDS 6 SERVINGS

DELICIOUS SPINACH BAKE

2 ready-made pie crusts	6 eggs
2 (10-ounce) packages frozen spinach, thawed and squeezed dry	1½ cups heavy cream
	1 cup milk
1 pound mushrooms, sliced	2 tablespoons all-purpose flour
¼ cup finely chopped onion	1 teaspoon salt
2 tablespoons butter	⅛ teaspoon cayenne pepper
1 cup cooked bacon or chopped ham, optional	⅛ teaspoon nutmeg
	⅓ teaspoon black pepper
8 ounces Swiss cheese, shredded	4 tablespoons butter, melted

Preheat oven to 425 degrees. Press pie crusts to line the bottom and sides of a 9x13-inch pan. Distribute spinach over crust. Sauté mushrooms and onions in butter until tender and scatter over spinach. Top with bacon and sprinkle with cheese. Beat together eggs and remaining ingredients until blended. Pour mixture over cheese. Bake 15 minutes. Reduce heat to 325 degrees and bake 40 minutes longer. Remove from oven and allow to set 10 minutes before serving.

YIELDS 9-12 SERVINGS

CHESAPEAKE BAY CRAB PIE

1 (9-inch) pie crust, unbaked	4 eggs
3-4 green onions, chopped	3 tablespoons grated Parmesan cheese
2 tablespoons chopped red or green bell pepper	½ teaspoon dried dill weed
	⅛ teaspoon black pepper
1-1½ tablespoons butter	⅛ teaspoon salt
2 cups crabmeat, drained and picked for shells	1½ cups half-and-half

Preheat oven to 400 degrees. Prick bottom and sides of pie crust with a fork every ½-inch. Cover outer edge of crust with foil or a pie ring to prevent burning. Bake 8-10 minutes; remove from oven and cool. Reduce oven temperature to 375 degrees. Lightly sauté onions and bell peppers in butter. Layer crabmeat and sautéed vegetables in cooled crust. In a separate bowl, lightly beat eggs. Mix in Parmesan cheese and remaining 4 ingredients until thoroughly blended. Pour mixture over crabmeat. Bake 35-45 minutes or until a knife inserted in the center comes out clean. Let stand 5-10 minutes before cutting.

YIELDS 6-8 SERVINGS

CREAM CHEESE BRAID

DOUGH

8 ounces sour cream, scalded	2 eggs
½ cup granulated sugar	2 packages dry yeast
½ cup butter or margarine, melted	¼ cup warm water
1 teaspoon salt	4-4½ cups all-purpose flour

FILLING

¾ cup granulated sugar	1 egg
2 (8-ounce) packages cream cheese	2 teaspoons vanilla

GLAZE, OPTIONAL

2 cups confectioners' sugar	2 teaspoons vanilla
4 tablespoons milk	

Heat sour cream and next 3 ingredients together in a saucepan over low heat; cool to lukewarm. Add eggs and mix well. Dissolve yeast in warm water according to package directions and add to mixture. Blend in flour. Cover dough tightly and refrigerate overnight. The next day, blend all filling ingredients; set aside. Divide dough into 4 equal portions. Knead each section 4-5 times. On a floured board, roll each section into an 8x12-inch rectangle. Spread one-fourth of filling over each rectangle. Roll up each, jelly roll fashion, into a log. Place logs, seam-side down, on a greased baking sheet. Pinch edges together and roll ends under to secure filling. Cut slits in each roll on an angle at 2-inch intervals, to resemble a braid. Cover and let rise 1 hour in a warm place; bread should double in size. When ready to bake, preheat oven to 375 degrees. Bake 15-20 minutes. To make glaze, blend ingredients in a medium bowl with an electric mixer. Apply glaze while bread is still warm.

YIELDS 4 BRAIDS

"This is a wonderful bread to serve at a brunch, with or without the glaze!"

LEMON OR ORANGE GLAZE

1 cup confectioners' sugar	1-1½ tablespoons lemon or orange juice
	4 tablespoons milk

Blend ingredients in a medium bowl using an electric mixer.

CHEESY-TOMATO HAM BAKE

6-8 slices bread, crusts removed	8 ounces shredded Swiss cheese
¾ pound coarsely shredded baked ham	6 eggs
3 small green onions with tops, finely chopped	2 cups heavy cream
	Salt and pepper to taste
½ cup drained and finely chopped sun-dried tomatoes	1 cup shredded mild Cheddar cheese

Arrange bread slices in a greased 9x13-inch baking dish. Layer ham, green onions, tomatoes and Swiss cheese on top of bread. Beat eggs in a mixing bowl. Blend in cream and season with salt and pepper. Stir in Cheddar cheese. Pour mixture over casserole. Cover and refrigerate overnight. When ready to bake, preheat oven to 375 degrees. Bake about 30-35 minutes.

YIELDS 9-12 SERVINGS

Always try to break eggs in a separate bowl before adding to your recipe so you can detect and retrieve any pieces of shell.

BEST EVER BRUNCH EGGS

6 tablespoons butter	6 tablespoons shredded Cheddar cheese
6 eggs	6 tablespoons cooked and crumbled bacon
1 tablespoon minced fresh parsley	Red or green leaf lettuce, optional
1 tablespoon minced fresh dill	3 medium tomatoes, sliced ¼-inch thick
Salt and pepper to taste	

Preheat oven to 350 degrees. Grease 6 muffin cups or individual custard cups. In each cup, place 1 tablespoon butter. Carefully break 1 egg into each cup over butter. Combine parsley and dill. Season each egg with salt, pepper and 1 teaspoon herb mixture. Top each egg with 1 tablespoon each cheese and bacon. Bake 15-20 minutes. To serve, place a lettuce leaf and tomato slice on each plate and top with an egg.

YIELDS 6 SERVINGS

If tomatoes are out of season, use seeded and chopped Roma tomatoes.

TOP O' THE MORNING BAKE

1	pound pork sausage, mild or spicy	8	ounces asparagus, cooked and cut into thirds
8	eggs	4-5	green onions, finely chopped
3	cups milk	1	red bell pepper, thinly sliced
1	teaspoon salt	1	cup shredded Swiss cheese
1	teaspoon dry mustard		
8	slices French bread, cut into cubes		

Brown sausage and drain; set aside. Beat together eggs and next 3 ingredients. In a greased 9x13-inch baking pan, layer bread cubes, cooked sausage, asparagus and remaining 3 ingredients. Pour egg mixture over top. Cover and refrigerate overnight. When ready to bake, preheat oven to 350 degrees. Bake 45 minutes or until bubbly and cheese is melted.

YIELDS 9-12 SERVINGS

APPLE PANCAKE GRANDE

3-4	medium apples, peeled and sliced	¼	cup water
4	tablespoons butter	½	cup chopped walnuts or pecans, optional
1	cup firmly packed dark brown sugar	1½	cups plain pancake batter
1	teaspoon cinnamon		

Preheat oven to 350 degrees. Using a 10-inch cast iron skillet or similar ovenproof skillet, cook apples in butter over medium heat until tender. Add brown sugar and next 3 ingredients. Cook until sugar is dissolved. Pour pancake batter over apples and place skillet in oven 10-15 minutes or until cake is golden brown on top. Invert pancake onto a plate.

YIELDS 4-6 SERVINGS

May omit the pancake batter and serve apples with vanilla ice cream for dessert.

> Always measure brown sugar tightly packed unless the recipe states otherwise.

BREAD & BREAKFAST

BACON AND ONION QUICHE

- 1½ tablespoons butter
- 2 medium onions, coarsely chopped
- ½ cup all-purpose flour
- 1½ cups milk
- 4 eggs, beaten
- 8 ounces Swiss cheese, shredded
- 12 ounces bacon, cooked crisp and crumbled

Preheat oven to 400 degrees. Melt butter in a skillet over medium heat. Add onions and cook until softened. Whisk flour and milk together in a medium bowl. Blend in sautéed onions, eggs, cheese and bacon. Pour mixture into a greased 9-inch pie pan. Bake 30-35 minutes or until golden brown.

YIELDS 6-8 SERVINGS

Quiche can be frozen after baking.

DID YOU KNOW?

You can prepare quiche a day ahead, remove from oven 15 minutes before fully cooked and refrigerate. Next day, bring to room temperature and finish cooking in preheated oven.

ELEGANT GRAND MARNIER™ TOAST

- 6 large eggs
- ⅔ cup orange juice
- ⅓ cup orange liqueur, such as Grand Marnier™
- ⅓ cup milk
- 3 tablespoons granulated sugar
- ¼ teaspoon vanilla
- ¼ teaspoon salt
- 8 (¾-inch thick) slices French bread
- Melted butter
- Confectioners' sugar

Blend together eggs and next 6 ingredients; this step can be done a day ahead and refrigerated until needed. Dip bread into egg mixture, coating both sides. In a skillet, cook bread slowly in melted butter for about 8 minutes on each side. Sprinkle with confectioners' sugar before serving.

YIELDS 6 SERVINGS

Sift confectioners' sugar after measuring to get rid of all the tiny lumps that develop in the package.

HEART OF THE HARBOR

MEXICAN CORN BREAD

1½ cups self-rising cornmeal	Pinch of salt
3 eggs	1 cup creamed corn
⅔ cup vegetable oil	Crushed red pepper flakes or cayenne pepper to taste
½ large green bell pepper, chopped	
½ large red bell pepper, chopped	1-2 cups shredded Cheddar cheese
1 cup buttermilk	

Preheat oven to 375 degrees. Mix all ingredients except cheese. Generously grease a 10- to 12-inch ovenproof skillet with oil and heat. Pour one-half to three-fourths of batter into hot skillet. Sprinkle cheese over top, then pour remaining batter over cheese. Bake 30-45 minutes or until golden brown.

YIELDS 10-12 SERVINGS

ZUCCHINI LOAF

2 eggs	3 cups all-purpose flour
2 cups granulated sugar	1 teaspoon baking soda
1 cup vegetable oil	½ teaspoon baking powder
2 cups grated unpeeled zucchini	½ teaspoon salt
1 teaspoon vanilla	1 tablespoon cinnamon

Preheat oven to 350 degrees. Beat eggs in a mixing bowl. Add sugar and oil and beat. Stir in zucchini and vanilla. Sift together flour and remaining 4 ingredients. Blend dry ingredients into zucchini mixture. Pour batter into 2 greased and floured 8½x4½-inch loaf pans. Bake 50-60 minutes or until a toothpick inserted in the center comes out clean.

YIELDS 2 LOAVES

STORING ZUCCHINI

In case your garden produced a bumper crop of zucchini squash and your family is desperate for new ways to eat the harvest, this recipe is guaranteed to turn even a picky eater into a zucchini lover. Fresh zucchini does not freeze well, but as a bread or casserole, it will last quite a long time in your freezer.

PUMPKIN BREAD

3 cups granulated sugar	1 teaspoon baking powder
1 cup vegetable oil	1 teaspoon nutmeg
4 large eggs, beaten	1 teaspoon allspice
1 (15-ounce) can pumpkin	1 teaspoon cinnamon
3½ cups all-purpose flour	½ teaspoon cloves
2 teaspoons baking soda	⅔ cup water
2 teaspoons salt	⅔ cup raisins, optional

Preheat oven to 350 degrees. Cream together sugar and oil. Blend in eggs and pumpkin. Sift together flour and next 7 ingredients. Add dry ingredients and water alternately to pumpkin mixture. Stir in raisins. Pour batter into two well greased and floured 9x5-inch loaf pans. Bake 1 hour, 30 minutes or until a toothpick inserted in the center comes out clean. Let stand 10 minutes before removing from pans to cool completely.

YIELDS 2 LOAVES

This bread freezes well and makes a great hostess gift!

ORANGE GLAZED CRANBERRY PUMPKIN BREAD

1 (15-ounce) can pumpkin	3½ cups all-purpose flour
1 (16-ounce) can whole berry cranberry sauce	2 teaspoons baking soda
	¼ teaspoon salt
4 eggs	1⅔ cups granulated sugar
⅔ cup vegetable oil	2 teaspoons pumpkin pie spice
¾ cup chopped nuts, optional	1 teaspoon baking powder

GLAZE

1 cup confectioners' sugar	⅛ teaspoon allspice
¼ cup orange juice concentrate	

Preheat oven to 350 degrees. Combine pumpkin and next 4 ingredients in a large bowl. Add flour and next 5 ingredients and mix well. Pour batter into 2 greased loaf pans. Bake 55-60 minutes or until a toothpick inserted in the center comes out clean. Cool in pan 10 minutes, then remove from pans and cool completely. Mix together all glaze ingredients and drizzle over cooled loaves.

YIELDS 2 LOAVES

ORANGE DATE MINI MUFFINS

¾	cup water	1½	teaspoons baking soda
1	cup chopped pitted dates	½	teaspoon cinnamon
2	cups all-purpose flour	½	cup chopped pecans
¾	cup granulated sugar	½	cup vegetable oil
1	tablespoon orange zest	1½	teaspoons vanilla
1½	teaspoons baking powder	2	eggs

Preheat oven to 375 degrees. Bring water to a boil in a small pan. Remove from heat and add dates; set aside to soften. In a large bowl, mix flour and next 6 ingredients. In a separate bowl, beat together oil, vanilla and eggs. Add liquid mixture to dry ingredients and stir well. Add dates with water and stir well. Spoon mixture into greased mini muffin tins. Bake 15 minutes or until golden brown on top, watching carefully to prevent overcooking or burning. Remove from pan and cool on a baking rack.

YIELDS 3-4 DOZEN

Keep these on hand in your freezer.

MORNING GLORY MUFFINS

2	cups all-purpose flour	½	cup chopped pecans or walnuts
1½	cups granulated sugar	¼	cup chopped apricots
2	teaspoons baking soda	½	cup shredded coconut
2	teaspoons cinnamon	1	apple, peeled and grated
½	teaspoon salt	3	eggs
2	cups shredded carrots	1	cup vegetable oil
½	cup raisins	2	teaspoons vanilla

Preheat oven to 350 degrees. In a large mixing bowl, combine flour and next 4 ingredients and blend well. Stir in carrots and next 5 ingredients. In a separate bowl, beat eggs with oil and vanilla. Stir egg mixture into flour mixture and blend well. Spoon batter into well greased muffin tins. Bake 20-25 minutes or until golden brown.

YIELDS 14 LARGE MUFFINS

Perfect for your overnight guests. Add extra fruit for larger muffins.

BREAD & BREAKFAST

CRANBERRY BREAD

2 cups sifted all-purpose flour	1 large egg, beaten
1½ teaspoons baking powder	1 teaspoon fresh orange zest
½ teaspoon baking soda	¾ cup orange juice
1 cup granulated sugar	1½ cups golden raisins
1 teaspoon salt	1½ cups fresh cranberries, chopped
4 tablespoons butter	

Preheat oven to 350 degrees. Sift flour and next 4 ingredients into a large bowl. Cut butter into dry ingredients until mixture is crumbly. Add egg, orange zest and orange juice all at once; stir just until mixture is evenly moist. Fold in raisins and cranberries. Spoon batter into a greased 9x5-inch loaf pan. Bake 1 hour, 10 minutes or until a toothpick inserted in the center comes out clean. Remove from pan and cool.

YIELDS 8 SERVINGS

SIMPLE BANANA BREAD

3 very ripe bananas, mashed	4 tablespoons butter or margarine, softened
1 cup sugar	1 teaspoon salt
1 egg	1 teaspoon baking soda
1½ cups all-purpose flour	Walnuts or mini chocolate chips, optional

Preheat oven to 325 degrees. Combine all ingredients in a medium bowl. Pour batter into a greased 8x4-inch loaf pan. Bake 55-65 minutes or until a toothpick comes out clean.

PEACH COFFEE CAKE

BATTER

- 1 (16-ounce) can peach pie filling
- 3 eggs
- 1 teaspoon almond extract
- ½ cup slivered almonds, toasted, optional
- 1 (18¼-ounce) package yellow butter cake mix

TOPPING

- ½ cup sugar
- ½ cup all-purpose flour
- 4 tablespoons butter, softened
- ½ teaspoon almond extract

Preheat oven to 350 degrees. Stir pie filling, eggs, extract and almonds into cake mix until well blended. Pour batter into a greased 9x13-inch cake pan.

Combine all topping ingredients with a fork or pastry blender until crumbly throughout. Sprinkle topping onto batter. Bake about 40 minutes.

YIELDS 12-15 SERVINGS

DRIED CHERRY SCONES

- 3 cups all-purpose flour
- ⅓ cup sugar
- 2½ teaspoons baking powder
- ½ teaspoon baking soda
- ¾ teaspoon salt
- ¾ cup butter, cut into pieces
- ¾ cup dried sweet cherries, softened in water and drained
- 1 teaspoon orange zest
- 1 cup buttermilk

Preheat oven to 400 degrees. Combine flour and next 4 ingredients in a large bowl. Cut in butter with a pastry blender until mixture resembles coarse cornmeal. Stir in cherries and zest. Pour in buttermilk and stir until blended. Gather dough into a ball and divide in half. Roll each half on a floured board into a flattened circle about 1 inch thick. Cut each circle into 8 wedges, leaving wedges intact in circle. Transfer to a lightly greased baking sheet. Bake 12-15 minutes or until a tester inserted in center comes out done.

COLONEL CRAWFORD'S COFFEE CAKE

- ½ cup butter, softened
- 1 cup granulated sugar
- 2 eggs
- 1 teaspoon vanilla
- 2 cups all-purpose flour
- 1 teaspoon baking powder
- 1 teaspoon baking soda
- ½ teaspoon salt
- 1 cup sour cream

STREUSEL
- ½ cup granulated sugar
- ½ cup chopped pecans
- 1 teaspoon cinnamon, or more to taste

Preheat oven to 375 degrees. Cream butter with next 3 ingredients. Sift together flour and next 3 ingredients. Add dry ingredients to creamed mixture alternately with sour cream. Pour batter into a greased tube pan. Combine all streusel ingredients and swirl into top portion of batter. Bake 35-40 minutes or until a toothpick inserted in the center comes out clean.

YIELDS 12 SERVINGS OR MORE

Variation: Just before pouring into pan, stir 6 ounces chocolate chips into batter.

Great with a cup of coffee and a good friend!

MONTEREY TOPPER FOR BREAD

- 1 loaf French bread
- 1 tablespoon Worcestershire sauce
- 1 medium onion, finely chopped
- 1 cup mayonnaise
- ½ cup grated Parmesan cheese

Preheat oven to 350 degrees. Slice bread in half lengthwise and heat in oven 4-5 minutes. Preheat broiler. Mix Worcestershire sauce and remaining 3 ingredients and spread over bread. Broil until golden brown. Slice and serve while warm.

YIELDS ABOUT 20 SERVINGS

FOCACCIA BREAD

3½ cups all-purpose flour, divided	1 cup water
1 tablespoon active dry yeast	2 tablespoons vegetable oil
1 teaspoon sugar	1 egg
1 teaspoon salt	3 tablespoons olive oil
2 teaspoons Italian seasoning	1 teaspoon dried rosemary, crushed
1 teaspoon garlic powder, optional	¾ teaspoon sea salt

Combine 1 cup flour, yeast and next 4 ingredients and mix well. Heat water and vegetable oil until warm and add to yeast mixture along with egg. Blend with an electric mixer on low speed until moistened. Beat 2 minutes longer. Beat in 1¾ cups flour until dough pulls away from side of bowl. Knead in remaining ¾ cup flour on a floured surface. Cover dough with a bowl and let stand 5 minutes. Roll out dough on a greased baking sheet into a 12-inch circle. Cover with greased plastic wrap and a cloth towel. Place in a warm place for 30 minutes. Uncover dough and poke holes in it with a spoon handle at 1-inch intervals. Drizzle olive oil on dough and sprinkle with crushed rosemary and sea salt.

When ready to bake, preheat oven to 400 degrees. Bake 17-25 minutes or until just golden. Remove from baking sheet and cool on a rack. Serve with dipping oils or soup.

Soups & Stews

TRINITY CHURCH

Erected in 1762 as the church for Portsmouth Parish, Trinity Episcopal Church is the oldest house of worship in the city. Located on the southwest corner of High and Court Streets, Trinity occupies the site designated for a church when Portsmouth was first laid out by its founder, Colonel William Crawford. Trinity's churchyard contains the graves of many of Portsmouth's earliest citizens and Revolutionary War Heroes.

DID YOU KNOW?

The officers of the *C.S.S. Virginia* (formerly the *U.S.S. Merrimack*) attended a special service at Trinity before sailing from Portsmouth into Hampton Roads to fight the *U.S.S Monitor* in March, 1862.

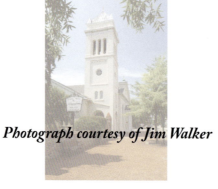

Photograph courtesy of Jim Walker

CREAMY ASPARAGUS SOUP

- 2 pounds asparagus
- ½ cup chopped onions
- 2 tablespoons butter
- 6 cups chicken broth
- ½ cup half-and-half or cream
- Curry powder to taste
- Salt and pepper to taste
- Sour cream and/or asparagus slices for garnish

Snap off tough ends from asparagus and cut into pieces. In a large saucepan, sauté onions in butter until translucent. Add broth and asparagus. Heat to a low boil and cook about 10 minutes. Cool slightly, then purée in a blender or food processor; return to saucepan. Bring to a simmer and whisk in cream. Season with curry and salt and pepper. Serve hot or cold. If desired, garnish with sour cream and/or asparagus slices. Freezes well.

YIELDS 4-6 SERVINGS

BORSCHT (COLD BEET SOUP)

- 2 (15-ounce) cans sliced beets
- 1 medium potato, baked and peeled
- Juice of 2 lemons
- 1 cup sour cream, divided
- 3¾ cups chicken broth
- Salt to taste
- Fresh chives for garnish

Drain beets, reserving juice in a large pitcher. Purée beets with potato and lemon juice in a food processor or blender. Add ½ cup sour cream and process until smooth. Pour mixture into beet juice. Blend in broth and season with salt; chill. Serve with a dollop of remaining sour cream and garnish with chives.

YIELDS 6-8 SERVINGS

This is wonderful warm or cold.

To cool soup properly, leave on counter to cool to 85 degrees, about 1 hour. Then, refrigerate without sacrificing other items in refrigerator due to hot soup.

SOUPS & STEWS

CHICKEN CHILI

- 4 cups chopped sweet onions (2 large)
- 4 tablespoons olive oil, divided
- 4-5 garlic cloves, minced
- 4 red, yellow or orange bell peppers, chopped
- 2 teaspoons chili powder
- 2 teaspoons ground cumin
- 2 teaspoons dried oregano
- ¼ teaspoon dried red pepper flakes, or to taste
- 2 teaspoons salt
- 4 (14½-ounce) cans petite diced tomatoes, undrained
- 2 (4-ounce) cans chopped green chiles
- ½ cup minced fresh basil leaves
- 4 split chicken breasts, cooked and chopped or shredded into bite-size pieces
- Toppings: Corn chips, shredded Monterey Jack or Cheddar cheese, sour cream

Sauté onions in 2 tablespoons olive oil over low heat for 10-15 minutes or until translucent. Add garlic and cook 1 minute. Add bell peppers and next 5 ingredients and cook 1 minute longer. Stir in tomatoes, chiles and basil. Bring to a boil. Reduce heat and simmer, uncovered, for 30 minutes, stirring occasionally. Add cooked chicken and simmer, uncovered, for 10-15 minutes. Serve immediately, or refrigerate overnight and reheat slowly. Serve with toppings on the side.

YIELDS 6-8 SERVINGS

To cook chicken, use bone-in breasts with skin on. Rub skin with olive oil and season with salt and pepper. Roast at 350 degrees for 20-25 minutes; chicken will finish cooking in pot. Skin and bone and cut or shred into bite-size pieces.

FLAVOR FOR CHICKEN

When preparing chicken, cooking with skin and bones intact will heighten the flavor.

SOUPS & STEWS

CHILLED WATERMELON SOUP

- 3 cups seeded and cubed watermelon
- 1 tablespoon lime juice
- ½ cup low-fat plain or vanilla yogurt
- 1 cup stemmed strawberries, fan-cut for garnish

Combine watermelon, lime juice and yogurt in a blender and process until smooth. Chill 1 hour before serving. Garnish with strawberries.

YIELDS 4-6 SERVINGS

Freeze leftovers in popsicle molds.

CHUNKY POTATO-CRAB CHOWDER

- 2 tablespoons butter
- 1 cup chopped onions
- ¾ cup chopped celery
- 1 garlic clove, minced
- 2½ cups diced red potatoes, cut into 1-inch cubes
- 3 tablespoons all-purpose flour
- 2½ cups milk
- 1-2 teaspoons chopped fresh thyme
- ½ teaspoon freshly ground black pepper
- ¼ teaspoon grated fresh nutmeg
- 1 (14¾-ounce) can cream-style corn
- 1 (14-ounce) can chicken broth
- 8 ounces lump crabmeat, or more
- 3 tablespoons chopped fresh parsley
- 1 teaspoon salt
- 2 tablespoons sherry, optional

Melt butter in a large saucepan over medium-high heat. Add onions, celery and garlic and sauté 4 minutes. Add potatoes and sauté 1 minute. Sprinkle with flour and cook 1 minute, stirring constantly. Stir in milk and next 5 ingredients. Bring to a simmer over medium heat, stirring frequently. Reduce heat, cover and simmer 20 minutes or until potatoes are tender, stirring occasionally. Stir in crab, parsley and salt. Cook 5 minutes, stirring occasionally. Stir in sherry.

YIELDS 6 SERVINGS

An apple stored with potatoes will prevent 'eyes' from growing on them.

HEART OF THE HARBOR

CRAB AND CORN BISQUE

- ½ cup butter
- ½ cup all-purpose flour
- 1 bunch green onions, chopped
- 2 (10½-ounce) cans chicken broth
- 1 quart half-and-half
- 2 (11-ounce) cans shoepeg corn, drained
- 2 tablespoons salt
- ½ teaspoon white pepper
- 1 pound crabmeat

Melt butter over medium heat in a 6-quart saucepan. Blend in flour and cook 2-3 minutes. Add onions and stir until softened. Whisk in broth, increase heat and bring to a boil. Add half-and-half and next 3 ingredients and return to a boil. Reduce heat to a simmer and fold in crabmeat. Adjust seasoning and thin with milk, if desired.

YIELDS 6-8 SERVINGS

> To thicken soup without adding flour or cornstarch, remove some of the ingredients and pulse in blender until puréed then add back to soup pot.

ITALIAN MEATBALL SOUP

- 1 egg white
- ½ cup soft bread crumbs
- ¼ cup finely chopped onion
- 1 garlic clove, minced
- 1 pound lean ground beef
- 2 Italian sausages, casing removed
- 2 (14-ounce) cans beef broth
- 1 (14-ounce) can diced Italian tomatoes, undrained
- 1 (15-ounce) can garbanzo beans, drained and rinsed
- 1 cup sliced mushrooms
- ½ cup water
- 1 cup cheese tortellini
- 3 cups torn spinach (10 ounces)
- Freshly grated Parmesan cheese

Combine egg white and next 3 ingredients in a mixing bowl. Add beef and sausage and mix well. Shape mixture into small meatballs. Sauté meatballs in a lightly greased skillet over medium heat until done; set aside. In a large pot, stir together broth and next 4 ingredients. Bring to a boil. Stir in tortellini, reduce heat and simmer until pasta is tender. Stir in meatballs and spinach. Cook 1-2 minutes or until spinach is wilted. Top each serving with Parmesan cheese.

YIELDS 8-10 SERVINGS

This is a delicious and hearty soup.

SOUPS & STEWS

HEARTY WINTER SOUP

- ¼ cup olive oil
- 3 cups diced smoked cooked ham
- 1½ pounds Polish sausage, such as kielbasa, cut into ½-inch slices
- 2 large yellow or Vidalia onions, chopped
- 2 garlic cloves, minced
- 2 cups chopped celery with leaves
- 1 large tomato, peeled and cut into wedges
- 1 pound lentils, washed
- 2-2½ quarts water, or enough to cover ingredients in pot by 2 inches
- 1 teaspoon hot pepper sauce, such as Tabasco
- 1-1½ teaspoons salt
- 1 (10-ounce) package frozen leaf spinach, thawed and loosely chopped

Heat oil in a 6-quart soup pot over medium heat. Add ham and next 3 ingredients and sauté for 5 minutes. Add celery and next 5 ingredients. Cover and cook over low heat 2 hours. Add spinach and cook 10 minutes longer.

YIELDS 12-14 SERVINGS

Great with a warm and crusty artisan loaf of bread on a brisk evening.

Never use wine in a recipe that you would not drink. It will not taste a bit better when cooked.

FAKI (GREEK LENTIL SOUP)

- 1 cup lentils, washed
- 6 cups water
- 1 large stalk celery, finely chopped
- 1 large carrot, finely chopped
- 3 garlic cloves, on a toothpick for easy removal
- 1 medium onion, finely chopped
- ½ cup olive oil
- ¾ cup tomato sauce
- 1 bay leaf
- ¼ teaspoon black pepper
- 1 teaspoon salt
- 2 tablespoons red wine vinegar

Place lentils in a large pot with enough water to cover. Bring to a boil and cook 3 minutes; drain and return to pot. Add water and next 9 ingredients. Return to a boil. Simmer, covered, 1 hour, 30 minutes, adding more hot water if needed. Add vinegar and cook 10 minutes longer.

YIELDS 4-5 SERVINGS

JUMPIN' JAMBALAYA

1	pound smoked sausage, kielbasa or smoked ham, cut into bite-size rounds
2	tablespoons olive oil
1	large onion, chopped
3	garlic cloves, minced
2-3	stalks celery, sliced
1	large green bell pepper, chopped
2	(28-ounce) cans diced tomatoes
1	tablespoon minced fresh parsley
1	teaspoon dried thyme
2	tablespoons salt
¼	teaspoon black pepper
	Hot pepper sauce to taste
1	cup long grain converted rice
1	pound large shrimp, shelled and deveined

Brown sausage in olive oil in a skillet over medium heat. Transfer sausage to a lightly greased 4- to 6-quart slow cooker, reserving drippings in skillet. Add onions and next 3 ingredients to skillet drippings and cook 6-8 minutes or until onions are softened; add to slow cooker. Stir tomatoes and next 6 ingredients into slow cooker. Cover and cook on low for 4-5 hours or until rice is done. Stir in shrimp and cook until shrimp are done. Adjust seasonings to taste.

YIELDS 6-8 SERVINGS

OREGON CRAB STEW

3	slices bacon, cut into ½-inch pieces
2½	pounds onions, chopped
1	pound carrots, chopped
1	pound celery, chopped
3	medium-size green bell peppers, diced
1½	pounds tomatoes, diced and crushed
	Garlic salt to taste
	Freshly ground black pepper to taste
1½	gallons hot water
¼	cup chicken stock base
1	(10-ounce) can whole clams, undrained
3	medium potatoes, peeled and diced
½	cup plus 2 tablespoons Worcestershire sauce
2	tablespoons fresh lemon juice
	Seafood seasoning, such as Old Bay, to taste
1½	pounds cooked crabmeat

Sauté bacon in a large saucepan until crisp. Add onion and next 3 ingredients and sauté 10-15 minutes or until lightly golden. Add tomatoes, garlic salt and black pepper. Gradually stir in hot water, chicken base and clams until well blended. Simmer 3-4 hours, uncovered, stirring occasionally. Add potatoes and next 3 ingredients. Simmer 30 minutes longer. Add crabmeat and cook until heated through. Serve hot.

YIELDS 1½ GALLONS

POTATO, LEEK AND ONION SOUP

¼ cup olive oil	4 (14-ounce) cans vegetable broth
1½ pounds russet potatoes, peeled and diced	Salt and pepper to taste
1 large white onion, chopped	½ cup chopped fresh chives or green onion tops for garnish
3 pounds leeks, including tops, thinly sliced	

Heat oil in a large pot over medium heat. Add potatoes, onions and leeks and sauté about 12 minutes. Stir in broth and bring to a boil. Reduce heat to medium-low and simmer 20 minutes; cool slightly. Working in small batches, purée soup in a food processor or blender. Return to pot and season with salt and pepper. Reheat or finish cooling, uncovered. Garnish with chives or green onions. Serve hot or cold.

YIELDS 6-8 SERVINGS

Don't store potatoes and onions together. Potatoes give off moisture causing onions to rot.

POTATO-CABBAGE SOUP

4 tablespoons butter	2 cups water
3 medium potatoes, peeled and diced	1 (13¾-ounce) can chicken broth
2 medium carrots, ¼-inch diced	1 teaspoon dried dill
1 bunch green onions, coarsely chopped	½ teaspoon black pepper
3 tablespoons all-purpose flour	4 ounces lean ham, ¼-inch diced
4 cups shredded cabbage	

Melt butter in a large saucepan over medium heat until hot but not smoking. Add potatoes, carrots and green onions and sauté 5 minutes or until green onions are wilted. Stir in flour and cook 1 minute, stirring constantly. Add cabbage and next 4 ingredients and bring to a boil. Reduce heat to low, cover and simmer 20 minutes, stirring occasionally. Just before serving, gently mash vegetables with a potato masher to thicken liquid, if desired. Stir in ham and heat through.

YIELDS 4 SERVINGS

// SOUPS & STEWS

ROASTED RED PEPPER SOUP

- 5 tablespoons butter
- 3-4 large garlic cloves, minced
- ¾ cup coarsely chopped celery
- ¾ cup coarsely chopped onions
- ¾ cup chopped carrots
- ¼ teaspoon kosher salt
- ⅛ teaspoon black pepper
- 1½ cups chicken broth
- ½ teaspoon ground basil
- ½ teaspoon ground thyme
- 1 (18-ounce) jar roasted red peppers, coarsely chopped
- 1½ cups heavy cream
- 2 tablespoons grated Parmesan cheese, or to taste

Melt butter in a 6-quart pot over medium-low heat. Add garlic and next 3 ingredients and sauté 10 minutes or until tender. Stir in salt and pepper. Whisk in broth and next 3 ingredients. Purée mixture in 2 batches in a blender until smooth; return batches to pot over low heat. Blend in cream and heat through. Whisk in Parmesan cheese until well blended. Just before serving, adjust seasoning to taste.

YIELDS 6 SERVINGS

Soup will keep in refrigerator for several days.

"For an elegant presentation, make 2 batches, one with red peppers and one with yellow peppers (you may have to roast your own yellow peppers.) At serving time, using 2 ladles or small measuring cups, pour both colors into bowls simultaneously. Swirl, if desired."

ROASTING BELL PEPPERS

Preheat broiler and set rack 3-4 inches below heat. Cut peppers in half lengthwise. Remove core, seeds and ribs. Place on a baking sheet, skin-side up and place pan under broiler. Watch carefully and, as they become black, turn so skins blacken uniformly. When skins are charred, using tongs, place peppers in a plastic bag. Seal bag and allow peppers to steam 15 minutes. Remove peppers and peel off skins. If not using right away, place in a jar and cover with olive oil. Cover and refrigerate for up to 1 week.

CRUSTACEAN SENSATION

¼	pound Polish sausage, such as kielbasa, cut into 1-inch pieces
¼	cup olive oil
1	cup chopped sweet onions
2	garlic cloves, chopped
2	cups chicken broth
1	(14½-ounce) can petite diced tomatoes
1	teaspoon ground cumin
⅛	teaspoon cayenne pepper, or to taste
¼	teaspoon salt
¼	teaspoon black pepper
2	bay leaves
1-1½	cups heavy cream
½	pound medium shrimp, peeled and deveined
½	pound sea scallops, cut into bite-size pieces
½	pound lobster meat, cooked, or imitation lobster meat
½	pound lump crabmeat or imitation crabmeat
2	tablespoons chopped fresh parsley
	Seafood seasoning to taste, such as Old Bay, optional

Sauté sausage in a large soup pot over medium-low heat until browned; remove sausage from pot and set aside. Add oil to pot along with onions and garlic and sauté until softened, scraping bottom to deglaze pan. Blend in broth and next 6 ingredients. Simmer 20-30 minutes. Stir in cream and next 4 ingredients. Simmer 1-2 minutes or until heated through or until shrimp are pink. Return sausage to pot and add parsley and seafood seasoning. Adjust seasonings as needed. Remove bay leaves.

YIELDS 4 SERVINGS

Soup may be made a day ahead and reheated over low heat, being careful not to further cook the seafood.

Soft shell crabs: Chesapeake Bay Blue Crabs shed their shell in response to water temperature and salinity. They make a sweet, delightfully tasting delicacy.

SUMMER HARVEST CORN SOUP

12	slices hickory-smoked bacon, cut into ½-inch pieces
4	quarts water
1½	large yellow onions, chopped
4	large vine-ripened tomatoes, peeled and cut into 2-inch pieces
10-12	ears fresh white sweet corn, such as Silver Queen or Super Sweet, cut off cob, reserving 4-5 stripped cobs, or 2 (12-ounce) bags frozen Super Sweet white corn kernels
	Salt and pepper to taste
¼	cup all-purpose flour
½	cup cold water

Sauté bacon in a 6-quart soup pot until fat is rendered but bacon is still limp. Add 4 quarts water, onions, tomatoes and stripped cobs. Simmer until onions are translucent. Remove cobs. Stir in corn kernels and season with salt and pepper. Simmer 8 minutes. Remove from heat. Blend flour with ½ cup cold water until smooth and stir into soup. Bring to a boil, then reduce heat and simmer until soup thickens.

YIELDS 12-14 SERVINGS

Like many soups, this one is best when made a day ahead.

TACO SOUP FOR A CROWD

6-8	boneless, skinless chicken breasts
2	(26-ounce) cans condensed cream of chicken soup
2	(29-ounce) cans tomato sauce
2	(10-ounce) cans Mexican-style Rotel tomatoes
2	(14¼-ounce) cans cream-style corn
2	(15¼-ounce) cans whole kernel corn, drained
1-2	(1¼-ounce) packages dry taco seasoning mix, or to taste
1-2	cups finely shredded sharp Cheddar cheese
8	ounces sour cream
	Tortilla chips, broken into small pieces

Cook chicken in 4 cups boiling salted water, reserving broth. Cut chicken into bite-size pieces. Combine chicken and 3 cups reserved chicken broth with condensed soup and next 5 ingredients in a large soup pot. Simmer over low heat 20-25 minutes. Top individual servings with cheese, sour cream and tortilla chips. Recipe may be halved; freezes well.

YIELDS 10-12 SERVINGS

SOUPS & STEWS

THREE ONION SOUP

- 3 tablespoons olive oil
- 4 large yellow onions, sliced
- 5 shallots, sliced
- 4 leeks, washed and diced
- 5 garlic cloves, minced
- 6 cups vegetable stock
- 1 (750 ml) bottle Cabernet or Merlot red wine
- 2 tablespoons red wine vinegar
- Kosher salt to taste
- Freshly ground pepper to taste
- 6 slices country-style bread, toasted
- ¾ cup freshly grated Parmesan cheese

Heat oil in a large soup pot over medium heat. Add onions, shallots and leeks and sauté, stirring occasionally, 10 minutes or until onions are softened. Add garlic and sauté 1 minute longer. Stir in stock and simmer, uncovered, for 30 minutes. Stir in wine, vinegar and season with salt and pepper. Place 1 slice toast in the bottom of each bowl. Ladle soup into bowls. Sprinkle cheese on top and serve immediately.

YIELDS 6 SERVINGS

TIDEWATER CLAM CHOWDER

- 3 slices bacon, chopped
- 1 large yellow onion, chopped
- 2 (8-ounce) bottles clam juice
- 2 (10-ounce) cans whole baby clams, undrained
- 2 (10-ounce) cans chopped clams, undrained
- 2-3 red potatoes, ¼-inch diced
- 2 cups heavy cream
- ½ cup cornstarch or all-purpose flour
- ¾-1 cup cold water
- ¾ teaspoon salt
- ¼-½ teaspoon freshly ground black pepper
- Bouquet garni
- 1 tablespoon chopped fresh parsley for garnish
- 1 tablespoon chopped fresh chives or green onion tops for garnish

Cook bacon in a large pot; remove bacon with a slotted spoon and set aside. Add onions to drippings in pot, reduce heat and cook until translucent, but not browned. Add cooked bacon, clam juice and next 4 ingredients. In a jar with a tight-fitting lid, shake cornstarch with cold water until well mixed. Blend mixture into chowder and season with salt and pepper. Add bouquet garni and bring to a boil. Reduce heat and simmer 8-10 minutes, stirring occasionally. Remove bouquet garni. Garnish individual servings with parsley and chives. Freezes well.

YIELDS 8-10 SERVINGS

Bouquet garni is a blend of thyme, bay leaf and parsley tied in cheesecloth for easy removal.

BISTRO TOMATO-BASIL SOUP

1 tablespoon olive oil	1 large garlic clove, crushed
1 bunch green onions, chopped	1 tablespoon tomato paste
1 medium onion, chopped	1 teaspoon firmly packed brown sugar
1 red bell pepper, chopped	½ teaspoon salt
1 cup chicken broth	Freshly ground black pepper to taste
1 cup half-and-half	2 bay leaves
1 (28-ounce) can chopped tomatoes, undrained	¾ cup fresh basil leaves
	Chopped fresh basil and chives for garnish
Juice of 1 orange	Croutons for garnish

Heat oil over medium heat in a 4-quart saucepan. Add green onions, onions and bell pepper and sauté until tender and golden. Stir in broth and next 9 ingredients. Cover and simmer 30 minutes, stirring occasionally. Discard bay leaves and purée soup in a blender or food processor. Return all except 1 cup soup to pan. Process basil with remaining 1 cup soup until basil is finely chopped. Add mixture to soup and cook over medium-low heat until heated through, stirring frequently. Ladle soup into individual bowls and garnish with fresh basil, chives and croutons.

YIELDS 4 SERVINGS

SPINACH SOUP WITH POT STICKERS

64 ounces chicken broth	10 pot stickers
2 large garlic cloves	4 cups fresh spinach
1 bay leaf	

Heat broth, garlic and bay leaf in a large pot. Simmer 10 minutes. Add pot stickers and simmer 10 minutes longer. Remove bay leaf and add spinach just before serving.

YIELDS 4 SERVINGS

Great as a main course with a salad and French bread.

WATERCRESS SOUP

6 cups chicken broth	1 large garlic clove, halved
2 yellow onions, coarsely chopped	6 tablespoons butter
3 stalks celery, coarsely chopped	4 bunches green onions, white part only, sliced
2 large carrots, cut into chunks	5 bunches watercress, ends trimmed
2 teaspoons dried thyme	6 red potatoes, peeled and thinly sliced
1½ teaspoons dried rosemary	Salt and pepper to taste
3 large bay leaves	1 cup heavy cream
15 peppercorns	Freshly shredded Parmesan cheese
8 sprigs parsley	

Pour chicken broth into a 4-quart saucepan. Add onions and next 8 ingredients and bring to a boil. Reduce heat, cover and simmer about 2 hours. Cool, strain and set aside. This may be done a day or two ahead and refrigerated. In same saucepan, melt butter. Add green onions, cover and cook slowly for 15 minutes or until softened. Stir in watercress and potatoes and cook, uncovered, for 10 minutes. Add chicken broth mixture. Cover and cook 45 minutes longer. Season with salt and pepper; cool. Purée cooled soup in a food processor or blender and return to pot. At this point, soup may be refrigerated overnight, if desired. Reheat soup, whisking in cream; avoid bringing to a boil. Serve in soup cups and top each with 1-2 teaspoons Parmesan cheese.

YIELDS 6 BOWLS OR 12 CUPS

"A wonderful soup that can be made in stages for hassle-free entertaining."

Fresh rosemary is very strong and the more it is chopped, the stronger the flavor. For just a hint of flavor, do not chop.

SOUPS & STEWS

GARLIC SOUP WITH SPINACH AND WHITE BEANS

1 tablespoon olive oil	1 (15-ounce) can white beans, drained and rinsed
1½ cups chopped onions	
6 garlic cloves, minced	1 teaspoon dried oregano
2 stalks celery, ¼-inch diced	¾ teaspoon chopped fresh rosemary
1 large carrot, ¼-inch diced	4 cups packed fresh spinach leaves (9 ounces)
1 tablespoon flour	
4 cups chicken broth	Kosher salt and freshly ground black pepper to taste
1 (14-ounce) can petite diced tomatoes	

Heat oil in a large saucepan over medium-high heat. Add onions and next 3 ingredients and stir to coat. Cook 6 minutes, stirring often, or until vegetables are softened. Add flour and cook, stirring constantly, for 2 minutes. Stir in broth and next 4 ingredients and bring to a boil. Reduce heat to medium-low and cook, uncovered and stirring occasionally, 20 minutes. Add spinach and cook, stirring, until spinach is wilted. Season with salt and pepper.

YIELDS 6 SERVINGS

Shelf life of dried herbs and spices depends on how you store them. Keep in an airtight container in a cool dry place. Many will last at least a year. Crush some in your hand. If you detect a fragrance you can use them but may need to use more than called for if you have had them awhile.

SOUPS & STEWS

EASY MINESTRONE

- 6 cups low-sodium chicken broth
- 1 (15½-ounce) can cannellini beans, drained and rinsed
- 1 (28-ounce) can diced tomatoes
- 3 tablespoons extra-virgin olive oil, plus extra for serving
- 2 onions, finely chopped
- 4 garlic cloves, minced
- ½ cup dry pasta, small such as orzo or ditalini
- 1 (16-ounce) bag frozen Italian blend vegetables; zucchini, carrots, broccoli, and beans
- ¼ cup minced fresh basil leaves
- Salt and pepper to taste

In a large saucepan, bring broth, beans and tomatoes to a boil. Meanwhile, heat oil in a Dutch oven over medium-high heat. Add onions and cook 5 minutes or until softened. Add garlic and cook 30 seconds or until fragrant. Stir in broth mixture and pasta and simmer 10 minutes or until pasta is tender. Stir in frozen vegetables and basil and cook 2 minutes or until heated through. Season with salt and pepper. Serve with additional olive oil for drizzling.

YIELDS 4-6 SERVINGS

SUMMER PEACH SOUP

- 1 cup dry white wine
- 1 cup peach schnapps
- ½ cup sugar
- 1 teaspoon chopped fresh mint leaves
- ½ teaspoon ground cinnamon
- ¼ teaspoon ground nutmeg
- 2 cups half-and-half
- 10 fresh ripe peaches, sliced

Place white wine and next 6 ingredients in a bowl. Stir until well blended and sugar is dissolved. Add sliced peaches, and transfer to a saucepan.

Cook over medium heat 15 minutes or until peaches are tender, stirring frequently. Reduce heat if needed to prevent scorching. Cool to a safe temperature for a blender. Pour mixture into blender or food processor and puree until completely smooth. Cover and refrigerate until ready to serve. Serve chilled.

Peel peaches, if desired. For easy peeling, dip peaches into boiling water, then immediately put in ice water and pull the peel off.

PORTUGUESE CHICKEN AND RICE SOUP (SOPA DE GALINHA)

1	(5-pound) whole chicken, remove cavity parts, if included
3	stalks celery with leaves, halved
1	bunch (6-8 stalks) green onions, ends trimmed
6-8	large sprigs parsley
3	bay leaves
3	garlic cloves, chopped
1½-2	teaspoons salt
½	teaspoon freshly ground black pepper
10	cups water
10	cups chicken broth, divided
1	cup diced celery
1½	teaspoons garlic salt
½	teaspoon dried sage
½	teaspoon dried basil
½	teaspoon dried mint
½	teaspoon ground cumin
2½	cups white rice
½	pound Kielbasa sausage, quartered
	Salt and pepper to taste

In an 8-quart soup pot, combine chicken and next 7 ingredients. Add water and 4 cups chicken broth and bring to a boil. Reduce heat to medium and simmer, partly covered, for 40 minutes or until chicken is cooked, occasionally skimming off fat. With a slotted spoon or tongs, remove chicken, celery stalks, green onions and parsley sprigs. Return broth to a boil. Add 4 cups chicken broth, diced celery and next 6 ingredients. Reduce heat and simmer, covered, for 25 minutes or until rice is tender. Meanwhile, remove chicken from bones and shred into bite-sized pieces, discarding any fatty or discolored parts. When rice is cooked, add chicken to soup along with sausage and remaining 2 cups chicken broth. Cook 10 minutes longer. Season with salt and pepper.

YIELDS 1½ GALLONS

Thin leftover soup as needed with water. Soup may be frozen in an airtight container for up to 3 months.

This recipe has been passed through my family for five generations. My mother, who's from the Azores (islands of Portugal), made it for my children and me, especially when we were sick. Now, my children and I make it for my parents and they love it.

Salads & Dressings

MEMORIAL DAY PARADE

Portsmouth is proud to host the oldest continuously held Memorial Day observance in the nation. Since 1884, Portsmouth has remembered the brave men and women of the military with a parade featuring marching bands and military units.

DID YOU KNOW?

Memorial Day was originally observed to honor those who died in the Civil War.

Photograph courtesy of Trish Halstead

SALADS & DRESSINGS

AVOCADO AND CRAB SALAD

- 1 medium-size ripe avocado
- 1 cup peeled, seeded and diced vine-ripened tomatoes
- 3 tablespoons finely chopped shallots
- 1½ teaspoons Dijon mustard
- ¼ cup extra virgin olive oil
- 2 tablespoons lime juice
- 1 teaspoon hot pepper sauce, such as Tabasco
- 1 pound lump crabmeat, thoroughly picked for shells
- Salt and pepper to taste
- Radicchio or Boston lettuce
- 2 tablespoons chopped fresh chives

Dice avocado into ¼-inch cubes. Combine avocado, tomatoes and next 6 ingredients, very gently folding in crabmeat. Season with salt and pepper. Refrigerate at least 30 minutes. Serve in a lettuce cup and garnish with chives.

YIELDS 4 SERVINGS

This delicious recipe can also be served on thin baguette slices as hors d'oeuvres. Yields 48 servings.

If avocados are ripe and you are not ready to use, store in refrigerator. To hasten ripening, place in brown bag with an apple and store at room temperature. This method will work with many unripened fruits.

BEET ASPIC

- 1 (15-ounce) can sliced beets, juice reserved
- 1½ teaspoons prepared horseradish
- ¾ cup cider vinegar
- ¾ cup granulated sugar
- 1 teaspoon grated onion
- 1 (3-ounce) package lemon gelatin

Combine drained beets and horseradish in a blender and purée. Pour reserved beet juice and vinegar into a saucepan and bring to a boil. Stir in sugar, onion, gelatin and beet purée. Pour mixture into a lightly greased 8x8-inch dish or into individual molds. Refrigerate until set. Double recipe if using a ring mold.

YIELDS 8 SERVINGS

"Rave reviews from the board of the Garden Club of Virginia at the annual Board of Governor's meeting in Portsmouth."

HEART OF THE HARBOR

BEET SALAD

- 1 (16-ounce) jar pickled beets, ¾ cup juice reserved
- ½ cup water
- 1 (3-ounce) package lemon gelatin
- 1 tablespoon minced onions
- 1½ teaspoons horseradish
- ¾ cup diced celery
- Lettuce leaves
- Mayonnaise or sour cream for garnish, optional

Combine ½ cup reserved beet juice and ½ cup water in a saucepan and bring to a boil. Pour boiling mixture over gelatin in a bowl and stir 2 minutes or until dissolved. Add beets, remaining ¼ cup reserved beet juice, onions, horseradish and celery. Pour mixture into a greased 8x8-inch dish and refrigerate until set. Serve on lettuce and top with mayonnaise or sour cream for garnish.

YIELDS 8-10 SERVINGS

This salad is quick, easy, delicious and pretty!

BEST SHREDDED CHICKEN SALAD

- 1 head lettuce, torn into pieces
- 1 head napa cabbage, shredded
- 1 deli rotisserie chicken, skinned, boned and meat shredded
- 8-10 grape tomatoes, halved
- 3-4 slices red onions, halved
- 2 green onions with tops, cut on bias
- ¼ cup dried sweetened cranberries or golden raisins
- ½ cup coarsely chopped peanuts
- ⅓ cup chopped fresh cilantro or parsley
- 5-6 ounces clementine orange segments, drained
- 1 avocado, thinly sliced
- Salad dressing of choice, such as Thai peanut, sesame or Asian ginger dressing
- Fried won ton strips or Chinese noodles

Combine enough lettuce and cabbage in a large salad bowl for 4-6 servings. Add chicken and next 8 ingredients to bowl and toss. Add dressing and toss. Sprinkle won ton strips or noodles on top and lightly toss.

YIELDS 4-6 SERVINGS

This is a great entrée that can be adapted to individual tastes. Serve with buttered crusty bread such as sourdough baguette.

BLACK BEAN SALAD OR SALSA

1 (15-ounce) can black beans, rinsed and drained	1 tablespoon minced fresh cilantro
1 red bell pepper, diced	¼ cup olive oil
1 green bell pepper, diced	¼ cup red wine vinegar
1 yellow or orange bell pepper, diced	½ cup lime juice
½ cup diced red onions	Salt and pepper to taste
1 (16-ounce) can corn, drained	Favorite leaf lettuce
1 garlic clove, minced	Tortilla chips

Combine beans and next 7 ingredients in a salad bowl and toss gently to mix. Add oil, vinegar and lime juice and season with salt and pepper. Mix until thoroughly blended; adjust seasonings as needed. Refrigerate before serving to blend flavors. Serve on lettuce leaves garnished with tortilla chips, or serve as a salsa with chips.

YIELDS 6 SERVINGS

RAISIN AND BROWN RICE-GINGER SALAD

4 cups brown rice	1-2 teaspoons chopped garlic
8 cups water	1 cup peeled and chopped fresh ginger
¾ cup vegetable oil	2 bunches green onions, sliced
¼ cup soy sauce	2 cups raisins
2 tablespoons lemon juice	1 cup salted peanuts
Black pepper to taste	

Cook rice in 8 cups water; drain and rinse well until water runs clear. Combine oil and next 5 ingredients; set aside. Mix drained rice with green onions, raisins and peanuts. Pour ginger sauce over rice mixture and stir well until rice is completely coated.

YIELDS 8-10 SERVINGS

This is the perfect salad for patio parties or barbecues. Can be made a day ahead and stored in an airtight container in the refrigerator.

BLUE CHEESE DRESSING

- 1 (3-ounce) package blue cheese
- 3 cups mayonnaise
- 1 pint sour cream
- 1 teaspoon garlic salt
- 1 tablespoon Worcestershire sauce
- 1 tablespoon dried parsley

Crumble blue cheese with a fork into a bowl. Add mayonnaise and remaining 4 ingredients and mix well. Dressing will hold in refrigerator up to 4 weeks.

YIELDS 5 CUPS

CAPRESE SALAD SURPRISE

- ¾ cup raisins
- ¼ cup olive oil
- 3 tablespoons balsamic vinegar
- ½ teaspoon dried thyme
- ½ teaspoon dried rosemary
- ½ teaspoon salt
- 1 pound fresh mozzarella cheese, cut into ¼-inch thick slices
- 3 medium tomatoes, cut into ¼-inch thick slices
- 1 cup packed fresh basil leaves
- Freshly cracked black pepper
- ½ cup pine nuts, toasted

Combine raisins and next 5 ingredients in a microwave-safe bowl. Microwave on high 30-45 seconds or until warm. Stir and refrigerate 30 minutes or until cool. Raisin dressing can be prepared up to 24 hours ahead and refrigerated. For salad, alternate overlapping slices of mozzarella, tomato and basil leaves on a large platter or individual plates. Spoon raisin dressing evenly over salad. Season with freshly cracked black pepper and sprinkle with pine nuts.

YIELDS 6-8 SERVINGS

A guaranteed hit! Mix red and yellow tomatoes for more color.

To toast pine nuts, spread in a single layer on a shallow baking pan. Bake at 350 degrees 3-5 minutes, checking often after 2 minutes.

To plump up dried up raisins, cover with boiling water and let stand about 5 minutes.

SALADS & DRESSINGS

CHILLED MARINATED SQUASH

5 medium-size yellow squash, thinly sliced	1 teaspoon salt
½ cup thinly sliced green onions	½ teaspoon black pepper
½ cup chopped green bell pepper	⅓ cup vegetable oil
½ cup thinly sliced celery	⅔ cup cider vinegar
2 tablespoons wine vinegar	1 garlic clove, crushed
¾ cup granulated sugar	

Combine squash and next 3 ingredients in a bowl. In a separate bowl, whisk together vinegar and remaining 6 ingredients and pour over vegetables. Chill 24 hours, stirring occasionally.

YIELDS 8 SERVINGS

DELUXE CORN SALAD

2 (20-ounce) packages frozen corn kernels	1 teaspoon dried thyme
1 cup chopped green onions, including tops	1 teaspoon ground cumin
⅔ cup chopped pimentos	1 tablespoon salt
½ cup red wine vinegar	Freshly ground black pepper to taste
¼ cup Dijon mustard	1 cup olive oil
2 tablespoons honey	¼ cup chopped fresh cilantro
2 teaspoons minced garlic	

Cook corn according to package directions; drain. Combine corn, green onions and pimentos in a large bowl. In a separate bowl, whisk together vinegar and next 7 ingredients. Add oil in a steady stream, whisking constantly to emulsify. Pour a little more than half the dressing over the corn. Stir in cilantro and toss until well mixed. Serve with extra dressing on the side.

YIELDS 10-12 SERVINGS

Leftover dressing can be used to marinate shrimp, chicken or flank steak.

Never boil honey but, if it becomes crystallized, correct by putting the container in warm water or microwave until crystals disappear.

HEART OF THE HARBOR

CRABMEAT MOUSSE

2	envelopes unflavored gelatin	1	small onion, grated
¼	cup cold water	1	tablespoon Worcestershire sauce
6	ounces cream cheese	½	teaspoon salt
1	(10¾-ounce) can condensed cream of mushroom soup	1	cup chopped celery
1	cup mayonnaise	1	cup crabmeat

Soften gelatin in cold water. Combine cream cheese and next 5 ingredients in a saucepan and melt over low heat, stirring until well blended. Remove from heat and stir in gelatin. Add celery and crabmeat. Pour mixture into a greased 6-cup mold and chill until set. Unmold on a bed of lettuce.

YIELDS 10 SERVINGS

Before using fresh crabmeat, always pick through meat for any shells that may have been missed.

CRANBERRY-ORANGE SALAD

1	(3-ounce) package black cherry gelatin	½	cup finely chopped celery, optional
1	cup boiling water	½	cup chopped nuts
½	cup Mandarin oranges, drained, juice reserved	8	ounces cream cheese, softened
½	cup whole berry cranberry sauce	1	cup sour cream
1	(8-ounce) can crushed pineapple with juice	¼	cup granulated sugar
		1	teaspoon vanilla

Dissolve gelatin in boiling water in a large bowl. Add reserved Mandarin juice and refrigerate until partially set. Add drained Mandarin oranges and next 4 ingredients. Mix well and pour into a 1- or 1½-quart greased baking dish and refrigerate until set. Using an electric mixer, blend cream cheese and remaining 3 ingredients. When salad is firm, spread cream cheese topping over salad to cover and refrigerate until ready to serve. When doubling recipe, it is not necessary to double topping.

YIELDS 6-8 SERVINGS

"This is a family favorite holiday recipe but it's great anytime!"

SALADS & DRESSINGS

CROWD PLEASING POTATO SALAD

- 10 medium-size red potatoes
- 6-8 eggs
- 1 cup finely chopped celery
- ½ cup finely chopped sweet pickles (about 8-10)
- 1½ cups mayonnaise
- 2 tablespoons prepared mustard
- 6 tablespoons pickle juice
- 1 (2-ounce) jar diced pimentos, drained
- 1 tablespoon granulated sugar
- Salt and pepper to taste
- Paprika for garnish

Boil potatoes in skins for 30-35 minutes; drain and cool. In a separate saucepan, boil eggs 10 minutes; set aside to cool. Peel and cube potatoes and eggs and place in a large plastic or glass salad bowl. Add celery and chopped pickles to bowl. In a separate bowl, blend together mayonnaise and next 4 ingredients. Pour mayonnaise dressing over potato mixture and mix with a wooden or plastic spoon. Season with salt and pepper. Transfer to a serving bowl and sprinkle with paprika. Cover and chill until ready to serve.

YIELDS 10-12 SERVINGS

Perfect salad for Fourth of July picnics!

CRUNCHY SPINACH SALAD

- 1 cup vegetable oil
- ¼ cup cider vinegar
- ½ cup catsup
- 1 tablespoon Worcestershire sauce
- 1 teaspoon salt
- 2 pounds fresh spinach, torn into bite-size pieces
- 1 (8-ounce) can sliced water chestnuts, drained
- 4 hard-cooked eggs, sliced
- 1 (16-ounce) can bean sprouts, drained
- ½ pound bacon, cooked crisp and crumbled

Combine vegetable oil and next 4 ingredients in a jar and shake well; chill dressing before serving. In a large bowl, combine spinach and remaining 4 ingredients and toss well. Shake chilled dressing well and drizzle sparingly over salad.

YIELDS 4-6 SERVINGS

DID YOU KNOW?
Older eggs are easier to peel than fresh ones.

CURRIED CHICKEN AND PEACH SALAD

6 tablespoons mayonnaise	8 cups torn lettuce
6 tablespoons sour cream	2 cups chopped cooked chicken
¾ teaspoon lemon juice	2 cups peeled and sliced fresh peaches
½ teaspoon curry powder, or to taste	½ cup raisins
⅛ teaspoon salt	Lettuce leaves for serving
⅛ teaspoon ground ginger	2 tablespoons chopped fresh chives
⅛ teaspoon cinnamon	

Thoroughly mix mayonnaise and next 6 ingredients in a bowl; set aside. In a separate bowl, combine lettuce and next 3 ingredients. Add dressing to taste and toss. Spoon 2 cups salad mixture onto each individual lettuce-lined plate and sprinkle with chives. Serve with extra dressing on the side.

YIELDS 4-6 SERVINGS

A unique combination of wonderful flavors.

ISLAND CHICKEN SALAD WITH CURRY

8 cups cooked shredded chicken	3 cups mayonnaise
1 (20-ounce) can water chestnuts, drained and sliced or diced	1 teaspoon curry powder
2 cups diced celery	2 teaspoons soy sauce
2 pounds seedless grapes, halved	1 (13-ounce) can pineapple chunks, drained
2-3 cups slivered almonds, toasted	Salt and pepper to taste

Mix chicken with water chestnuts in a large bowl. Add celery, grapes and about two-thirds of almonds. In a small bowl, mix mayonnaise, curry powder and soy sauce. Add mayonnaise dressing and pineapple to chicken mixture and stir thoroughly until chicken is coated. Season with salt and pepper. Sprinkle with remaining almonds.

YIELDS 8-12 SERVINGS

A tangy chicken salad with a touch of curry.

To toast almonds, spread in a single layer on a baking sheet. Bake at 350 degrees for 3-5 minutes, shaking or stirring several times or until golden brown.

SALADS & DRESSINGS

WILDLY DELICIOUS STEAK SALAD

MARINADE AND STEAK

- ½ cup vegetable oil
- 3 tablespoons soy sauce
- ¼ cup lemon juice
- 1½ teaspoons Worcestershire sauce
- 1½ tablespoons Dijon mustard
- 2 garlic cloves, minced
- Salt and pepper to taste
- 1½-2 pounds flank steak

SALAD

- 8 ounces small red potatoes, skins on, halved or quartered, depending on size
- 8 ounces fresh green beans
- ¼ cup julienned Gruyère cheese
- ¼ cup finely chopped celery
- ¼ cup finely chopped red onions
- Grape tomato halves to taste
- 3 tablespoons mayonnaise
- 2 tablespoons Dijon mustard
- 1½ tablespoons red wine vinegar
- ½ teaspoon dried tarragon
- Salt and pepper to taste
- 1 cup oil of choice

Combine vegetable oil and next 6 ingredients and blend well. Pour marinade over steak and marinate 8-24 hours. Grill steak to medium-rare; cool. This step may be done a day ahead. Thinly slice meat across grain; set aside. For salad, cook potatoes in boiling water 6-8 minutes or until barely done. Rinse immediately to stop cooking; drain thoroughly. Blanch beans 1-2 minutes and plunge immediately into cold water to stop cooking and preserve color; drain thoroughly. Combine steak, potatoes and beans in a large bowl. Add cheese and next 3 ingredients. In a food processor, blend mayonnaise and next 3 ingredients. Season with salt and pepper. With processor running, gradually add oil. Gently fold mayonnaise dressing into salad to taste. Adjust seasoning and chill 4-5 hours. Serve at room temperature.

YIELDS 4-6 SERVINGS

"This is also 'wildly' different."

The term "cutting across the grain" in a recipe, refers to cutting perpendicular across the length of the parallel fibers (the grain) which make up the meat. This makes tougher cuts easier to chew, such as flank steak or skirt steak.

LETTUCE DRESS FOR DINNER

- ½ cup granulated sugar
- ½ teaspoon salt
- 1 teaspoon dry mustard
- 1 tablespoon cornstarch
- 1 egg, beaten
- ½ cup cider vinegar
- ½ cup water

Mix sugar and next 3 ingredients in a bowl. Blend in egg. Gradually add vinegar and water and cook over medium heat until dressing thickens.

YIELDS ABOUT 1¼ CUPS

This is an old Eastern Shore recipe that can be served warm or cool over any type of lettuce, but is especially delicious over home-grown lettuce with chopped hard-cooked eggs.

DO AHEAD COMPANY SALAD

- ¾ cup mayonnaise
- 3 tablespoons granulated sugar
- 3 tablespoons red wine vinegar
- Salt to taste
- 1 (5-ounce) package mixed greens of choice
- ½ medium-size sweet onion, sliced
- ¼ red onion, sliced
- ¼ cup raisins
- 6 slices bacon, cooked and crumbled
- 1 (11-ounce) can Mandarin oranges, drained

Mix mayonnaise and next 3 ingredients for dressing and refrigerate at least 24 hours before serving. When ready to serve, toss mixed greens with remaining 5 ingredients. Gradually drizzle dressing to taste over salad and toss.

YIELDS 4-6 SERVINGS

Especially good with spinach/romaine mix or broccoli.

DID YOU KNOW?
Romaine lettuce has much more vitamins A and C than iceberg.

EUROPEAN SALAD

DRESSING

- ¾ cup oil
- ¼ cup unsweetened pineapple juice
- 1 teaspoon lemon zest
- 2 tablespoons fresh lemon juice
- 1 tablespoon chopped fresh mint
- ¾ teaspoon salt
- ½ teaspoon dry mustard

SALAD

- 1 large avocado, cut into 1-inch cubes
- 2 cups sliced celery
- 4 kiwis, sliced
- 1 (5-ounce) package salad mix
- 1 (11-ounce) can Mandarin oranges, drained, optional

Combine all dressing ingredients and refrigerate overnight. Place all salad ingredients in a large bowl. Add dressing to taste and toss lightly to mix. Serve on a lettuce-lined platter.

YIELDS 6 SERVINGS

A great combination of flavors and ingredients make this a truly special salad.

GREAT GRAPE SALAD

- 8 ounces cream cheese, softened
- 1 cup sour cream
- ¼ cup granulated sugar
- 1 teaspoon vanilla
- 2 pounds seedless grapes, green and red mix
- 1 cup pecans, toasted and chopped
- 1 cup firmly packed light brown sugar
- Lettuce cups for serving

Blend cream cheese and next 3 ingredients in a bowl until smooth. Place grapes in a separate bowl and fold in desired amount of cream cheese mixture. Combine pecans and brown sugar. In a 9x13-inch pan, layer half the grape mixture, then half the pecan mixture. Repeat layers, ending with pecans. Refrigerate at least 2 hours. Serve in lettuce cups.

YIELDS 8-10 SERVINGS

A sure hit with adults and children. They will love this combination.

Freezing grapes is easy and fun. Wash, dry and remove stems. Pack in airtight containers. The natural high sugar content and acid level act as a preservative. Eat right from freezer. If making preserves, thaw before cooking just until crushable.

SALADS & DRESSINGS

EASY FAUX CRABMEAT SALAD

- 1 pound imitation crabmeat
- ½ large lemon
- 1 onion, chopped
- 3-4 stalks celery, chopped
- 1 (8-ounce) can sliced water chestnuts, quartered
- ¼ cup chopped fresh parsley
- ¾ cup frozen peas, thawed
- Seafood seasoning to taste, such as Old Bay
- Black pepper to taste
- ¼ cup mayonnaise

Break up crabmeat into a large bowl. Squeeze lemon juice over crab and toss to blend thoroughly. Add onions and next 4 ingredients and mix well. Season with seafood seasoning and pepper. Gradually mix in mayonnaise to taste. Adjust seasonings and chill until ready to serve.

YIELDS 4-6 SERVINGS

A great filling for stuffing tomatoes when they are at their peak. Try throwing in some small shrimp.

MANGO CHICKEN SALAD

- ¾ cup plain low-fat yogurt
- ½ cup chopped fresh cilantro
- 2 tablespoons fresh lime juice
- 2 tablespoons mango chutney
- 1 tablespoon Dijon mustard
- 1 teaspoon ground turmeric
- ¼ teaspoon cayenne pepper, or to taste
- Coarse salt and ground pepper to taste
- 4 cups shredded cooked chicken
- 1 very ripe mango, peeled, seeded and diced
- Spinach or lettuce of choice
- ½ cup sweetened shredded coconut, toasted

Whisk together yogurt and next 6 ingredients in a bowl. Season with salt and pepper. Add chicken and mango and toss to mix. Serve on spinach or lettuce. Sprinkle with coconut.

YIELDS 4 SERVINGS

To toast coconut, spread on a baking sheet. Bake at 350 degrees, tossing occasionally, 8-10 minutes or until golden brown; watch carefully to not burn.

FIVE CUP SALAD

- 1 cup Mandarin oranges, drained
- 1 cup crushed pineapple, drained
- 1 cup miniature marshmallows
- 1 cup shredded coconut
- 1 cup sour cream

Mix all ingredients together in a medium bowl. Cover and chill 2 hours before serving.

YIELDS 4-6 SERVINGS

"Incredibly easy and guaranteed to be a favorite with children."

GARDEN CLUB CHICKEN SALAD

- 4-5 boneless, skinless chicken breasts
- 3 ounces pitted small black olives, sliced lengthwise
- 5 ounces grape tomatoes, whole or halved, depending on size
- 1 (16-ounce) can artichoke hearts, drained and quartered
- 3 ounces crumbled feta cheese
- 4 ounces non-creamy Caesar salad dressing, such as Ken's or Paul Newman's

Cook chicken, cool and cut into bite-size pieces. Mix chicken in a bowl with olives and next 3 ingredients. Just before serving, toss salad with dressing to taste. Serve on lettuce.

YIELDS 8-10 SERVINGS

A favorite of the Testing Committee

GRILLED ROMAINE

- 3 heads hearts of romaine lettuce
- Olive oil
- ¾ cup crumbled feta cheese
- ¼ cup aged balsamic vinegar
- ½ cup pine nuts, toasted

Preheat grill to high. Cut heads of romaine in half lengthwise, making six portions and leaving stem intact to hold leaves together. Drizzle romaine with olive oil and place on grill. Cook 3 minutes or until slightly charred. Remove quickly and sprinkle with feta. Drizzle with vinegar, about 2 teaspoons per portion. Sprinkle with pine nuts.

YIELDS 6 SERVINGS

BEAUTIFUL HOLIDAY SALAD

- 1 large head Boston lettuce, washed, dried and torn
- 1 ripe pomegranate, seeded
- ½ cup pecan halves
- ½ cup Gorgonzola cheese
- ½ cup thinly sliced red onions
- Dressing of choice, such as oil and vinegar, lemon or poppy seed dressing

Combine all ingredients except dressing. Lightly dress with dressing of choice. If preparing ahead, do not assemble until ready to serve.

YIELDS 4-6 SERVINGS

A beautiful addition to your holiday table!

> To seed a pomegranate, submerge quartered fruit in cold water; pulp and seeds will separate easily under water. Drain seeds. Children love doing this. Pomegranates will keep in refrigerator for up to 2 months.

HOT SPINACH SALAD

- 8 slices bacon
- 10 ounces fresh spinach, washed, dried and torn
- 2 hard-cooked eggs, chopped
- ½ cup chopped green onions
- ½ cup red wine vinegar
- ¼ teaspoon dry mustard
- 1 teaspoon granulated sugar
- Salt and pepper to taste

Cook bacon until crisp; drain, reserving fat. Crumble bacon into a salad bowl along with spinach, eggs and green onions. Combine 2-4 tablespoons warm bacon fat with vinegar, mustard and sugar and pour over salad. Toss lightly.

YIELDS 6 SERVINGS

Great do-ahead recipe. Prepare first 4 ingredients and refrigerate in separate zip-top bags. Mix dressing and reheat just before serving.

LUSCIOUS LEMON SALAD

- 3 (8-ounce) cans crushed pineapple with juice
- 2 (3-ounce) packages lemon gelatin
- 2 cups buttermilk
- 1 (8-ounce) container frozen nondairy whipped topping, thawed
- ½ cup chopped pecans

Heat undrained pineapple in a saucepan over medium heat. When bubbles begin to form, stir in gelatin until completely dissolved. Remove from heat and cool until mixture begins to gel. Stir in buttermilk and fold in whipped topping and pecans. Transfer to a 9x13-inch dish and refrigerate at least 3-4 hours before serving.

YIELDS 8-10 SERVINGS

Salad or dessert? You decide!

FAMILY FAVORITE MARINATED BEAN SALAD

- 1 (15½-ounce) can black beans, drained
- 1 (15½-ounce) can kidney beans, drained
- 1 (15½-ounce) can chickpeas, drained
- 1 medium onion, thinly sliced
- ¼ cup chopped red or green bell peppers
- ¼ cup granulated sugar
- ½ cup vegetable or canola oil
- ⅓ cup red wine vinegar
- ½ teaspoon celery seed

Combine black beans and next 4 ingredients in a large bowl. In a separate bowl, combine sugar and remaining 3 ingredients and mix well. Pour dressing mixture over beans and stir gently to blend. Cover and refrigerate 8 hours or overnight, stirring occasionally.

YIELDS 8 SERVINGS

May delete onions and/or bell peppers and add chopped roasted red peppers.

"My brother-in-law brings this to family gatherings where it is enjoyed by everyone, especially my daughter who is vegetarian."

NAPA CABBAGE SALAD

2 tablespoons soy sauce	2 bunches green onions with tops, chopped
¾ cup olive oil	Butter or margarine
½ cup granulated sugar	2 (3-ounce) packages ramen noodles, broken into small pieces
¼ cup wine vinegar	
1 large or 2 small heads napa cabbage, shredded	4 ounces sliced almonds
	½ cup sesame seeds

Combine soy sauce and next 3 ingredients in a saucepan. Bring to a boil and cook 1 minute. Cool and refrigerate until ready to use. Mix cabbage with green onions in a very large bowl and refrigerate until ready to assemble. Melt butter in a large skillet. Add noodles, almonds and sesame seeds and cook, stirring often, until brown. Cool and store in a zip-top bag until needed. Just before serving, add noodles to cabbage mixture. Shake dressing well and toss with salad, adding a little at a time to taste.

YIELDS 10-12 SERVINGS

ORANGE-CUCUMBER SALAD

1 small seedless cucumber (wrapped in plastic)	1½ tablespoons drained and chopped oil-packed sun-dried tomatoes
1 (11-ounce) can Mandarin oranges, drained	¼ teaspoon salt
¼ cup extra virgin olive oil	⅛ teaspoon black pepper
1 tablespoon cider vinegar	¼ teaspoon ground cumin
1 tablespoon honey	Pinch of cayenne pepper, or to taste
1 teaspoon oil drained from tomatoes	

Halve cucumber lengthwise, then halve lengthwise again. Cut crosswise into pieces about the size of orange segments. Place cucumber pieces and drained orange segments in a bowl. Whisk together oil and remaining 8 ingredients and toss with cucumber mixture. Serve on a bed of red leaf lettuce.

YIELDS 4 SERVINGS

ORZO SALAD WITH BLACK BEANS AND ARTICHOKES

- 8 ounces orzo
- 1 (0.7-ounce) package dry Italian dressing mix, such as Good Seasons
- Balsamic vinegar
- Olive oil
- 1 (2¼-ounce) can sliced black olives, drained
- 2 (6-ounce) jars marinated artichoke hearts, drained and chopped
- 1 (15½-ounce) can black beans, drained and rinsed
- ½ cup chopped red or sweet onions
- 3 green onions, sliced
- ½ cup chopped green bell pepper
- ½ cup seeded and chopped cucumber
- 1 tomato, seeded and chopped
- 2-3 small garlic cloves, minced
- ½ cup chopped fresh parsley
- Salt and pepper to taste

Cook orzo until al dente, rinse in cold water and drain; set aside in a large salad bowl. Prepare dressing according to package directions using balsamic vinegar, olive oil, ground black pepper and salt. Add olives and remaining ingredients to orzo in bowl. Pour dressing over salad and gently mix. Refrigerate until ready to serve.

YIELDS 6-8 SERVINGS

REFRESHING PEAR SALAD

- 5 cups fresh spinach, washed, blotted dry and torn
- 1 fresh pear, peeled and sliced
- 10 fresh strawberries, sliced
- ½ cup chopped walnuts
- 3 ounces goat cheese, crumbled
- Light balsamic vinaigrette to taste

Toss together spinach, pears and strawberries. Add walnuts and goat cheese. Add dressing to taste and toss.

YIELDS 4 SERVINGS

Incredibly easy and guaranteed to be a hit.

APPLE HARVEST SALAD

LEMON DRESSING

- ⅔ cup olive oil
- 2 tablespoons red wine vinegar
- Juice of 3 lemons
- ½ teaspoon dry mustard
- ½ teaspoon salt
- ½ teaspoon paprika
- Black pepper to taste
- 1 teaspoon garlic salt
- 1 teaspoon granulated sugar

SALAD

- 1 Gala apple, sliced
- ½ cup chopped walnuts
- ½ cup dried cranberries
- ½ cup crumbled Gorgonzola cheese
- 1 (5-ounce) package spring mix greens

Mix all dressing ingredients in a jar and shake well. Chill before serving. Combine all salad ingredients in a large bowl. Toss salad lightly with dressing. Serve immediately.

YIELDS 4 SERVINGS, 1 CUP DRESSING

The dressing is good with fruit or greens. A packaged Italian dressing mix made with red wine vinegar may be substituted.

DID YOU KNOW?

Cranberries got their name from the pilgrims, who called them cranberries because their long-necked pink blossoms resembled the head of a crane.

WALDORF COLE SLAW

- ½ cup thinly sliced celery
- ½ cup thinly sliced sweet onions
- ½ cup dried sweetened cranberries
- ½ Braeburn apple, unpeeled and thinly sliced
- ½ cup chopped walnuts
- Sea salt to taste
- Freshly ground black pepper to taste
- ¼ cup light slaw dressing, Marzetti's recommended
- 1 (16-ounce) package angel hair cabbage slaw

Combine all ingredients except cabbage and toss until thoroughly coated. Add cabbage and toss until well coated. Refrigerate until ready to serve. May be prepared in the morning for an evening meal.

YIELDS 4-6 SERVINGS

SALADS & DRESSINGS

ARTICHOKE-RICE SALAD

- 1 (6.9-ounce) package chicken-flavored rice mix
- 1 (4-ounce) jar marinated artichokes
- ⅔ cup mayonnaise
- 1-2 teaspoons curry powder
- 10 small pimento-stuffed olives, sliced into fourths
- 4 green onions with tops, sliced
- Parsley sprigs for garnish, optional

Prepare rice mix according to package; cool to room temperature and refrigerate 1 hour. While rice cools, chop artichokes, discarding any woody or tough pieces; reserve half the artichoke marinade. Blend mayonnaise, curry powder and reserved artichoke marinade. Add artichokes, olives and green onions and stir until combined. Add artichoke mixture to cooled rice and blend well. Refrigerate overnight. Garnish with parsley.

YIELDS 6-8 SERVINGS

This is truly special!

ASPARAGUS SALAD

VINAIGRETTE

- 1 cup olive or vegetable oil
- 2 tablespoons red wine vinegar
- 1 tablespoon balsamic vinegar
- 1 tablespoon Dijon mustard
- Salt and pepper to taste

SALAD

- 1 pound asparagus
- ⅓ cup coarsely chopped sweet onions
- 10 grape tomatoes, halved
- ¼ cup crumbled blue cheese

Combine all vinaigrette ingredients in a jar or blender and blend until all mustard is incorporated; set aside. For salad, snap tough ends off asparagus and discard. Cut spears into 2-inch pieces. Cook asparagus in boiling salted water 2-3 minutes or until still slightly crunchy. Quickly drain and rinse under cold water or plunge into ice water to stop cooking and retain color; drain on paper towels to remove all water. Transfer asparagus to a large bowl with onions, tomatoes and blue cheese. Toss with vinaigrette to taste. To make ahead, refrigerate prepared asparagus, onions and tomatoes in separate containers up to 24 hours.

YIELDS 6 SERVINGS

ATHENIAN ORZO SALAD

SALAD

- 12 ounces orzo
- 2 tablespoons olive oil
- 1½ cups crumbled feta cheese
- 1 cup chopped red bell pepper
- 1 cup chopped yellow bell pepper
- ¾ cup sliced kalamata olives
- 4 green onions, chopped
- 2 tablespoons capers, drained

DRESSING

- 3 tablespoons fresh lemon juice
- 1 tablespoon white wine vinegar
- 1 tablespoon minced garlic
- 1½ teaspoons dried oregano
- 1 teaspoon Dijon mustard
- 1 teaspoon ground cumin
- ½ cup olive oil
- Salt and pepper to taste
- 3 tablespoons pine nuts, toasted, for garnish

Cook orzo in boiling salted water until tender; drain, rinse with cold water and drain again. Transfer orzo to a large bowl and toss with remaining salad ingredients; set aside. For dressing, combine lemon juice and next 5 ingredients in a small bowl. Gradually whisk in olive oil. Season with salt and pepper. Toss dressing with salad. Adjust seasonings and garnish with pine nuts.

YIELDS 10-12 SERVINGS

To toast pine nuts, spread in a single layer on a baking sheet. Bake at 350 degrees 3-5 minutes or until golden brown, checking early and often as they will burn quickly. Pine nuts will continue to brown for a few seconds after removing from oven.

TORTELLINI SALAD WITH SHRIMP

- 1 pound cheese tortellini, cooked al dente
- 3 large stalks celery, coarsely chopped
- ½ cup chopped onions
- 1 cup fresh broccoli florets
- 1 (0.7-ounce) package dry Italian dressing mix, Good Seasons recommended, prepared
- 1 (0.4-ounce) package buttermilk ranch dressing mix, Hidden Valley recommended, prepared
- 2 pounds medium shrimp, cooked, peeled and deveined
- 1-1½ cups coarsely shredded mozzarella cheese

Combine tortellini and next 3 ingredients in a large bowl. Add enough prepared Italian dressing to cover and marinate several hours or overnight. Before serving, drain thoroughly. Add prepared ranch dressing to taste and toss with shrimp and cheese.

YIELDS 8 SERVINGS

OVERNIGHT PASTA SALAD WITH CREAMY BASIL DRESSING

DRESSING

- 2 cloves garlic
- 2 egg yolks
- ¼ cup white wine vinegar
- ¾ teaspoon salt
- Freshly ground black pepper to taste
- ¾ cup packed fresh basil
- ¾ cup olive oil
- ¾ cup canola oil

SALAD

- 2 pounds tortellini, cooked and drained
- 1 red bell pepper, chopped
- 1 yellow bell pepper, chopped
- ¾ cup chopped red tomatoes
- ¾ cup chopped yellow tomatoes
- 1½ cups shredded Asiago cheese
- 2-3 (6-ounce) jars marinated artichoke hearts, drained and coarsely chopped
- ½ cup chopped Italian parsley leaves
- Salt and pepper to taste

Using a food processor or blender, combine all dressing ingredients except the oils. With unit running, slowly add oils until well blended. To prepare salad, toss tortellini with half of dressing. At this point, salad can be covered and refrigerated overnight. When ready to serve, add remaining salad ingredients. Add more dressing and adjust seasoning as needed with salt and pepper.

YIELDS 10 SERVINGS

SWEET AND SAUERKRAUT SALAD

- ½ large green bell pepper, thinly sliced
- ½ large red bell pepper, thinly sliced
- 1 cup thinly sliced celery, cut on bias
- 2 (14-ounce) cans sauerkraut, undrained
- ½ cup thinly sliced onions
- ½ cup vegetable oil
- ½ cup cider vinegar
- ¼ cup water
- 1½ cups granulated sugar

Mix green pepper and next 4 ingredients in a large bowl. Heat oil and next 3 ingredients in a saucepan over medium heat until sugar dissolves. Pour mixture over vegetables and blend well. Refrigerate, covered, overnight. Salad will keep a week or more in refrigerator.

YIELDS 4-6 SERVINGS

TANGY GREEK SALAD

2 tablespoons chopped fresh basil	1½ cups olive oil
¾ tablespoon chopped fresh chives	Sugar to taste, optional
½ tablespoon chopped fresh thyme	8-12 ounces mixed lettuce greens
¾ tablespoon chopped fresh rosemary	¼ cup thinly sliced red onions
1 tablespoon chopped fresh oregano	½ cup crumbled feta cheese
Salt and pepper to taste	2 tablespoons capers, drained
5 garlic cloves, pressed	½ cup chopped tomatoes
⅓ cup fresh lemon juice	¼ cup sliced kalamata olives
¼ cup white wine vinegar	

Combine basil and next 4 ingredients in a small bowl. Stir in salt and pepper and next 3 ingredients. Slowly drizzle in oil, whisking to emulsify. If dressing is too tangy, whisk in sugar to taste. Combine lettuce and remaining 5 ingredients in a large bowl. Toss salad with dressing just prior to serving.

YIELDS 6 SERVINGS

POOLSIDE STRAWBERRY AND SPINACH SALAD

ALMONDS

1 tablespoon butter	½ cup sliced almonds
¼ cup granulated sugar	

DRESSING

2 teaspoons minced onions	¼ teaspoon Worcestershire sauce
½ cup olive oil	¼ teaspoon paprika
¼ cup cider vinegar	2 teaspoons poppy seeds
½ cup granulated sugar	

SALAD

6 ounces fresh spinach	2 cups sliced strawberries, cut lengthwise

Stir butter and sugar in a pan over medium heat until melted and well mixed. Stir in almonds and simmer, stirring occasionally, until sugar is caramelized and almonds are coated. Transfer almonds to a sheet of foil to dry; separate almonds when cool. Mix together all dressing ingredients and set aside. In a salad bowl, combine spinach, strawberries and almonds. Toss salad with dressing and serve.

YIELDS 6-8 SERVINGS

"A refreshing summertime salad and a favorite of our book club!"

SALADS & DRESSINGS

SEARED SCALLOPS ON BACON AND SPINACH SALAD

- 1 cup apple cider or juice
- 2 teaspoons granulated sugar
- 5 slices bacon
- ¼ cup chopped shallots
- 1 tablespoon cider vinegar
- ¾ teaspoon salt, divided
- ¼ teaspoon freshly ground black pepper
- 1½ cups thinly sliced Granny Smith apples
- ⅓ cup thinly sliced red onions
- 1 (6- to 8-ounce) package fresh baby spinach
- ¼ teaspoon curry powder
- ⅛ teaspoon cayenne pepper
- 18-20 sea scallops
- 2 teaspoons olive oil

Combine cider and sugar in a small saucepan over medium-high heat. Bring to a boil and cook 9 minutes or until reduced to ¼ cup; remove from heat. Cook bacon in a nonstick skillet over medium-high heat until crisp. Drain bacon, reserving 1 teaspoon drippings in pan. Add shallots to pan and sauté 1 minute. Remove from heat and stir in cider mixture, vinegar, ¼ teaspoon salt and pepper; set aside. In a large bowl, combine apples, onions and spinach. Crumble bacon on top. In a small bowl, combine remaining ½ teaspoon salt, curry and cayenne pepper. Sprinkle spice mixture evenly over both sides of scallops. Heat oil in a large nonstick skillet over medium-high heat. Add scallops to skillet and cook 3 minutes on each side or until done. Drizzle cider mixture over spinach mixture in bowl and toss gently to coat. Place salad on individual plates and top each serving with scallops.

YIELDS 4-6 SERVINGS

An elegant first course or late night supper.

SEAWALL SHRIMP AND PEA SALAD

- 1 cup sour cream
- ½ cup mayonnaise
- 1 tablespoon fresh lemon juice
- ½ teaspoon salt
- ½ teaspoon dried dill
- 4 hard-cooked eggs, chopped
- ¼ cup chopped sweet pickles or sweet relish
- 2 tablespoons chopped green onions
- 1 cup chopped celery
- 1 pound cooked shrimp, peeled, deveined and cut bite-size
- 4 cups fresh or frozen peas, cooked

Combine sour cream and next 4 ingredients in a large bowl. Stir in eggs and next 3 ingredients. Add shrimp and stir well. Gently fold in peas and refrigerate, covered, overnight. Serve on a lettuce leaf-lined platter.

YIELDS 4-6 SERVINGS

TROPICAL SALAD WITH CURRIED CHICKEN

Juice of ½ lime	1 red bell pepper, sliced and cut into 1-inch pieces
¾ cup ranch dressing, prepared from Hidden Valley Buttermilk dressing mix	½ cup sweetened dried cranberries
1 teaspoon curry powder	1 pound boneless, skinless chicken breasts
1 large garlic clove, pressed	2 tablespoons coarsely chopped fresh cilantro or parsley
½ small red onion, thinly sliced	1 large Granny Smith apple, unpeeled
1 large stalk celery, thinly sliced on angle	1 (10-ounce) package baby spinach
1 carrot, thinly sliced on angle	½ cup sliced almonds, toasted, divided

Whisk together lime juice and next 3 ingredients in a small bowl; set dressing aside. In a separate bowl, combine onions and next 4 ingredients; cover and refrigerate. Pound chicken breasts to ½-inch thick and cut into ½-inch cubes. In a lightly greased large skillet, sear chicken without stirring in a single layer over medium-high heat for 2 minutes or until no longer pink. Remove from heat and add cilantro and ¼ cup of dressing, tossing to coat. Core apple and cut into small pieces. Combine apple, spinach and half the almonds with other salad ingredients. Toss with remaining dressing. Serve salad topped with chicken and remaining almonds.

YIELDS 8 SERVINGS

To toast almonds, spread in a single layer on a shallow baking pan. Bake at 350 degrees 3-5 minutes or until golden brown. Check often as almonds can quickly burn.

SALAD IN A POCKET

2 (7-ounce) cans tuna	8 ounces cheese of choice, shredded
1 cup cherry or grape tomato halves	⅓ cup oil and vinegar dressing of choice
1 medium-size green bell pepper, diced	2 teaspoons crushed fresh basil
¼ cup chopped red onions	6 whole-wheat pita bread rounds, halved
½ cup sliced black olives	

Combine all ingredients except bread. Toss and stuff into pita pockets.

YIELDS 6 SERVINGS

Great for tailgating!

PORTOBELLO SALAD WITH ROASTED RED PEPPERS

- 3 tablespoons olive oil
- 12 ounces Portobello mushrooms, sliced
- 2 tablespoons balsamic vinegar
- ½ teaspoon dried basil or Italian seasoning
- 1 pound asparagus, ends trimmed and cooked al dente
- 1 head red or green leaf or romaine lettuce, torn bite-size
- 1 (12-ounce) jar roasted red peppers, cut into bite-size pieces
- ½ cup pine nuts, toasted
  balsamic and basil vinaigrette, such as Wishbone, Ken's or homemade
- 4 ounces goat cheese

Heat oil in a medium skillet over medium-high heat. Add mushrooms and sauté 3 minutes. Drizzle vinegar over mushrooms and add basil. Sauté 3 minutes longer, adding more oil if needed; remove from heat. Cut asparagus into halves or thirds. Toss lettuce with asparagus, mushrooms, roasted peppers and pine nuts. Gradually blend in vinaigrette to taste. Top with goat cheese.

YIELDS 6 SERVINGS

To toast pine nuts, spread on a shallow baking sheet and bake at 350 degrees 3-5 minutes, checking often.

KALEIDOSCOPE SALAD

- 1 sweet onion, chopped
- 2 (15-ounce) cans whole kernel corn, drained
- 3-4 tomatoes, seeded and chopped, optional
- ½ red bell pepper, chopped
- ½ green or orange bell pepper, chopped
- 1 (15-ounce) can pitted black olives, quartered
- 2-3 green onions with tops, chopped
- ¼ teaspoon salt, or to taste
  Black pepper to taste
- ¼ cup chopped fresh parsley
  Italian dressing to taste, Good Seasons recommended
- 1 avocado, sliced just before serving

Combine all ingredients except dressing and avocado. Toss salad with dressing. Salad may be made a day or 2 ahead and refrigerated until serving. Serve on a bed of lettuce leaves with avocado slices.

YIELDS 8-10 SERVINGS

POPPY SEED SALAD

DRESSING

- 1 cup salad oil
- ½ cup granulated sugar
- ⅓ cup white balsamic vinegar
- Dash of salt
- 1 teaspoon prepared mustard
- 1 teaspoon onion powder
- 2 tablespoons poppy seeds

SALAD

- 6 cups torn romaine lettuce
- 1 cup pecans, coarsely chopped
- 1 cup diced Havarti cheese with dill
- 1 cup dried sweetened cranberries

Whisk together all dressing ingredients; set aside. Toss all salad ingredients together in a large bowl. Slowly add dressing to salad to taste.

YIELDS 4-6 SERVINGS

Sugared pecans make this salad even better! Melt 1 tablespoon butter in a skillet. Stir in 2 tablespoons brown sugar. Add chopped pecans and sauté quickly over medium heat, being careful not to burn. Cool before adding to salad.

STEWED TOMATO ASPIC

- 1 (14½-ounce) can stewed tomatoes
- 1 (3-ounce) package lemon gelatin
- 2 tablespoons cider vinegar
- ½ teaspoon salt
- Dash of Worcestershire sauce
- ½ cup chopped celery
- ½ cup chopped green olives
- ½ cup water

In a saucepan, cut through large pieces of tomatoes and boil 2 minutes. Add gelatin and stir until completely dissolved. Remove from heat and stir in vinegar and remaining 5 ingredients. Pour mixture into individual molds or a shallow 1½- to 2-quart baking dish. Refrigerate overnight or until set.

YIELDS 8 SERVINGS

Olives can be omitted and amount of celery doubled.

SPINACH TORTELLINI SALAD WITH SUGARED PECANS

SALAD

- 1-1½ cups cheese tortellini
- 1-1½ pounds fresh spinach
- ½ cup sliced red onions
- ¾ cup shredded carrots
- ½ cup cherry or grape tomatoes
- 3 ounces crumbled feta or blue cheese
- ½ cup dried cranberries
- 1 cup chopped fresh basil
- 1 cup sugared pecans (recipe below)

DRESSING

- ½ cup olive oil
- ½ cup balsamic vinegar
- ½ cup white wine
- ½ teaspoon salt
- ½ teaspoon black pepper
- ½ cup granulated sugar

Cook tortellini according to package directions; drain and cool completely. Mix tortellini with remaining salad ingredients and toss. Blend all dressing ingredients together. Add dressing sparingly to salad before serving.

YIELDS 8 SERVINGS

Make a meal of this salad by adding shredded rotisserie chicken and chopped cooked bacon.

Sugared pecans: Melt 1 tablespoon butter in a skillet. Add pecans and 2 tablespoons light brown sugar. Sauté quickly over medium heat, being careful not to burn.

PREPARING GREEN SALAD AHEAD

Wash, dry and tear greens. Store in a zip-top bag lined with paper towels. Prepare all other salad ingredients, except nuts, in a bowl and add dressing to taste. Cover and refrigerate. When ready to serve, toss greens well with dressed vegetables. It usually will not need additional dressing. This is a good way to prevent "over dressing" your salads.

SALADS & DRESSINGS

PECAN CHICKEN SALAD

- 4 boneless, skinless chicken breasts
- Chicken broth or water, optional
- 2 stalks celery, diced
- 1 cup pecan pieces
- 1 cup sliced seedless green grapes
- ½ cup mayonnaise
- ½ cup ranch dressing
- ½ teaspoon sea salt
- ⅛ teaspoon white pepper
- 12 small or 6 large croissants

Cook chicken in a large skillet in broth or water 20-30 minutes or until no longer pink. Dice cooked chicken and place in a medium bowl. Add celery, pecans and grapes and toss to mix. Blend in mayonnaise and next 3 ingredients. Serve salad on croissants.

YIELDS 6 LARGE OR 12 SMALL SERVINGS

BALSAMIC VINAIGRETTE

- 1 cup sugar
- 1 cup balsamic vinegar
- 1 cup extra virgin olive oil
- 1 (0.7-ounce) package dry Italian dressing mix, such as Good Seasons

Bring all ingredients to a boil and cook until sugar dissolves. Store in refrigerator up to 2 weeks.

YIELDS 2 CUPS

MOTHER'S SLAW DRESSING

- 2 eggs, beaten with fork
- ¾ cup granulated sugar
- ½ cup cider vinegar
- 1 teaspoon prepared mustard
- 4 tablespoons butter (do not substitute)
- Pinch salt

Do not double recipe. Combine all ingredients in a saucepan and cook over medium heat, stirring constantly, until mixture just begins to boil. **Do not allow to boil.** Pour into a container and chill well before using.

YIELDS 2 CUPS

This dressing is especially good on cabbage, spinach and tomatoes.

Meat, Seafood & Poultry

LIGHTSHIP PORTSMOUTH

Built in 1915, the lightship Portsmouth has been a waterfront icon since 1964. The Lightship Service, now part of the United States Coast Guard, protected maritime traffic from shoals and other hazards by anchoring lightships to mark the locations. Beacons atop tall masts acted as seagoing lighthouses, manned by crews for months at a time. Now a museum, the Portsmouth honors the brave men who served aboard her and her sister vessels.

DID YOU KNOW?

The name of a lightship, written in large letters on each side of the vessel, was changed whenever she was restationed to reflect her new location.

Photograph courtesy of Jim Walker

MEAT, SEAFOOD & POULTRY

TEXAS BRISKET

1	(5- to 7-pound) beef brisket	½	cup lemon juice
2	cups catsup	2	cups water
3	tablespoons liquid smoke	2	teaspoons salt
½	cup Worcestershire sauce	2	teaspoons celery seed

Preheat oven to 450 degrees. Brown meat in a roasting pan in oven for 30 minutes. Mix together catsup and remaining 6 ingredients. Remove meat from oven and drain fat from pan. Reduce oven temperature to 250 degrees. Pour sauce over meat. Bake 4 hours, uncovered, basting often. Serve meat sliced on a platter with sauce drizzled over the top.

YIELDS 8-10 SERVINGS FROM A 7-POUND ROAST

After cooking meat, always let it rest for about 10 minutes. Most juices will be retained resulting in more flavor and tenderness.

LAMB KABOBS WITH GREEN OLIVE AND MINT SAUCE

¾	pound boneless lamb shoulder chops	½	teaspoon kosher salt
3	tablespoons extra virgin olive oil, divided	2	teaspoons red wine vinegar
1	teaspoon minced garlic, divided	1	teaspoon honey
1	teaspoon ground cumin, divided	2	tablespoons chopped green olives
	Pinch of dried red pepper flakes	2	tablespoons chopped fresh mint

If using wood skewers, soak in water a minimum of 30 minutes to prevent burning. Trim excess fat from meat and cut into 1-inch cubes. In a medium bowl, combine lamb with 1 tablespoon oil, ½ teaspoon garlic, ½ teaspoon cumin, pepper flakes and salt. Toss to coat and set aside. Prepare a hot grill or preheat broiler to high heat with the top oven rack set so broiler pan is 2-3 inches away from the heat source. In a small bowl, combine vinegar, honey and olives with remaining 2 tablespoons oil, ½ teaspoon garlic and ½ teaspoon cumin. Stir in mint. Thread lamb onto 4 small skewers. Broil or grill, turning once, 3-4 minutes per side or until browned and sizzling. Transfer skewers to plates and spoon mint sauce over the top.

YIELDS 2-4 SERVINGS

"Our guests raved how the kabobs were tender, unique and delicious!"

HEART OF THE HARBOR

PERFECTLY GRILLED LAMB CHOPS

- ⅓ cup olive oil
- ⅓ cup dry white wine
- 2½ tablespoons fresh lemon juice
- 4 green onions, finely chopped
- 3 large garlic cloves, minced
- 1 tablespoon chopped fresh rosemary
- 2 tablespoons chopped fresh parsley
- ¼ teaspoon dried red pepper flakes, or more to taste
- Seasoned salt to taste, such as Lawry's
- 4 (1- to 1½-inch thick) lamb loin chops

Combine all ingredients except lamb and blend well. Place lamb in a zip-top bag and add marinade. Seal bag and refrigerate 8-24 hours, turning often. When ready to cook, preheat grill. Grill lamb 7-8 minutes per side for 1-inch chops, 8-10 minutes per side for 1½-inch chops.

YIELDS 2-4 SERVINGS

GRILLED MARINATED LEG OF LAMB

- ½ cup soy sauce
- ½ cup olive oil
- ½ cup sesame oil
- ½ cup fresh parsley leaves
- 2 garlic cloves, crushed
- 1 tablespoon chopped fresh thyme
- 1 teaspoon chopped fresh rosemary
- 1 teaspoon dry mustard
- 1 teaspoon mace
- ½ teaspoon dried oregano
- 1 boneless leg of lamb, any size
- 1 cup red Zinfandel wine

Mix all ingredients except lamb and wine. Pour mixture over lamb and marinate overnight. When ready to cook, preheat grill. Grill lamb, basting often with marinade, until a meat thermometer reaches 160 degrees for medium and 170 degrees for well done; cooking time will vary depending on grill. Combine remaining marinade and wine in a saucepan and bring to a simmer. Serve wine sauce on the side.

YIELDS 8-10 SERVINGS

For the best and most delicate flavor, do not buy a bone-in leg of lamb that weighs more the six pounds. American lamb is considered to have a better flavor than Australian or New Zealand varieties.

MEAT, SEAFOOD & POULTRY

CROCKPOT NORTH CAROLINA STYLE BBQ

- 1 (4- to 6-pound) pork shoulder or Boston butt
- 2 cups cider vinegar
- ¼ cup Worcestershire sauce
- 2 tablespoons granulated sugar, or to taste
- 2 tablespoons salt
- 2 tablespoons dried red pepper flakes
- 2 tablespoons liquid smoke

Combine all ingredients in a large crockpot, cutting meat if needed to fit in pot. Cover pot and cook on high 6 hours or until meat falls apart easily when prodded with a fork. Turn off pot and cool. Cover and refrigerate overnight. Remove fat that has hardened on top and shred meat, removing any fat and tough parts. To serve, reheat in a saucepan or microwave, adding more sauce from crockpot to keep meat moist. Leftover meat can be stored in refrigerator for up to 4 weeks, or in freezer for up to 4 months.

YIELDS 15 SERVINGS

FLEMISH PORK CHOPS

- 6 pork chops
- 4 tablespoons butter, divided
- 1 large onion, sliced
- ¾ cup vermouth
- ¾ cup chicken broth
- Salt and pepper to taste
- 2 tablespoons flour
- 1 tablespoon Dijon mustard

Preheat oven to 300 degrees. Brown pork chops in 2 tablespoons butter in a large skillet. Transfer pork chops to a covered casserole dish, reserving drippings in skillet. Add onions to skillet and cook until transparent. Add vermouth and broth and season with salt and pepper. Cook 1 minute. Pour mixture over chops. Bake 1 hour, 30 minutes. Remove chops and onions to a serving platter. Melt remaining 2 tablespoons butter and whisk in flour. Blend butter mixture into pan juices and simmer until thickened. Stir in mustard and pour sauce over chops.

YIELDS 6 SERVINGS

If you are substituting a glass pan for baking, remember to reduce the oven temperature by 25 degrees.

COMPANY VEAL SHANKS

6-8 tablespoons olive oil, divided	Salt and pepper to taste
18 shallots, peeled	All-purpose flour
1 pound white mushrooms, thickly sliced	3 (14-ounce) cans chicken broth
6 garlic cloves, chopped	¾ ounce dried mixed wild mushrooms, rinsed
1 tablespoon minced fresh rosemary	
2 teaspoons chopped fresh thyme	1 (15-ounce) can diced tomatoes, drained
6 (10-ounce, 1½-inch thick) veal shanks	

Preheat oven to 350 degrees. Heat 4 tablespoons oil in a large heavy pan over medium-high heat. Add shallots and sauté 7 minutes or until they start to brown. Using a slotted spoon, transfer shallots to a plate and set aside. Add white mushrooms and next 3 ingredients to pan and sauté 5 minutes or until mushrooms begin to brown. Transfer mixture to a bowl. Add remaining olive oil to pan. Season veal with salt and pepper and coat with flour. Sauté veal in hot oil 5 minutes on each side or until brown. Transfer veal to a separate plate. Add 2 tablespoons flour to pan and stir 1 minute or until mixture is golden. Add broth and bring mixture to a boil, scraping up brown bits. Return veal and any accumulated juices from plate to pan. Add dried mushrooms, tomatoes and mushroom mixture to pan and bring to a boil. Cover pan and place in oven. Bake 30 minutes. Add shallots, cover and bake 30 minutes longer. Uncover and bake 20 minutes more or until veal is tender and sauce thickens. Transfer to a platter.

YIELDS 6 SERVINGS

This dish may be made a day ahead and reheated over medium heat.

An oven thermometer is a good investment. Many ovens vary as much as 25 or more degrees and that much difference can ruin a meal or baked goods.

SWEET AND SAVORY PORK ROAST

1 cup whole berry cranberry sauce	1-2 teaspoons crushed rosemary
1 (10- to 12-ounce) jar apricot preserves	1 (3- to 4-pound) center-cut boneless pork loin roast
1½ tablespoons spicy mustard	1 teaspoon salt
1 cup chicken broth	1 teaspoon black pepper
3 large garlic cloves, minced	
2 tablespoons ground or crushed thyme	

Preheat oven to 425 degrees. Stir together cranberry sauce and next 6 ingredients in a medium saucepan. Bring to a boil over medium heat. Reduce heat and simmer 5 minutes. Season pork with salt and pepper and place on a rack in a foil-lined roaster. Pour sauce over meat. Bake 40-45 minutes or until a meat thermometer reaches 155 degrees, basting several times during roasting. Remove from oven and let rest 10 minutes before slicing. Drizzle some sauce over pork slices and pass remaining sauce on the side.

YIELDS 8 SERVINGS

SAVORY SPAGHETTI SAUCE WITH ITALIAN SAUSAGES

4 Italian sausages	2 tablespoons maple syrup or honey, optional
1 tablespoon olive oil	1 teaspoon black pepper
1 tablespoon dried red pepper flakes	1 teaspoon salt
2 garlic cloves, minced	3 tablespoons minced fresh basil
½ cup diced zucchini	1 tablespoon minced fresh oregano
½ cup diced yellow squash	2 tablespoons chopped fresh parsley
2 (14½-ounce) cans stewed or diced tomatoes with basil and oregano	1 tablespoon cornstarch
¼ cup red wine	¼ cup water
	1 pound thin spaghetti, cooked and drained

Brown sausages in oil in a saucepan; set aside. In same pan, stir in red pepper flakes and garlic and cook 2 minutes. Add zucchini and squash and cook 10 minutes. Stir in tomatoes and next 7 ingredients and cook 20 minutes. Dissolve cornstarch in water and stir into sauce. Cook about 5 minutes or until thickened. Serve spaghetti topped with sausages and sauce.

YIELDS 2-4 SERVINGS

PORK CHOPS WITH SWEET ONION AND CAPERS

- 4 (1- to 1½-inch thick) boneless pork chops
- Kosher salt
- Freshly ground black pepper
- ⅓ cup all-purpose flour
- 1 tablespoon olive oil
- 2 tablespoons unsalted butter, divided
- 1 large sweet onion, thinly sliced
- ½ cup dry vermouth
- ¼ cup water
- 1 cube chicken bouillon, crushed
- 2 tablespoons capers, rinsed and drained
- 2 tablespoons cream
- 2 tablespoons chopped flat-leaf parsley for garnish

Season chops with salt and pepper and dredge lightly in flour, shaking off excess. Heat oil and 1 tablespoon butter in a large skillet over medium-high heat. Sear chops, turning once, for 2 minutes per side or until lightly browned; transfer to a plate. Add remaining tablespoon butter to skillet. Add onions and sauté, stirring, 3-4 minutes or until onions are barely tender and golden. Add vermouth and water and simmer 3 minutes or until liquid is reduced to ¼ cup. Stir in bouillon and capers. Return chops to skillet on top of onions. Reduce heat to a gentle simmer, cover and cook 8 minutes; be sure to maintain a low simmer. Turn chops and cook 4-5 minutes longer or until pork is just barely pink inside and firm to the touch (145-155 degrees). Transfer chops to a plate and cover loosely with foil. Increase heat to high and bring skillet juices to a boil. Stir in cream and boil, stirring occasionally, 1-2 minutes or until reduced by half to a sauce consistency. Adjust seasoning as needed with salt and pepper. Stir accumulated pork juices into sauce. Spoon sauce over chops and garnish with parsley.

YIELDS 4 SERVINGS

Make sure your cooking thermometers are accurate. Put tip of thermometer in boiling water; if it reads 212 degrees it is fine. If not, adjust thermometer according to package directions. New electronic thermometers shouldn't need adjusting.

PORK CHALUPAS

1	(1-pound) package dried pinto beans
1	(3-pound) pork loin roast
1	(4-ounce) can diced green chiles
2	tablespoons cumin seeds
1	tablespoon salt
2	garlic cloves, chopped
1	teaspoon dried oregano
	Corn chips, such as Fritos
	Chopped onions
	Shredded Cheddar cheese
	Shredded lettuce
	Diced tomatoes
1	(7½-ounce) jar jalapeño relish or taco sauce

A day ahead, if desired, rinse beans and place in a saucepan. Cover with water and boil 2 minutes. Remove from heat and let stand in same water for 1 hour; drain. If boiling ahead, refrigerate until ready to use. Combine drained beans and next 6 ingredients in a large pot or Dutch oven. Add enough water to cover. Simmer 6 hours, stirring occasionally, adding water as needed. Remove roast, cut meat from bone and break meat apart with hands. Return meat to pot and cook, uncovered, 1 hour to 1 hour, 30 minutes or until mixture is thickened. To serve, place corn chips on each plate. Top with meat mixture, onions, cheese, lettuce and tomatoes. Serve with jalapeño relish or taco sauce.

YIELDS 8-10 SERVINGS

This is great on tortillas, too.

PEPPERCORN SAUCE FOR BEEF TENDERLOIN OR STEAK

½	cup Merlot
1	shallot, minced
2	tablespoons coarsely crushed four-peppercorn mix
1¾	cups chicken stock
1¾	cups beef stock
4	tablespoons butter, softened
¼	cup milk
1	tablespoon cornstarch

Bring wine, shallots and peppercorns to a boil in a saucepan. Reduce heat and simmer 5 minutes or until reduced by half, stirring frequently. Stir in chicken and beef stocks and bring to a boil. Boil lightly 20-25 minutes or until sauce reduces to about 2 cups. Stir in butter and milk. Sift cornstarch into mixture and whisk until smooth. Cook 4 minutes or until sauce coats the back of a spoon, stirring constantly. Serve over tenderloin or steak. Sauce can be made ahead, covered and refrigerated until ready to use; bring to room temperature and reheat before serving.

YIELDS ABOUT 2½ CUPS

This wonderful sauce will really perk up your steaks.

ONE POT SPAGHETTI SAUCE

2 pounds ground beef	2 (14½-ounce) cans diced tomatoes
1 large onion, minced	1 (4-ounce) can mushrooms
1 teaspoon Italian seasoning	1 green bell pepper, minced
Salt and pepper to taste	Minced garlic to taste
3 (15-ounce) cans tomato sauce	Garlic salt to taste
1 (12-ounce) can tomato paste	Hot Italian sausage, cooked and crumbled

In deep pan, brown ground beef and onion. Sprinkle in Italian seasoning and salt and pepper. Add tomato sauce and next 6 ingredients. Stir in Italian sausage. Cook over low heat for several hours; the longer the better!

MUSTARD HORSERADISH SAUCE FOR BEEF TENDERLOIN

⅔ cup sour cream	½ teaspoon salt
¼ cup Dijon mustard	¼ teaspoon freshly ground black pepper
1 cup mayonnaise, Hellmann's recommended	2 tablespoons horseradish

Combine all ingredients in a small bowl and blend well. Adjust seasonings as needed.

YIELDS 2 CUPS

PERFECT BEEF TENDERLOIN

Before using this method, you should know your oven thermometer is accurate. Preheat oven to 450 degrees. Prepare whole tenderloin as desired and place in oven 20 minutes. Turn off oven. DO NOT OPEN OVEN DOOR. Leave meat in 45 minutes longer. Remove from oven. Meat will be medium-rare.

OSSO BUCO

6	(2- to 3-inch thick) center-cut veal shanks	2	sprigs fresh thyme
	Salt and pepper to taste	1	large sprig fresh rosemary
½	cup all-purpose flour	1	large pinch dried marjoram
4	tablespoons butter	¼	cup finely chopped Italian parsley
4	tablespoons olive oil	1	cup good dry Marsala or other dry red wine
2	large onions, chopped		
3	large stalks celery, chopped	2½	cups chicken stock
3	large carrots, chopped	4	tomatoes, peeled, seeded and chopped
4	large garlic cloves, chopped		Gremolata, optional (see below)

Pat veal shanks dry and season all over with salt and pepper. In a bag or bowl, toss meat with flour to coat, shaking off excess. In a large heavy skillet or Dutch oven, melt butter and oil together over medium heat. Brown veal on all sides, adding more butter or oil as needed; remove meat and set aside. Add onions and next 7 ingredients to skillet drippings and cook vegetables until al dente. Season mixture with salt and pepper. Increase heat to high and stir in wine to deglaze pan. Return veal to skillet along with stock and tomatoes. Drizzle with olive oil and reduce heat to low. Cover and simmer, stirring occasionally, 1 hour, 30 minutes or until meat is tender. Uncover and simmer 10-20 minutes to reduce sauce. Spoon sauce over meat and sprinkle with gremolata.

YIELDS 4-6 SERVINGS

To make gremolata, mix together the zest of 1 orange and 1 lemon, 2 minced garlic cloves and 2 tablespoons chopped Italian parsley. This is a great flavor enhancer for this and other meat dishes.

Many good cooks will take a look at the number of ingredients or length of instructions and just "keep going" when searching for a recipe. This is particularly true of soup recipes. In most cases, the recipe is worth the extra effort. Before passing by a recipe of interest, look again and consider whether much of the preparation can be done a day or two ahead. Often it can be a matter of chopping and storing.

LONDON BROIL

- 1 (1½-pound) flank steak or top round
- ⅓ cup cider vinegar
- ⅓ cup vegetable oil
- 3 tablespoons brown sugar
- 3 tablespoons soy sauce
- 2 medium onions, chopped
- ½ teaspoon coarse black pepper

Place meat in a shallow glass baking dish or zip-top bag. Mix vinegar and remaining 5 ingredients well and pour over meat. Cover and refrigerate 8 hours or overnight. When ready to cook, preheat broiler or grill. Remove meat from marinade and broil or grill until rare or medium-rare, basting with marinade during cooking. Heat remaining marinade to a boil. Thinly slice meat at an angle across the grain. Serve sliced meat on a platter with heated marinade drizzled on top.

YIELDS 6 SERVINGS

CAROLINA-STYLE RIBS

- 4 racks baby back ribs
- 24 ounces beer of choice
- 2 cups vinegar
- 2 cups catsup
- 4 tablespoons hot sauce, such as Texas Pete
- 1 cup honey mustard, such as Texas Pete
- ½ cup teriyaki sauce
- Juice of 2 limes

Cut racks into 2-rib sections. Boil ribs in a mixture of beer and vinegar and enough water to cover for 30-60 minutes or until most fat is gone and meat is tender. Whisk together catsup and remaining 4 ingredients in a large saucepan and bring to a boil. Using a basting brush, cover ribs completely with sauce. For juiciest ribs, baste ribs immediately after removing from boiling liquid. Grill coated ribs 10-15 minutes.

YIELDS 8 SERVINGS

JEZEBEL SAUCE FOR PORK

- 1 cup apple jelly
- 1 cup pineapple-orange marmalade or pineapple preserves
- 1 (6-ounce) jar prepared mustard
- 1 (5-ounce) jar prepared horseradish
- ¼ teaspoon black pepper

Whip apple jelly with an electric mixer. Add marmalade and remaining 3 ingredients and blend well. Excellent for basting pork roast or drizzling over pork chops.

YIELDS 3 CUPS

MARINADE FOR PORK, LAMB OR PHEASANT

- ½ cup oil, any kind
- ½ cup soy sauce
- 2 tablespoons Dijon mustard
- 4 garlic cloves, minced

Combine all ingredients in a jar with a lid. Cover and shake well. Pour mixture over meat and marinate a few hours or overnight.

YIELDS 1 CUP

When grilling meat, use tongs to turn as forks will pierce meat allowing juices to run out. This creates a less flavorful and less tender result.

ROCK N' ROCKFISH (STRIPED BASS)

1 (8-pound) rockfish, scaled and cleaned	1½-2 cups frozen raw peeled small shrimp, thawed
Salt and pepper to taste	½ lemon, thinly sliced
Seafood seasoning to taste, such as Old Bay	4 onion slices
1 (6-ounce) package cornbread stuffing mix	2 slices bacon, halved

Preheat oven to 350 degrees. Line a large baking pan with foil and grease foil. Place fish on foil in pan. Cut four (2- to 2½-inch wide) diagonal slits on top side of fish; the knife should cut through skin and slightly into flesh of fish. Season fish cavity with salt, pepper and seafood seasoning. Prepare stuffing according to package directions. Thoroughly pat shrimp dry and mix with stuffing. Pack stuffing into fish cavity. Place lemon, onion and bacon in and over cuts on top of fish. Bake 1 hour, 30 minutes or until fish flakes easily with a fork.

YIELDS 6-8 SERVINGS

TARTAR SAUCE

1 cup mayonnaise	Lemon juice to taste
1 tablespoon drained sweet pickle relish	Salt and pepper to taste
1 tablespoon grated onion	

Combine all ingredients. Best if made a few hours ahead.

YIELDS 1 CUP

Try adding 1 tablespoon chopped fresh parsley, ½ teaspoon Worcestershire sauce, 2 teaspoons small drained capers and 1 pressed garlic clove.

Food should not sit at room temperature more than 2 hours. When cleaning up, discard food that has been out for 2 hours or more.

FIX AHEAD COMPANY SHRIMP

24	medium shrimp, peeled and deveined		Minced garlic to taste
16	crackers, or ¾ cup panko	¾	cup dry sherry or white wine
6	tablespoons butter		Parsley
¼	cup Worcestershire sauce		Paprika
2-3	tablespoons dried or fresh minced onions		

Preheat oven to 325 degrees. Place 12 shrimp into each of two ovenproof 8-ounce ramekins. Crumble 8 crackers over each dish. In a saucepan, combine butter and next 4 ingredients and heat just until butter is melted. Spoon equal amounts of butter mixture over top of each ramekin. Top with parsley and paprika. Dish can be prepared earlier in the day and refrigerated, covered, until ready to bake. Bake 40 minutes or until shrimp are pink and crackers are slightly browned. Serve with crusty bread for dipping. Double or triple recipe as needed.

YIELDS 2 SERVINGS

SIMPLE CRAB CAKES

1	large egg	1	teaspoon country Dijon mustard, Grey Poupon recommended
2	tablespoons mayonnaise, Hellmann's recommended	1	pound lump crabmeat
			Butter

Whisk together egg, mayonnaise and mustard. Very gently fold in crabmeat. Form mixture into small cakes for appetizers, medium-size cakes for entrées or large cakes for sandwiches. Cover and chill at least 1 hour; do not skip this step as the cakes must be thoroughly chilled in order to hold together. Sauté cakes in butter over medium heat until heated through and golden brown on both sides.

YIELDS 4 SERVINGS

CRABMEAT PREP

Always check for shells in fresh crabmeat. Place crabmeat in a large container and, very gently, pick through small amounts at a time in your palm to feel for missed shell. If you use a stainless steel bowl, you can often hear the shell scrape the surface.

SHRIMP AND FETA CHEESE WITH PASTA

- 3 pounds medium-large shrimp, peeled and deveined
- Salt and pepper to taste
- ½ cup plus 2 tablespoons extra virgin olive oil
- 1 cup chopped onions
- 1 pound mushrooms of choice, sliced
- 6-8 plum tomatoes, seeded and chopped
- 1 cup chopped fresh basil
- 1 cup chopped fresh parsley
- 6 large garlic cloves, minced
- ½ teaspoon dried red pepper flakes, or to taste
- 5-6 ounces crumbled feta cheese
- 5-6 ounces grated Parmesan cheese
- 1 pound linguine or spaghetti, cooked and drained
- Fresh parsley for garnish, optional

Season shrimp all over with salt and pepper. Heat 4 tablespoons oil in a large, heavy skillet over medium-high heat. Add shrimp and sauté 3 minutes or until just opaque; do not overcook. With a slotted spoon, remove shrimp, cover and set aside. Add 4 tablespoons oil to same skillet. Add onions and sauté 3-4 minutes. Add mushrooms and sauté 5-6 minutes or until tender. Add tomatoes and next 4 ingredients and cook until heated through. Blend in cheeses. Add tomato sauce to drained pasta and toss to coat. Adjust seasonings and transfer to a large serving bowl. Top with shrimp and garnish with parsley.

YIELDS 8 SERVINGS

SCALLOPS AND SHRIMP IN HERBED CREAM SAUCE

- 14 ounces fresh sea scallops
- Salt and pepper to taste
- ¼ cup flour
- 3 tablespoons olive oil
- 1½ tablespoons minced fresh garlic
- 1½ cups heavy cream
- ½ cup dry white wine
- 1 pound large shrimp, peeled and deveined
- 3 tablespoons chopped fresh basil
- 3 tablespoons chopped fresh parsley
- ¾ cup seeded and diced tomatoes

Season scallops with salt and pepper and toss with flour until lightly coated. Heat oil in a nonstick pan over medium heat. Add scallops and sauté 1½ minutes on each side. Add garlic and cook 1 minute longer; do not brown garlic. Remove scallops from pan and set aside. Add cream to pan and bring to a boil. Cook until reduced by half. Add wine and continue to reduce. Stir in shrimp, basil and parsley. Cook until shrimp are pink and opaque. Return scallops to pan and adjust seasoning. Add tomatoes just before serving.

YIELDS 4-6 SERVINGS

SHRIMP AND BROCCOLI SAUTÉ

2	tablespoons butter	1¼	cups heavy cream
1	tablespoon olive oil	5-6	tablespoons tomato paste
2	cups broccoli florets	¼	teaspoon salt
¾	cup coarsely chopped sweet onions	¼	teaspoon black pepper, or to taste
	Salt and pepper to taste	½	cup chopped tomatoes
1	pound shrimp		Freshly grated Parmesan cheese

Heat butter and oil in a large nonstick skillet. Add broccoli and onions and sauté over medium-high heat about 3 minutes. Season with salt and pepper. Add shrimp and sauté, tossing to mix, 1 to 1½ minutes; do not allow shrimp to fully cook. Remove all from pan, set aside and cover. Return skillet to medium heat. Pour cream into skillet. Gradually whisk in tomato paste to taste. Season with ¼ teaspoon salt and ¼ teaspoon pepper and remove from heat until ready to serve. At serving time, return sauce to medium heat. Add shrimp and broccoli mixture and cook, stirring constantly, just long enough to finish cooking shrimp. Serve over pasta or rice, if desired. Top with chopped tomatoes and Parmesan cheese.

YIELDS 4 SERVINGS

CARB-CONSCIOUS

At home or dining out, consider substituting fresh dark green curly leaf spinach for pasta. Many cream sauce recipes are excellent over these raw greens and restaurants can often accommodate this request.

SALMON IN WHITE WINE WITH TARRAGON

4	salmon steaks	¼	cup dry white wine
	Salt and pepper to taste	½	teaspoon dried tarragon
2	tablespoons butter, softened	1	tablespoon chopped fresh parsley
2	tablespoons fresh lemon juice		

Preheat oven to 450 degrees. Season salmon steaks with salt and pepper. Place salmon in a greased baking dish and rub with butter. Combine lemon juice and remaining 3 ingredients and pour over steaks. Bake 10 minutes per inch thickness or until done.

YIELDS 4 SERVINGS

SAVORY SEAFOOD SAILBOAT

1 French bread loaf, partially baked	6 ounces medium shrimp, peeled and deveined, cut if needed
½ cup butter, cut into pats	
2½ tablespoons fresh parsley	2 ounces salmon fillet, cut into pieces
2 garlic cloves, finely chopped	4 sea scallops, cut into pieces
1 medium shallot, finely chopped	2 plum tomatoes, peeled and chopped
2 tablespoons white wine, sherry or brandy	¼ teaspoon each dried herbs of choice: dill, thyme, rosemary or tarragon, optional
Salt and pepper to taste	Lemon wedges for garnish

Preheat oven to 400 degrees. Slice top one-third off bread loaf and set aside. Hollow out loaf with a spoon or fork, leaving a 1-inch border around the sides and bottom. Break hollowed-out bread into small pieces and set aside. In a food processor, blend butter and next 4 ingredients to make 'snail' butter. Season with salt and pepper. Spread mixture on inside bottom and sides of loaf and underside of removed top. Alternate layers of seafood, bread pieces, chopped tomatoes and herbs of choice. Replace top of bread to cover loaf and place on a baking sheet. Bake 20 minutes or until seafood is cooked and bread is nicely browned. Slice and serve with lemon wedges.

YIELDS 4 SERVINGS

Substitute individual loaves, rolls or English muffins. Use any combination of seafood.

For maximum flavor, fresh herbs should be added near the end of the recipe while dried may be added near the beginning.

MEAT, SEAFOOD & POULTRY

SALMON WITH LEMON-MUSTARD SAUCE

- 4 garlic cloves, finely chopped
- Juice of 1 small lemon
- 2 tablespoons white wine
- 1 cup heavy cream
- 1 tablespoon Dijon mustard
- ½ teaspoon Worcestershire sauce, or to taste
- Tabasco sauce to taste, optional
- Salt and pepper to taste
- 1 (2-pound) salmon fillet (generous 1-inch at center)
- Olive oil
- 1 lemon, halved

Preheat oven to 375 degrees. To prepare sauce, combine garlic, lemon juice and wine in a saucepan over medium heat. Cook until very little liquid is left. Add cream and bring to a boil. Reduce heat and simmer 10-12 minutes or until sauce is thickened. Add mustard, Worcestershire sauce and Tabasco sauce and season with salt and pepper; set aside. Remove skin from salmon with a sharp fillet knife, if desired. Rub fillet all over with olive oil and season liberally on both sides with salt and pepper. Place salmon in a shallow pan and squeeze lemon juice on top. Bake 15 minutes or until fish flakes easily with a fork. Serve with lemon-mustard sauce.

YIELDS 6 SERVINGS

Variation: Spread pesto sauce over salmon on platter and drizzle with lemon-mustard sauce. Makes a delicious and attractive entrée or buffet selection.

CUCUMBER-DILL SAUCE

- 1 large cucumber, seeded and diced
- ¾ cup mayonnaise
- 3 tablespoons chopped onions
- 1 tablespoon chopped fresh dill, or 1 teaspoon dried
- Salt and pepper to taste
- Water

Combine cucumber and next 3 ingredients. Season with salt and pepper. Gradually add water to desired consistency. Cover and chill. Serve on baked salmon.

YIELDS 2-3 SERVINGS

RISOTTO FIT FOR A PRINCE

- 3 tablespoons olive oil
- 2 tablespoons butter
- 1 cup chopped onions
- 4 cups dry Arborio rice
- ½ cup chopped fennel
- 8-10 cups chicken or fish stock, heated
- 1 cup medium shrimp, peeled and deveined, halved if desired
- ½ cup bay scallops
- ½ cup shucked clams
- 1 cup sautéed mushrooms, combination of choice
- 4 tablespoons combined mixture minced parsley, thyme and chives
- 2 tablespoons minced fennel leaves

Heat oil and butter in a heavy saucepan. Add onions and cook until translucent. Stir in rice and fennel and cook until rice is opaque. Begin adding hot stock, ½ cup at a time, stirring rice continuously until stock is absorbed before adding more. After one-third of stock is added, add shrimp and next 3 ingredients. Continue adding stock until all is used. After last addition of stock, stir in herbs. Risotto should be creamy, almost soupy, and rice should be slightly firm in the center. Serve immediately.

YIELDS 8 SERVINGS

PRINCELY FARE

In 1990, a number of fine restaurants in Charleston, South Carolina, were patronized by then personal secretary to Prince Charles. The prince was planning a visit to the USA and Charleston would be one of his stops. The secretary left with copies of the best recipes and made his recommendations to the prince, who then selected one restaurant for entertaining an elite group of businessmen. Prince Charles liked this recipe so much that it is the only dish, of the entire trip, that he asked to be served again the next day.

PAELLA

2½ cups chicken broth	1½ cups dry short-grain rice, or 2 packages Arborio rice Milanese-style with saffron
1 bay leaf	
¼ cup dry white wine	1 tablespoon minced fresh parsley
¼ teaspoon saffron threads	2 tomatoes, peeled and finely diced
4 tablespoons olive oil, divided	1-1½ pounds medium shrimp, peeled and deveined
4 chicken thighs, cut into 1-inch pieces	
Salt and pepper to taste	12-18 mussels, scrubbed and debearded, or frozen mussels
1 small onion, finely chopped	
1 small red bell pepper, finely chopped	12-18 littleneck (small) clams, scrubbed
3 garlic cloves, minced	½ cup shelled fresh or frozen peas
	1 lemon, cut into wedges

Preheat oven to 400 degrees. Bring broth and next 3 ingredients to a boil in a small saucepan. Reduce heat to a simmer and keep hot until needed. In a large oven-proof skillet or paella pan, heat 1 tablespoon oil over medium-high heat. Season chicken with salt and pepper and cook in hot oil 5-7 minutes or until golden brown; poultry will still be rare. Remove chicken from skillet and set aside. Reduce heat to low and add remaining 3 tablespoons oil to skillet. Add onions, peppers and garlic and sauté, stirring often, for 3 minutes or until onions are translucent. Stir in rice and sauté several minutes. Add parsley and tomatoes. Ladle hot broth over rice, stir to mix and spread evenly in skillet. Bring to a boil; do not stir again. Place chicken in a ring about 2 inches from the side of skillet. Add shrimp, mussels and clams. Scatter peas on top and return to a boil. Carefully transfer skillet to oven and bake 20-25 minutes or until rice has absorbed broth so mixture is moist but not wet and clams and mussels have opened. Remove skillet from oven and let rest 5 minutes. Serve with lemon wedges.

YIELDS 4 SERVINGS

DID YOU KNOW?

Saffron comes from the stamen of a small purple crocus. Saffron is the most expensive spice in the world.

OVEN BAKED CATFISH

- ¼ heaping cup mayonnaise
- ½ teaspoon dried dill weed
- 1 teaspoon dried minced onions
- ½ teaspoon lemon juice
- 1 pound catfish fillets or other mild white fish, such as tilapia or haddock
- 8 saltine crackers, crushed
- 1-2 tablespoons butter
- Sliced almonds or chopped pecans, optional

Preheat oven to 400 degrees. Mix together mayonnaise and next 3 ingredients. Place washed and dried fish fillets in an ovenproof dish and spread mayonnaise mixture on top. Sprinkle with cracker crumbs and dot with butter. Top with nuts. Bake 20-30 minutes.

YIELDS 3-4 SERVINGS

ORANGE ROASTED TILAPIA

- 6 tablespoons olive oil, plus extra for baking
- 2 fennel bulbs, thinly sliced
- 6 garlic cloves, crushed
- 3 green onions, thinly sliced
- ¾ cup white wine
- ½ cup orange juice
- 6 slices orange peel
- Sea salt to taste
- Freshly ground black pepper to taste
- 6 tilapia fillets
- 3 oranges, peeled and sliced into rounds
- 1 cup mixed pitted black and kalamata olives
- 6 bay leaves
- 1 orange, sliced or cut into wedges, for garnish

Preheat oven to 400 degrees. Heat 6 tablespoons oil in a large roasting pan on stovetop over medium heat. Add fennel, garlic and green onions and sauté, stirring occasionally, until vegetables are softened. Stir in wine and boil 1 minute. Add orange juice and orange peel. Reduce heat and simmer 2 minutes; remove from heat. Season with salt and pepper and allow to cool. Season tilapia fillets with salt and pepper and place in same pan, spooning cooled mixture over top. Marinate 1 hour or more, basting occasionally. Drizzle a few teaspoons olive oil over each fillet. Place orange rounds, olives and bay leaves on top and around fillets. Bake 15-20 minutes or until fish is cooked through. Remove from oven to a serving platter. Baste fish with liquid from pan, discarding bay leaves. Garnish with orange slices or wedges and serve hot.

YIELDS 6 SERVINGS

ORANGE BALSAMIC BROILED SALMON

4 (2-inch) salmon fillets	2 tablespoons balsamic vinegar
⅓ cup dry sherry	1 tablespoon soy sauce, regular or low salt
2 tablespoons orange marmalade	

Preheat broiler. Remove any bones from fillets. Place salmon in a bowl with sherry and marinate 30 minutes. Mix marmalade, vinegar and soy sauce to form a glaze. Spread half of glaze over salmon before broiling. Broil 3 minutes. Turn and brush with remaining glaze. Broil 2-3 minutes or until done; do not overcook.

YIELDS 4 SERVINGS

Quick, easy and delicious!

MUSTARD RUBBED TUNA WITH TOMATO MINT RELISH

½ teaspoon cumin seeds	½ teaspoon chopped fresh mint
Olive oil	½ teaspoon chopped fresh parsley
3 tablespoons spicy mustard	½ teaspoon fresh lemon juice
½ teaspoon honey	1 tablespoon extra virgin olive oil
½ teaspoon dried thyme	¼ teaspoon lemon zest
½ teaspoon chopped fresh mint	½ teaspoon kosher salt
6 tuna steaks or cod	½ teaspoon freshly ground black pepper
6 Roma tomatoes, seeded and ¼-inch dice	¼ cup pine nuts, lightly toasted

Sauté cumin seeds in a small amount of oil over medium heat for 3 minutes or until fragrant; transfer seeds to a small bowl. Add mustard and next 3 ingredients to seeds and mix well. Rub mixture over tuna steaks. Arrange tuna in a single layer in a 9x13-inch baking dish. Cover pan tightly and refrigerate several hours. In a separate bowl, combine tomatoes and next 7 ingredients. Cover and let stand at room temperature 1-2 hours. Place a large nonstick skillet over high heat until almost smoking. Add enough olive oil to cover bottom of pan. Remove steaks from marinade and season with salt and pepper. Place steaks in hot skillet and sear 3-4 minutes per side; steaks should have a pink ring around outside edges. Transfer tuna to a warm serving platter. Add pine nuts to relish and spoon over each serving.

YIELDS 6 SERVINGS

To toast, spread pine nuts in a single layer on a baking sheet. Toast at 350 degrees for 3-5 minutes, stirring occasionally, and checking often after 2 minutes.

MEAT, SEAFOOD & POULTRY

MUSSELS MARINERS' STYLE

- 4 quarts mussels, scrubbed and debearded
- 6 tablespoons chopped fresh parsley, divided
- 3 tablespoons butter, divided
- 2 garlic cloves, minced
- 1 small onion, chopped
- 1 bay leaf
- ¼ teaspoon dried thyme
- 2 cups white wine
- Lemon slices for garnish

Discard mussels that do not close when handled or that have broken shells; set mussels aside. Combine ¼ cup parsley, 2 tablespoons butter and next 5 ingredients in a large pot and bring to a boil. Reduce heat and cook 2 minutes. Add mussels to pot. Cover and cook 2-4 minutes or just until shells open; do not overcook. Remove mussels from sauce and place in bowls, discarding any unopened shells. Strain liquid and return to pot. Add remaining 2 tablespoons parsley and 1 tablespoon butter and heat until butter melts. Pour liquid over mussels and serve with lemon slices.

YIELDS 4 SERVINGS

May add a shot of cream to sauce.

PREPARING MUSSELS

Discard any mussels that are chipped, broken or do not close when handled. To purge mussels of sand, place in cold water, mix in a handful of flour or cornmeal and let stand 15-20 minutes. Rinse in clear water and scrub with a stiff brush. When ready to use, debeard by grasping with a dry towel and giving a sharp yank out and toward the hinge end. This will not kill the mussel. If you pull toward the opening end, it will kill the mussel and must be discarded.

KEY WEST SAUTÉ

Peel and clean 8 jumbo shrimp per person. Sauté in garlic butter over medium heat 3-5 minutes or until opaque. Remove shrimp from pan and turn heat up to high. Blend chopped parsley and sherry into garlic butter and sear 30 seconds. Pour over shrimp and serve.

MIXED BERRY SALSA FOR FISH

- ¼ cup minced red onion
- 3 tablespoons minced yellow bell pepper
- 3 tablespoons minced red bell pepper
- 3 tablespoons minced green bell pepper
- 3 tablespoons minced fresh cilantro
- ½ cup sliced strawberries
- 3 tablespoons fresh orange juice
- 1 tablespoon olive oil
- 1 fresh jalapeño pepper, seeded and minced, optional
- 1 fresh chile pepper, seeded and minced, optional
- 4 fish fillets, such as tuna

Mix together all ingredients except fish in a small bowl. Place half of mixture in a zip-top bag and add fish; set aside remaining mixture for salsa. Marinate fish in refrigerator 2 hours. When ready to cook, oil grill rack generously and preheat grill over medium heat. Remove fish from marinade, discarding marinade, and place on hot grill. Grill about 4-5 minutes on each side. Garnish with reserved salsa and serve.

YIELDS 4 SERVINGS

MEDITERRANEAN SHRIMP OVER PASTA

- 2 tablespoons olive oil
- 1 medium onion, finely diced
- 1 green bell pepper, chopped
- 2 garlic cloves, pressed or finely diced
- ¼ cup diced oil-packed sun-dried tomatoes, drained
- 2 (14½-ounce) cans diced tomatoes
- 1 tablespoon dried oregano
- 1 tablespoon dried basil
- 1 teaspoon black pepper
- ½ teaspoon salt
- 1½ teaspoons dried red pepper flakes
- 1 tablespoon capers
- ⅓ cup dry white wine
- 1½ pounds small-medium shrimp, peeled and deveined
- 1 pound thin spaghetti, cooked and drained

Heat oil in a large skillet. Add onions, peppers and garlic and sauté until onions are translucent. Add sun-dried tomatoes and next 7 ingredients. Cover and cook 30 minutes over medium heat. Uncover and cook 15 minutes longer. Blend wine into sauce. Add shrimp and cook 5-7 minutes or until shrimp are done. Serve over spaghetti.

YIELDS 4 SERVINGS

LOBSTER WITH TARRAGON SAUCE

- 1 pound vermicelli, cooked according to package
- ½ cup plus 1 tablespoon butter, divided
- 3-4 leeks, white and light green parts only
- 1 cup dry white wine, divided
- 1 tablespoon finely chopped fresh tarragon, plus extra leaves for garnish
- 1 cup heavy cream
- Salt and freshly ground black pepper to taste
- 1 medium-large beet, peeled and coarsely shredded
- 1¼ teaspoons fresh lemon juice
- 1 pound cooked lobster meat

Drain cooked vermicelli in a colander and place wax paper or plastic wrap directly on surface of vermicelli to prevent drying out; set aside. Cut leeks in half lengthwise, clean and thinly slice crosswise. Melt 3 tablespoons butter in a large saucepan or skillet. Add leeks and cook over medium heat 5-7 minutes or until just tender. Add ½ cup wine and tarragon and cook 2-3 minutes. Add cream and salt and pepper and cook, partially covered, over low heat 10 minutes or until mixture starts to thicken. Transfer mixture to a blender and purée until smooth. Return to pan, adjust seasoning to taste, cover and keep warm. Melt 1 tablespoon butter in a small pan. Add shredded beet and cook over medium-high heat, stirring constantly, 7-9 minutes or until tender. Stir in lemon juice and set aside. In a saucepan over low heat, melt remaining 5 tablespoons butter. Add lobster and stir until just heated through. Remove lobster and set aside. Whisk remaining ½ cup wine into butter in saucepan. Pour boiling water over pasta, tossing to reheat. Add pasta to warm tarragon sauce along with warmed wine-butter. Serve on plates or in pasta bowls topped with lobster and garnished with beets and extra tarragon leaves.

YIELDS 6 SERVINGS

To prepare a day ahead, refrigerate sauce, beets, lobster and pasta in separate containers. Before serving, heat lobster in butter as directed and continue with instructions. Beets may be warmed or at room temperature. Use a fork to place beets on top of lobster to strain any excess liquid.

Always read a recipe carefully before embarking upon it. Set out ingredients and proper equipment prior to preparation as well. This will take away frustration if you don't have something you need on hand.

BAKED SALMON WITH SPINACH AND CARROTS

- ⅓ cup mayonnaise
- 2 teaspoons Dijon mustard
- 2 tablespoons white wine
- 5 cups fresh spinach
- 2 medium carrots
- 1 (2-pound) salmon fillet
- 1 teaspoon drained capers
- 4 tablespoons butter, melted
- 1 lemon, thinly sliced

Preheat oven to 400 degrees. Whisk together mayonnaise, mustard and wine in a small bowl; set aside. Place spinach in a greased 9x13-inch baking dish. With a vegetable peeler, shave carrot over spinach. Cut salmon into serving size pieces, if desired, and place over vegetables. Spread mayonnaise mixture over salmon. Scatter capers on top and drizzle melted butter over all. Top with lemon slices. Bake 10-12 minutes or to desired doneness.

YIELDS 4-6 SERVINGS

This recipe is elegant enough for guests and easy enough to become a weekly family entrée. It is also excellent with halibut.

BOURBON BASTED SALMON

- ¼ cup firmly packed brown sugar
- 1 green onion, chopped
- 2 tablespoons soy sauce
- 1 tablespoon grated fresh ginger
- 2 tablespoons olive or sesame oil
- 3 tablespoons bourbon
- 1 (1½-pound) salmon fillet, or 4 salmon steaks
- 2 tablespoons sesame seeds

Preheat oven to 350 degrees. Combine all ingredients except salmon and sesame seeds in a zip-top bag and mix well. Add salmon and marinate in refrigerator several hours. Place salmon in a lightly greased baking dish, reserving marinade for basting. Sprinkle salmon with sesame seeds. Bake 10-12 minutes or until opaque, basting occasionally and turning once. Fish may be grilled over medium heat on a well oiled grill rack 7 minutes per side, basting occasionally. Serve hot or cold.

YIELDS 4 SERVINGS

A great summer dish!

BAKED CRABMEAT

1 large white onion, chopped	½ teaspoon dried thyme
4 tablespoons butter	2 dashes hot pepper sauce, or to taste
2 generous tablespoons mayonnaise	1 pound lump crabmeat
2 tablespoons Worcestershire sauce	½ cup panko bread crumbs

Preheat oven to 350 degrees. Sauté onions in butter in a large skillet. Add mayonnaise and next 3 ingredients. Gently fold in crabmeat. Spoon mixture into 6 greased scallop-shaped baking shells or a greased shallow 2-quart baking dish. At this point, dish can be refrigerated until ready to bake; bring to room temperature before proceeding. Top with bread crumbs. Bake 20 minutes or until heated through.

YIELDS 6 SERVINGS

TROPICAL CRAB CAKES

1 pound backfin crabmeat	1 tablespoon mayonnaise
1½ cups shredded zucchini	Butter, optional
1 egg	½ ripe banana
¼ cup Italian bread crumbs	1 cup prepared mango or peach salsa

Preheat oven to 350 degrees. Combine crabmeat and next 4 ingredients and shape into patties. Bake 15 minutes, or sauté in butter in a pan until golden brown. For sauce, mash banana and mix with salsa. Serve with crab cakes.

YIELDS 6 SERVINGS

For a crowd, place cakes on baking sheets and cover with plastic wrap. Stack pans in refrigerator and they are ready to pop in oven as needed.

The best way to thaw seafood is overnight in the refrigerator. Place wrapped package on a shallow pan or plate and allow 8-10 hours. Thawing at room temperature or in warm water is sure to reduce quality of flavor and texture.

TUNA WITH ASIAN SEARING SAUCE

¼	cup firmly packed brown sugar	2	tablespoons soy sauce
¼	cup rice wine vinegar	2	green onions with tops, minced
2	garlic cloves, minced	1	fresh jalapeño pepper, seeded and minced, optional
1	tablespoon minced fresh ginger		
½	teaspoon freshly ground black pepper	6	tuna or swordfish steaks
2	tablespoons Asian sesame oil		

Combine brown sugar and vinegar in a small saucepan and bring to a boil, stirring constantly. Remove from heat and stir in garlic and next 6 ingredients; cool. In a shallow glass dish, arrange fish in a single layer. Pour marinade evenly over fish. Cover and refrigerate 2 hours. Remove from marinade and pat dry. Heat a skillet over medium heat. Sear fish in skillet, turning once, 4-5 minutes on each side or until lightly browned. Serve immediately.

YIELDS 6 SERVINGS

SWORDFISH EN PAPILLOTE

1	tablespoon olive oil	4	cups coarsely shredded carrots
½	teaspoon fennel seeds, crushed	12	asparagus spears, trimmed
4	garlic cloves, thinly sliced	4	(6-ounce) swordfish steaks
¼	cup lemon juice	¼	teaspoon salt

Preheat oven to 375 degrees. Heat oil in a small skillet over medium heat. Add fennel seeds and garlic and sauté 3 minutes. Remove from heat. Cool slightly and stir in lemon juice; set aside. Cut four (15-inch) squares of parchment paper. Fold each square in half, then open. Place 1 cup carrots and 3 asparagus spears near each fold. Top each with a steak. Spoon 1½ tablespoons garlic mixture over each steak and sprinkle with salt. Fold paper and seal edges with narrow folds. Place packets on a baking sheet. At this point, packets can be refrigerated up to 4 hours; bring to room temperature before proceeding. Bake 20-23 minutes or until paper is puffy and lightly browned. Transfer packets to individual plates and cut open; serve immediately. If well done vegetables are preferred, cook vegetables slightly before placing in packet.

YIELDS 4 SERVINGS

When served this dish, guests are always excited with anticipation of what's inside!

SWORDFISH WITH BROWNED BUTTER AND ROASTED RED PEPPER-CAPER SAUCE

4	(8-ounce, 1-inch thick) swordfish or halibut steaks
1/3	cup minced fresh flat-leaf parsley, divided
1/3	cup extra virgin olive oil
4	garlic cloves, minced
	Large pinch of dried red pepper flakes or chili powder
2	tablespoons fresh lemon juice
	Freshly ground black pepper
6	tablespoons unsalted butter
6	large garlic cloves, thickly sliced
1	(12-ounce) jar roasted red peppers, drained, dried and thinly sliced
1/4	cup capers, drained and rinsed
	Kosher salt
1	tablespoon balsamic vinegar

Heat broiler with rack in position closest to heat source, or heat gas grill, covered, to high heat. Trim steaks of any skin or dark flesh. Arrange steaks in a 9x13-inch dish. Combine half of parsley with next 4 ingredients and season generously with black pepper. Spread mixture evenly over fish; set aside. Melt butter in a 12-inch skillet over medium heat until hot and bubbling. Reduce heat to medium-low and cook butter gently 2 minutes or until milk solids begin to turn light golden brown. Add sliced garlic and cook, stirring occasionally, 2-3 minutes or until garlic is golden; do not let garlic or butter solids burn. Stir in roasted peppers and capers, then remove from heat; set aside. Sprinkle both sides of fish with salt. Place steaks on a cold broiler pan or on hot grill. Broil 4 minutes, turn and broil 6 minutes longer. If grilling, grill 6 minutes, turn and grill 4 minutes more. Transfer fish to a warmed serving platter. Reheat caper sauce over medium heat until sizzling. Stir in vinegar, remaining parsley and black pepper to taste. When hot, spoon over steaks and serve immediately.

YIELDS 4 SERVINGS

Non-reactive cookware is often called for in recipes with acidic foods which will chemically react with certain metals and produce off-flavors in foods and will even stain your pans. Enamelware, glass, stainless steel and glazed ceramic are all examples of non-reactive cookware. Aluminum, copper and cast iron are examples of reactive cookware.

LINGUINE WITH TUNA, CAPERS AND RAISINS

12	ounces linguine	½	teaspoon black pepper, or to taste
¼	cup extra virgin olive oil	2	(6-ounce) cans tuna in olive oil, undrained
1	cup chopped onions	⅓	cup drained capers
1	tablespoon finely chopped garlic	¾	cup golden raisins
½	teaspoon salt, or to taste	½	cup chopped fresh flat-leaf parsley

Cook pasta al dente in 6-8 quarts boiling salted water. Reserve 1 cup pasta water, then drain and return pasta to pot. Heat oil in a heavy 12-inch skillet over high heat until hot but not smoking. Add onion and garlic with salt and pepper and cook, stirring occasionally, until golden. Stir in reserved pasta water, undrained tuna and remaining 3 ingredients. Toss with pasta and serve.

YIELDS 4 SERVINGS

LINGUINE WITH SHRIMP SCAMPI

1	(16-ounce) package linguine	½	cup chopped fresh parsley
3	tablespoons butter		Zest of ½ lemon
2	tablespoons minced garlic	¼	cup fresh lemon juice
¼	cup olive oil	¼	lemon, sliced into thin rounds
1	pound (16/20-count) shrimp, peeled and deveined	¼	teaspoon dried red pepper flakes, or to taste
2	teaspoons kosher salt	1	tablespoon seafood seasoning, such as Old Bay
½	teaspoon black pepper		

Cook pasta al dente, drain and return to pot. Melt butter in a 12-inch skillet over low heat. Add garlic and sauté 1 minute, being careful not to burn. Add olive oil. When hot, add shrimp, salt and pepper. Sauté, stirring often, 2-5 minutes, depending on size, or until shrimp are pink and opaque. Remove from heat and stir in parsley and next 5 ingredients, blending well. Add drained pasta and toss.

YIELDS 4 SERVINGS

DID YOU KNOW?

The best quality seafood is often frozen. Quality does not improve once it leaves the water, it can only be maintained. Therefore, if high technology freezing has been employed, it may be fresher tasting than what you find at the grocery store.

A SHRIMP CAPER

- 3 tablespoons capers
- 3 tablespoons chopped shallots
- 3 garlic cloves, minced
- 3 tablespoons chopped fresh parsley
- Sea salt to taste
- Cracked black pepper to taste
- Hot pepper sauce to taste, such as Tabasco
- 1 teaspoon Worcestershire sauce
- 1 cup butter, divided
- 1 tablespoon olive oil
- 2 pounds (16/20-count) shrimp, peeled and deveined
- ¼ cup white wine
- 2 lemons, quartered
- 1 loaf crusty bread, toasted

Combine capers and next 7 ingredients in a bowl. In a large sauté pan, slowly melt ½ cup butter with olive oil. When hot, add capers mixture and sauté until shallots are translucent. Add remaining ½ cup butter. When butter starts to sizzle, add shrimp and toss to coat. Remove from heat and add wine. Return pan to heat and cook over medium heat until wine starts to reduce and shrimp are opaque. Serve shrimp in a large bowl with lemon quarters. Place pan drippings in individual bowls for dipping with crusty bread.

YIELDS 4-6 SERVINGS

Vermouth (white and red) keeps indefinitely in the refrigerator. If you do not keep wine on hand, the vermouth will always be on hand for those recipes calling for wine.

GOSPORT JUMBO CRAB CAKES

- 1 egg, lightly beaten
- 3 tablespoons mayonnaise
- 1 teaspoon Dijon mustard
- 1 teaspoon seafood seasoning, such as Old Bay or Prudhomme
- 1½ tablespoons finely chopped onions
- 1 pound jumbo lump crabmeat, checked for shells
- ¼ cup Japanese panko bread crumbs, or dried plain bread crumbs
- Canola oil or margarine for frying

Mix egg and next 4 ingredients together well. Gently mix in crabmeat and bread crumbs. Shape mixture into 4 large patties. Cover and refrigerate for at least 1 hour. Fry patties in oil or margarine over medium heat about 4-5 minutes per side. Serve with cocktail or tartar sauce.

YIELDS 4 SERVINGS

IRISH SHELLFISH DELIGHT

16	sea scallops
16	large shrimp, peeled and deveined
¼	cup olive oil
½	cup Irish Mist liqueur
1	large garlic clove, minced
6	tablespoons chopped onions
1	cup sliced mushrooms
2	cups heavy cream
	Salt and pepper to taste
2	tablespoons chopped fresh parsley
3-4	teaspoons chopped fresh tarragon
	Seafood seasoning to taste, Old Bay recommended

Pat scallops and shrimp dry with paper towels. Heat oil and liqueur in a large skillet. Sear seafood in skillet 3 minutes or until almost done, turning once. Remove from skillet and set aside. Add garlic, onions and mushrooms to same skillet and sauté until limp. Stir in cream and cook gently until reduced and slightly thickened. Season with salt and pepper. Return seafood to skillet and cook 2 minutes or until done. Stir in parsley and tarragon and season to taste with seafood seasoning. Serve over pasta, rice or fresh dark green curly leaf spinach.

YIELDS 4 SERVINGS

FLOUNDER ITALIANO

2	(4- to 5-ounce) flounder fillets
3	tablespoons bread crumbs
3	tablespoons Parmesan cheese
⅛	teaspoon chopped fresh oregano
¼	cup chopped fresh parsley
2	tablespoons chopped garlic
	Salt and pepper to taste
2-3	tablespoons olive oil
2-3	tablespoons fresh lemon juice

Preheat broiler. Place fillets on a broiler pan. Mix bread crumbs and next 4 ingredients and season with salt and pepper. Sprinkle mixture over fillets and drizzle with oil and lemon juice. Broil close to heat source 3-4 minutes on each side.

YIELDS 2 SERVINGS

CALYPSO FISH FILLETS

3	tablespoons vegetable oil, divided	1½	tablespoons Asian fish sauce
⅓	cup finely chopped shallots	1	tablespoon granulated sugar
1	(2- to 3-inch) fresh red or green chile pepper, minced, seeds removed according to desired level of heat	¼	teaspoon salt
		2	tablespoons fresh lime juice
2	large firm-ripe mangoes, peeled and ½-inch diced	4	fish fillets, such as tilapia, striped bass or mahi-mahi
			Salt and pepper to taste

Heat 2 tablespoons oil in a large nonstick skillet over medium-low heat. Add shallots and cook, stirring occasionally, 3-5 minutes or until golden. Add chile pepper and cook 1 minute or until softened. Add mangoes and next 3 ingredients and cook, stirring occasionally, 7 minutes or until mangoes are softened and mixture is slightly thickened. Remove from heat and add lime juice. Transfer salsa to a bowl and set aside. Pat fish fillets dry and season with salt and pepper. In a clean skillet, heat remaining tablespoon oil over medium-high heat until it just begins to smoke. Add fish, skin-side down and cook, turning once, until golden and just cooked through. Serve topped with salsa.

YIELDS 4 SERVINGS

Salsa is also good with chicken or pork.

EASY FOIL BAKED SALMON

6	ounces salmon fillet	¼	onion, thinly sliced
	Salt and pepper to taste		Fresh or dried dill
	Butter		Fresh lemon juice

Preheat oven to 400 degrees. Season salmon all over with salt and pepper. Place a square of foil on a baking sheet and fold up sides. Add 1 tablespoon butter to foil and melt in oven. Remove from oven and place fillet on melted butter. Top with onion slices, a pat of butter and dill. Squeeze lemon juice over all. Wrap tightly, place foil on oven rack and bake 20 minutes. Quick and easy!

YIELDS 1 SERVING

CRAB EILEEN

- 1 quart cream
- 2 ears fresh corn, roasted in husk, shucked and kernels cut off cob
- 4 ounces country ham or smoked sausage, diced size of corn kernels
- 1 medium-size sweet potato, peeled and diced small, blanched in salted water
- 1 tablespoon sherry, brandy or chardonnay
- Pinch of cayenne pepper
- Pinch of nutmeg
- Salt and pepper to taste
- 3 pounds crabmeat, jumbo or colossal, picked for shells
- 2 tablespoons chopped fresh chives
- 1 tablespoon chopped fresh parsley, tarragon or sage

Bring cream to a medium boil and reduce until thickened. Lower heat and stir in corn kernels and next 5 ingredients. Season with salt and pepper. Fold in crabmeat and cook until heated through. Add herbs just before serving. Serve with crêpes, or over buttered angel hair pasta or your favorite fish.

YIELDS 6 SERVINGS

A very versatile recipe.

CITRUS ZEST FOR FISH

- 1 teaspoon lime zest
- 3 tablespoons fresh lime juice
- 2 teaspoons grapefruit zest
- 3 tablespoons fresh grapefruit juice
- 1 teaspoon orange zest
- 3 tablespoons fresh orange juice
- ½ cup olive oil
- ½ cup thinly sliced red onions
- 2 garlic cloves, minced
- 1 fresh jalapeño pepper, seeded and minced, optional
- Salt and pepper to taste
- 4 fish fillets

Whisk together all ingredients except fish in a small bowl. Set aside half of mixture and place other half in a zip-top bag. Add fish to bag. Refrigerate 1-2 hours. When ready to cook, generously oil a grill rack and preheat grill to medium. Remove fillets from marinade, discarding marinade in bag. Grill fish, turning once, 4-5 minutes per side. Serve with reserved marinade on the side.

YIELDS 4 SERVINGS

This recipe is also good with chicken. Adjust cooking time.

CAJUN SHRIMP PASTA

- ¾ cup butter
- 2 garlic cloves, finely chopped
- ½ bunch green onions, chopped
- 2½ pounds raw shrimp, peeled and deveined
- 1½ tablespoons Cajun seasoning
- 8 ounces heavy cream
- ¼ cup sherry
- 1 pound angel hair pasta, cooked and drained
- Freshly chopped parsley for garnish

Melt butter in a large skillet over low heat. Add garlic and onions and sauté until tender. In a bowl, toss shrimp with Cajun seasoning and add to skillet. Cook 3-4 minutes or until shrimp are pink. Add cream and sherry and stir until warm. Serve sauce over pasta and garnish with parsley.

YIELDS 8 SERVINGS

BOILED SEAFOOD POT

- 1 (16-ounce) package Italian sausage links, halved or whole
- 2 pounds small red potatoes, whole or cut depending on size
- 5 onions, peeled and quartered
- Dried herb blend (equal amounts of basil, oregano and thyme)
- Salt and pepper to taste
- Seafood seasoning, such as Old Bay to taste
- 5 ears corn, fresh or frozen, halved or whole
- 1 bunch celery hearts, chopped
- 5 pounds jumbo shrimp, in shell

Place sausage, potatoes and onions in pot and sprinkle with herb blend, salt, pepper and seafood seasoning. Cover with water and bring to a rolling boil for 5 minutes. Add corn and celery, repeat seasonings and cook 10 minutes. Add shrimp, sprinkle with seasonings and cook 3-4 minutes or until shrimp are pink and opaque. Transfer to a large platter, choose what you like and enjoy.

SERVES 10

This is a crowd pleaser as well as a fun meal with family and friends.

SUNSHINE SNAPPER WITH PINEAPPLE SALSA

- 2 red snapper fillets, skin on
- ¼ cup fresh orange juice
- 1½ teaspoons olive oil
- 1½ teaspoons salt
- ¼ teaspoon freshly ground black pepper
- ¼ teaspoon paprika
- 3 garlic cloves minced

SALSA

- 1½ cups fresh pineapple, peeled, cored and quartered
- 1½ cups chopped red bell pepper
- 1½ cups chopped green bell pepper
- 1½ cups chopped yellow bell pepper
- 2 hot peppers, seeded and chopped
- ¼ cup chopped fresh cilantro
- ¼ cup chopped fresh parsley
- 1 small onion, chopped
- 3 green onions, chopped
- ¼ cup vegetable or olive oil
- ¼ teaspoon sugar
- 2 tablespoons fresh lime juice
- Salt to taste

Rinse fish and pat dry. Combine orange juice and next 5 ingredients in a zip-top bag. Add fish and seal tightly; turning to coat fish. Marinate in refrigerator 2 hours.

To make salsa, preheat oven to broil. Place pineapple in single layer on a baking pan. Broil pineapple until warm, but not brown. Remove from oven, drain and chop. Combine pineapple and all remaining salsa ingredients in large bowl; set aside.

Preheat grill and brush rack generously with oil. Remove fish from marinade. Place fish skin-side down and grill 5 minutes. Turn fish over and grill 4 minutes longer. Remove from grill. Serve with salsa.

Salsa can be covered and refrigerated up to 7 days. It is also good served over poultry, game or pork.

ITALIAN CHICKEN

- ½ (1-ounce) envelope dry Italian salad dressing mix
- ½ cup Italian seasoned bread crumbs
- ¼ cup freshly grated Parmesan cheese
- 1 teaspoon dried oregano
- ¼ cup all-purpose flour
- ¼ teaspoon garlic powder
- 6 boneless chicken breasts
- 1 egg, beaten
- Olive oil

Combine dressing mix and next 5 ingredients. Dip chicken in egg, then dredge in dry mixture. Heat olive oil in large skillet over medium heat. Add chicken and cook 3-4 minutes on each side or until golden brown.

YIELDS 6 SERVINGS

SMOKED TURKEY BREAST WITH HERB BARBECUE SAUCE

½ cup butter or margarine	1 teaspoon salt
1 garlic clove, minced	3 tablespoons brown sugar
1 medium onion, minced	Fresh ground black pepper to taste
¾ cup tarragon vinegar	1 (7- to 8-pound) turkey breast
Sprigs of fresh rosemary, thyme, marjoram and parsley, chopped, or 2 teaspoons dried herbs	

To make barbecue sauce, combine all ingredients except turkey in a small sauce pan and simmer gently for about 5 minutes.

Place turkey in a roasting pan and brush with sauce.

To grill over charcoal, cover pan loosely with a single sheet of foil and grill over medium heat for 2½ hours with grill covered. Remove foil and baste again with barbecue sauce. Add damp hickory chips to the fire and continue cooking 1 hour in covered grill, basting occasionally with sauce.

To grill with a gas grill, add about 2 teaspoons liquid smoke seasoning to sauce. Follow instructions above for charcoal grilling, adding damp hickory chips for the last hour if grill is suited for that.

To serve, slice turkey and place on platter. Add remaining barbecue sauce to roasting pan drippings dissolved in a little water and bring to a boil. Serve sauce on the side with turkey. This turkey is great for sandwiches or for dinner.

SLOW COOKER MOROCCAN CHICKEN

2 tablespoons olive oil	¼ cup honey
2 garlic cloves, crushed	1½ teaspoons cumin
1½-2 cups prepared salsa, hot or mild	1½ teaspoons cinnamon
⅔ cup water	3 boneless, skinless chicken breasts
¼ cup currants or raisins, chopped	

Combine all ingredients except chicken in a slow cooker. Add chicken. Cover and cook on low medium heat 2-3 hours or until chicken is done. Serve over rice.

YIELDS 4 SERVINGS

Halfway through cooking, add some chopped celery, carrots, apricots or apples.

HERBED CORNISH HENS

4	(1½-pound) Cornish hens	1	tablespoon chopped fresh parsley
¼	cup raspberry vinegar, divided	1	teaspoon chopped fresh thyme
1	teaspoon salt	1	tablespoon chopped fresh chives
½	teaspoon freshly ground black pepper	1	teaspoon fresh tarragon
1	tablespoon extra virgin olive oil	4	large garlic cloves, peeled and halved

Rinse and dry hens. Sprinkle 3 tablespoons vinegar on the inside and outside of hens, then sprinkle with salt and pepper. In a small bowl, combine remaining 1 tablespoon vinegar with oil and next 4 ingredients. Slip herb mixture under skin of hens and place garlic halves in hen cavities. Tie legs of each hen together with a string. Cover and refrigerate at least 1 hour or up to 24 hours. Remove hens from refrigerator and uncover 30 minutes prior to roasting. When ready to bake, preheat oven to 400 degrees. Arrange hens in a roasting pan. Bake 1 hour, covering loosely with foil after 45 minutes if skin starts to overbrown. Split each hen in half. Transfer hens to a platter. Skim fat from pan juices and serve juices on the side.

YIELDS 8 SERVINGS

GARLIC CHICKEN WITH ARTICHOKES AND SUN-DRIED TOMATOES

4	boneless, skinless chicken breasts	1	tablespoon spicy mustard
	Salt and pepper to taste	½	teaspoon dried thyme
1	teaspoon olive or vegetable oil	1	(14-ounce) can artichoke hearts, drained and halved
1	cup chicken broth		
3	garlic cloves, pressed	⅓	cup dried sun-dried tomatoes, coarsely chopped

Season chicken with salt and pepper. Heat oil in a large nonstick skillet over medium-high heat. Add chicken to skillet and brown 2-3 minutes on each side. In a medium bowl, whisk together broth and next 3 ingredients until well blended. Add artichoke hearts, tomatoes and broth mixture to chicken in skillet, making sure all tomatoes are immersed in broth. Bring to a boil. Reduce heat to low, cover and simmer 15-20 minutes or until chicken is cooked through. Remove chicken to a serving platter. Boil sauce 2 minutes longer and pour over chicken. Serve with rice or pasta.

YIELDS 4 SERVINGS

MEAT, SEAFOOD & POULTRY

SHERRY-HONEY GLAZED CHICKEN

- ½ cup dry sherry
- ⅓ cup honey
- 1 teaspoon cinnamon
- 2 tablespoons vegetable oil
- 2 tablespoons lemon juice
- 1 teaspoon salt
- 1 (3½- to 4-pound) chicken, cut up

Preheat oven to 350 degrees. Blend together all ingredients except chicken. Pour mixture over chicken, cover and marinate overnight in refrigerator. Bake 1 hour or until browned meat juices run clear when pierced with a fork. This is also good cooked on a grill.

YIELDS 6 SERVINGS

To pre-season a chicken, dissolve 1-cup kosher salt in 2-quarts water. Submerge whole or cut up chicken for 30 minutes. A great flavor enhancer! Don't try this formula with chicken tenders.

ZESTY LEMON CHICKEN

- 2 large boneless, skinless chicken breasts
- ¾ cup flour
- Salt and pepper to taste
- 3 tablespoons butter
- 3 tablespoons vegetable oil
- Juice and zest of 1 lemon
- ½ cup white wine or vermouth
- ½-¾ cup chicken broth
- 1 tablespoon capers, drained
- ½ cup chopped mushrooms, optional
- Chopped parsley for garnish
- Lemon slices for garnish

Cut chicken into strips; this is easier if partially frozen. Mix flour, salt and pepper in a bag. Coat strips, a few at a time, in seasoned flour. Shake off excess and place on a plate, in a single layer. Heat butter and oil in a heavy saucepan until foamy. In batches, sauté chicken strips very quickly, about 30 seconds on each side, then remove; do not overcrowd pan or overcook, chicken will finish cooking later. Sprinkle each batch with lemon zest. Deglaze pan with wine. Add broth and cook until liquid is reduced by half. Return chicken to pan and add capers, lemon juice and mushrooms. Reheat very slowly. Garnish with parsley and lemon slices.

YIELDS 4 SERVINGS

GREEK QUESADILLAS

4	(7- to 8-inch) flour tortillas	¼	cup cherry or grape tomatoes, halved
1	cup shredded roasted chicken	¼	cup pitted kalamata olives, halved
½	cup crumbled feta cheese	2	tablespoons whole flat-leaf Italian parsley
¼	cup thinly sliced red onions	1	tablespoon chopped fresh oregano
¼	cup chopped cucumbers	¼	cup vinaigrette dressing of choice

Coat one side of each tortilla with cooking spray. Place tortilla, sprayed-side down, on wax paper. Sprinkle with chicken and next 7 ingredients. Drizzle dressing over top and fold in half, pressing gently. Heat a large skillet over medium heat. Cook two at a time, 2-3 minutes per side or until light brown and heated through; may be kept warm in oven until ready to serve.

YIELDS 4 SERVINGS

Speed preparation by using deli rotisserie chicken or canned chicken breast chunks.

MEXICANO CHICKEN

1	tablespoon salt	4	tablespoons butter, melted
½	tablespoon black pepper	¼	teaspoon dried marjoram
2	tablespoons chili powder	1	cup sliced onions
½	teaspoon dried oregano	½	cup pimento-stuffed green olives
½	cup all-purpose flour	1	cup red wine, such as port or claret
4	boneless, skinless chicken breast halves	½	cup broken pecans or almonds

Preheat oven to 350 degrees. Combine salt and next 4 ingredients in a zip-top bag. Add chicken and toss to coat. Place chicken in a greased 9x13-inch baking dish. Pour melted butter over chicken. Bake 25-30 minutes. Remove from oven and sprinkle with marjoram. Top with onions, olives and wine. Bake 20-25 minutes longer. Before serving, scatter nuts on top. Serve over egg noodles.

YIELDS 4 SERVINGS

"This is a family favorite originally given to me by my mother. Delicious as a leftover!"

Never stuff a turkey before you are ready to cook it. It can harbor bacteria that is never fully cooked and killed. Always remove all stuffing after the turkey has rested before carving for the same reason.

CREAMY CHICKEN ENCHILADAS

- 4 large boneless, skinless chicken breasts
- 4 cups fresh spinach, or 5 ounces frozen chopped, thawed and drained
- 2 green onions, chopped
- ¼ cup chopped onions
- 1 (10¾-ounce) can cream of chicken soup
- 1⅓ soup cans sour cream
- ¼ teaspoon salt
- ¼ teaspoon black pepper
- ¼ teaspoon dried red pepper flakes
- 1 (4-ounce) can diced green chiles, drained
- 6 (7-inch) flour tortillas
- ⅓ cup shredded Monterey Jack cheese
- Salsa or chopped fresh tomatoes for garnish

Preheat oven to 350 degrees. Place chicken in a 3-quart saucepan with enough water to cover. Bring to a boil. Reduce heat and simmer, covered, 10-15 minutes. Remove chicken from pan and cool. Place fresh spinach in a steamer basket over boiling water. Reduce heat and steam, covered, 3-5 minutes; drain well. Shred chicken with a fork. Combine chicken, spinach and onions in a bowl. In a separate bowl, blend together soup and next 5 ingredients. Divide mixture into 2 equal portions. Mix 1 portion with chicken mixture; set other portion aside. Spoon equal amounts of chicken mixture on each tortilla, spreading 1 inch from edge. Roll tortillas and place, seam-side down, in a lightly greased 2-quart baking dish. Spoon reserved cream mixture over tortillas. Bake, uncovered, 20-25 minutes or until heated through. Remove from oven and sprinkle with cheese. Let stand 5 minutes. Garnish with your favorite salsa or chopped tomatoes.

YIELDS 4 SERVINGS

To prepare ahead, cover filled tortillas and refrigerate up to 24 hours. Store sauce separately. Before baking, spoon sauce over tortillas. Add 10-15 minutes to baking time.

KICKIN' CHICKEN CURRY

- 1 large white onion, medium diced
- 2-3 tablespoons olive oil
- 1 (14½-ounce) can petite-diced tomatoes, undrained
- 1 (15-ounce) can LeSueur peas, undrained, or frozen
- Curry paste to taste, such as Patak's
- 1 (3-pound) whole chicken, cooked on the bone
- Chicken broth as needed

In a large soup pot, sauté onion in oil until soft. Add tomatoes and peas with liquids, then season with curry paste. Remove skin and bones from cooked chicken and cut meat into bite-size pieces. Add chicken to pot and simmer until chicken is heated through; be careful not to over-stir or chicken will shred and thicken the dish. If needed, thin with chicken broth. Serve with Basmati or jasmine rice.

YIELDS 4 SERVINGS

CHICKEN SATAY

½ cup finely ground or pulverized unsalted or lightly salted peanuts	3 Thai chiles or small hot peppers, minced, or canned jalapeño peppers
½ cup unrefined peanut oil	Zest of 1 lime
1½ tablespoons fish sauce	3 large boneless, skinless chicken breasts
3 tablespoons raw cane sugar or firmly packed brown sugar	Juice of 1 lime
1 medium-size white onion, minced	1 tablespoon yellow turmeric
9 large garlic cloves, minced	1 (13½-ounce) can coconut milk, shaken

For marinade, combine peanuts and next 7 ingredients in a bowl, blending well. Cut chicken into 1- to 1½-inch lengthwise strips. Add chicken to marinade, making sure meat is well coated. Cover bowl or transfer all to a zip-top bag and refrigerate 1-3 hours, or overnight. In a shallow dish, soak 9 bamboo skewers in lime juice or water for 30 minutes; this keeps skewers from burning on the grill. Once marinated, thread chicken onto skewers and return to refrigerator. When ready to cook, preheat grill to hot and oil top rack. Cook chicken, covered, 1 minute. Carefully turn skewers and, if using a gas grill, reduce heat. If using a charcoal grill, test early and often. Cook 3-5 minutes total and transfer to a serving plate; do not overcook. For sauce, pour remaining marinade into a medium saucepan and stir in turmeric. Add half of shaken coconut milk to pan and boil 1 minute. Reduce heat and keep warm. Just before serving, add remaining coconut milk. Remove chicken strips from skewers and serve. Especially tasty served over saffron rice and drizzled with sauce.

YIELDS 4-6 SERVINGS

This recipe is also a great appetizer. Cut chicken strips into smaller pieces and serve on skewers with sauce for dipping.

Always soak wooden skewers in water 30 minutes before using to prevent them from burning.

CHICKEN IN SHERRY CREAM SAUCE

¼	cup all-purpose flour	¼	cup cornstarch
2½	teaspoons salt	3	cups half-and-half, divided
1	teaspoon paprika	½	cup sherry
12	boneless, skinless chicken breasts	1	cup shredded Swiss cheese
½	cup butter	½	cup chopped fresh parsley
⅓	cup chicken broth		

Preheat oven to 350 degrees. Combine flour, salt and paprika in a shallow dish. Coat chicken breasts with flour mixture. Melt butter in a large skillet. Add chicken and cook until lightly browned. Add broth and simmer, covered, 15-20 minutes or until chicken is almost tender. If pan becomes too dry, add more broth. Arrange chicken in a greased 9x13-inch baking dish. Mix cornstarch with ¼ cup half-and-half and add to same skillet, stirring well. Cook over low heat, gradually adding remaining cream, until mixture thickens. Blend in sherry. Pour sauce over chicken and bake, covered, 20-25 minutes. Uncover and sprinkle with cheese and parsley. Bake, uncovered, until cheese bubbles.

YIELDS 12 SERVINGS

This dish may be frozen after adding sauce. Thaw and bring to room temperature before baking.

BLACK BEAN AND CHICKEN QUESADILLA

1	(15-ounce) can black beans, rinsed and drained	1½	teaspoons chili powder
		8	(6-inch) flour tortillas
2	(5-ounce) cans chunk chicken breast, drained	1	(8-ounce) package shredded Mexican blend cheese
¾	cup salsa		Sour cream

Combine beans and next 3 ingredients in a medium bowl and stir to mix well. Cover and refrigerate overnight. When ready to cook, preheat oven to 400 degrees. Coat a large baking sheet with cooking spray and place 4 tortillas on sheet. Spread bean mixture over each tortilla and sprinkle evenly with cheese. Top with remaining 4 tortillas and coat tops with cooking spray. Bake 10-12 minutes or until cheese is melted. Cut each in half, if desired, and serve with sour cream.

YIELDS 4 QUESADILLAS

CHICKEN LETTUCE WRAPS

STIR-FRY SAUCE
- ¼ cup granulated sugar
- ½ cup water
- 2 tablespoons light soy sauce
- 2 tablespoons rice wine vinegar
- 2 tablespoons catsup
- 1 tablespoon lemon juice
- ⅛ teaspoon sesame oil
- 1 teaspoon cornstarch

HOT SAUCE
- 2 teaspoons very hot water
- 2 teaspoons minced garlic
- 1 teaspoon dried red pepper flakes

STIR-FRY
- 2 tablespoons light soy sauce
- 2 tablespoons firmly packed brown sugar
- ½ teaspoon rice wine vinegar
- 3 tablespoons sesame oil
- 2 boneless, skinless chicken breasts
- 3 tablespoons chopped onions
- 1 (8-ounce) can water chestnuts, drained and coarsely chopped
- ⅔ cup coarsely chopped mushrooms
- 1 teaspoon minced garlic
- 2-3 leaves iceberg lettuce, separated

Stir together all stir-fry sauce ingredients in a small bowl until sugar dissolves; set aside. Combine hot sauce ingredients; set aside. To make stir fry, combine soy sauce, brown sugar and vinegar in a small bowl; set aside. Heat sesame oil in a skillet over medium heat. Add chicken and sauté 4-5 minutes, turning once. Cool and cut into small bite-size pieces. In a bowl, combine chicken, onions and next 3 ingredients. Reheat skillet over medium-high heat, adding more oil if needed. Add chicken and stir-fry sauce to skillet and stir until heated through. Adjust flavor by adding brown sugar mixture to taste. Spoon chicken mixture into center of each lettuce leaf. Drizzle with hot sauce and roll up.

YIELDS 2-3 SERVINGS

Raw meat is easier to cut for stir-fry or other recipes when partially frozen.

PENNE PASTA WITH CHICKEN AND TOMATOES

4 chicken breasts	1 tablespoon all-purpose flour
¼ cup dry white wine	⅛ teaspoon dried red pepper flakes
1 tablespoon Italian seasoning	1 (12-ounce) can evaporated skim milk
3 tablespoons chopped shallots	1 (14½-ounce) can diced tomatoes, drained
1¼ cups chopped mushrooms	1 tablespoon chopped fresh basil
½ cup fresh or frozen peas	1 (16-ounce) package penne pasta, cooked and drained
2-3 teaspoons extra virgin olive oil	
5 garlic cloves, minced	10 black olives, thinly sliced, for garnish

Preheat oven to 350 degrees. Combine chicken and wine in a lightly greased 9x13-inch shallow baking dish. Sprinkle with Italian seasoning. Bake 15-20 minutes. Remove chicken and pour cooking juices into a large skillet. When cool, shred chicken and set aside. Add shallots, mushrooms and peas to pan juices and sauté until liquid is absorbed and vegetables are tender. Remove skillet from heat and cover. Place a medium saucepan over medium heat for 1 minute. Add olive oil to coat bottom of pan. Add garlic, flour and pepper flakes. Blend in milk, whisking constantly. Bring to a boil and cook 5 minutes. When thickened, add diced tomatoes and basil. Add milk mixture and chicken to skillet with sautéed vegetables. Serve over pasta, garnished with olives.

YIELDS 4 SERVINGS

POLYNESIAN CHICKEN

4 tablespoons butter	1 onion, sliced
½ cup all-purpose flour	½-1 cup pimento-stuffed olives
Salt and pepper to taste	1 pound (41-60 count) shrimp, peeled and deveined
6-8 boneless chicken breasts	
1 (20-ounce) can pineapple chunks, juice reserved	1 (10¾-ounce) can condensed tomato soup
1 green bell pepper, sliced	¼ cup chili sauce

Preheat oven to 375 degrees. Melt butter in a greased 9x13-inch baking dish. Combine flour and salt and pepper in a separate dish or zip-top bag. Coat chicken in flour mixture and place in baking dish. Bake 25-30 minutes. Remove baking dish from oven and turn chicken over. Place pineapple chunks on top of chicken. Top with bell peppers, onions, olives and reserved pineapple juice, reserving ¼ cup of juice. Bake 15 minutes longer. Chicken can be prepared ahead up to this point. Place shrimp over chicken. Combine soup, chili sauce and reserved ¼ cup pineapple juice. Mix well and pour sauce over chicken dish. Cover with foil and bake 15-20 minutes or until shrimp are done. Serve with rice.

YIELDS 6-8 SERVINGS

SOUTHWESTERN PIZZA

- 1 (10-ounce) baked pizza crust
- 1¼ cups fresh or prepared salsa, drained
- 1¾ cups shredded sharp Cheddar cheese
- ¾ teaspoon ground cumin
- 1½ cups shredded cooked chicken
- ½ cup thinly sliced red onions, quartered
- 2 large jalapeño chiles, seeded and chopped, or 1 (4-ounce) can diced green chiles, drained
- ⅓ cup frozen corn kernels, thawed
- ½ cup chopped cilantro or parsley

Preheat oven to 425 degrees. Place pizza crust on a rimless baking sheet. Spread half of salsa over crust, leaving a ¾-inch border around edge. Place cheese in a bowl and toss well with cumin. Layer 1 cup cheese on salsa. Add chicken and onion layers. Scatter chiles, then half the corn and half the cilantro over onions. Top with remaining salsa, corn, cheese and cilantro. Bake 12-15 minutes or until crust is crisp and topping is heated through.

YIELDS 8 SLICES

Substitute cooked, crumbled Italian sausage for the chicken.

CROCKPOT LEMON CHICKEN TAGINE

- 4 boneless, skinless chicken breasts, cut into strips
- 1 large onion, chopped
- 3 carrots, chopped
- 3 stalks celery, chopped
- 1-2 yellow squash, seeded and chopped
- 1 cup chicken broth
- 1 cup dry white wine
- ¼ cup fresh lemon juice
- 1 teaspoon ground cumin
- ½ teaspoon turmeric
- ½ teaspoon ground ginger
- ¼ teaspoon saffron
- 1 pinch cayenne pepper
- 1 (16-ounce) can garbanzo beans
- ¼ cup chopped flat-leaf parsley
- ¼ cup chopped cilantro
- Hot picante sauce, such as Tapatio, to taste

Combine chicken and next 12 ingredients in a crockpot. Cook on high for 2½ hours. Remove lid; add beans and parsley, continue cooking for 30 minutes. Just before serving, stir in cilantro. Serve over couscous or rice, with hot sauce on the side.

YIELDS 10 SERVINGS

DIPPING SAUCE FOR CHICKEN OR PORK

½	cup water	3	tablespoons fresh orange juice
3	tablespoons red wine vinegar	1	tablespoon catsup
½	cup thinly sliced green onions	2	teaspoons unsulfured molasses
1	tablespoon minced peeled fresh ginger	½	tablespoon Oriental sesame oil
4	teaspoons sugar	1	tablespoon cornstarch, dissolved in ¼ cup cold water
2	tablespoons soy sauce		

In a saucepan, stir together water and next 4 ingredients. Bring to a boil and simmer, covered, for 5 minutes. Stir in soy sauce and next 4 ingredients. Stir cornstarch mixture and add to sauce. Simmer and stir 2 minutes. Chill, covered, about 20 minutes. May be made 2-3 days ahead. Serve with any prepared chicken or pork.

YIELDS 1¼ CUPS

"I took this with chicken nuggets for a picnic at Wolftrap. Delicious and easy to serve."

FAST AND EASY CHICKEN WITH PEPPERS

4	boneless, skinless chicken breasts	1	medium onion, thinly sliced
	Salt and pepper to taste	4	large garlic cloves, minced
2	tablespoons olive oil, divided	3	tablespoons balsamic vinegar
2	tablespoons butter, divided	¼	cup chopped fresh basil, divided
4	cups thinly sliced bell peppers (mix any colors)	½	cup thinly sliced fresh mushrooms

Season chicken with salt and pepper. Heat 1 tablespoon each oil and butter in a large skillet over medium heat. Sauté chicken 6-8 minutes total or until golden on both sides, turning once. Remove chicken to a plate. Add remaining oil and butter to skillet and sauté peppers and onions until al dente. Add garlic and cook, stirring, about 1 minute. Stir in vinegar and 2 tablespoons basil. Reduce heat to medium-low and return chicken with any accumulated juices to skillet. Add mushrooms and simmer 2-3 minutes or until chicken is cooked through. Stir in remaining 2 tablespoons basil.

YIELDS 4 SERVINGS

CHICKEN BOURSIN WITH SPINACH AND PROSCIUTTO

- 6 slices lean prosciutto
- 6 boneless, skinless chicken breasts, pounded to ½-inch thick
- 1 (5-ounce) bag baby spinach, cleaned, dried and stems removed
- 1 (5.2-ounce) package Boursin cheese
- 2 eggs, lightly beaten with 1 tablespoon water
- 1½ cups packaged bread crumbs or panko bread crumbs
- 4 tablespoons butter, melted

SAUCE
- 1 cup half-and-half
- 1 (5.2-ounce) package Boursin cheese

Preheat oven to 350 degrees. Line a baking pan with greased foil for easy cleanup. Place a slice of prosciutto on each chicken breast and cover with spinach. Divide cheese into six equal parts and place a piece at the end of each breast. Roll breast tightly and secure with toothpicks. Dip each chicken breast into egg mixture and then roll in bread crumbs, covering completely. Brush each with melted butter. Bake about 30-35 minutes, depending on size of breasts; do not overcook.

For sauce, heat half-and-half in a small saucepan over medium heat. Crumble in cheese and stir until cheese is melted and sauce is hot; do not scorch. Spoon sauce over chicken breasts and serve.

YIELDS 6 SERVINGS

GRILLED CHICKEN WITH ROSEMARY MUSTARD CREAM

- 4 teaspoons whole-grain Dijon mustard, divided
- 1 tablespoon olive oil
- 1 teaspoon chopped fresh rosemary
- ¼ teaspoon salt
- ¼ teaspoon black pepper
- 4 (6-ounce) boneless, skinless chicken breasts
- 3 tablespoons light mayonnaise
- 1 tablespoon dry white wine or water
- Rosemary sprigs, optional

Preheat grill and coat grill rack with cooking spray. Combine 1 teaspoon mustard, olive oil and the next 3 ingredients in a small bowl. Brush mixture over chicken. Grill chicken 6 minutes on each side or until done. Combine remaining 3 teaspoons mustard, mayonnaise and wine in a bowl. Serve mayonnaise mixture over chicken. Garnish with rosemary sprigs.

YIELDS 4 SERVING

DRY RUB CHICKEN WITH SPICY PEACH CHUTNEY

- 1 tablespoon black pepper
- 1 tablespoon white pepper
- 1 tablespoon sugar
- 2 teaspoons cayenne pepper
- 2 tablespoons chili powder
- 1 tablespoon ground cumin
- 1 tablespoon garlic powder
- 1 tablespoon brown sugar
- 1 tablespoon ground oregano
- ¼ cup paprika (the sweet kind — not the hot kind)
- 1 teaspoon dry mustard
- 1 tablespoon celery salt
- 1 tablespoon salt

Thoroughly combine all ingredients in a bowl. Rub mixture into chicken, wrap tightly with plastic wrap and refrigerate 8 hours or overnight. Store leftover mixture in an airtight jar or in freezer.

When ready to bake, preheat oven to 350 degrees. Bake 30 minutes or cook on a grill. Serve with Spicy Peach Chutney.

SPICY PEACH CHUTNEY

- 1 tablespoon dried red pepper flakes, or to taste
- 2 pounds peaches, peeled and chopped
- 2 cups garlic herb vinegar
- 1¼ cups brown sugar
- ¼ cup fresh lemon juice
- 1 medium onion, minced
- ½ cup golden raisins
- 2 teaspoons yellow mustard seeds
- 1 teaspoon ground ginger
- 1 teaspoon ground cinnamon
- ¼ teaspoon ground allspice

Combine all ingredients in 4-quart saucepan and bring to a boil. Reduce heat to low and simmer, stirring occasionally, for 45 minutes or until mixture thickens. Skim off any foam that forms. Serve warm or cold. May also be served with fish or pork.

YIELDS 4 CUPS

SUPER GRILLED CHICKEN FOR TWO

- 1 (0.7-ounce) package dry Good Season's Italian dressing mix
- 1½-2 tablespoons teriyaki sauce, recommend La Choy sauce and marinade
- Dried red pepper flakes to taste, optional
- 2 boneless, skinless chicken breasts

Prepare dressing mix according to package directions. Add teriyaki sauce to taste and shake or whisk to blend well. Blend in pepper flakes. Pierce chicken with a fork and place in zip-top bag with of ½ cup marinade mixture, reserving remaining marinade for serving. Refrigerate 8 hours or overnight, turning bag occasionally.

When ready to cook, preheat grill. Grill 3-4 minutes per side or until just cooked through; do not overcook. Let rest 5 minutes and slice across the grain. Serve over pasta or rice and drizzle with reserved marinade.

YIELDS 2 SERVINGS

Pasta & Rice

PORTSMOUTH NAVAL SHIPYARD MUSEUM

Founded on the grounds of the Norfolk Naval Shipyard in Portsmouth in 1949, the Naval Shipyard Museum was moved in 1963 to its present location on the waterfront at High Street Landing. The museum's exhibits relate the history of America's oldest naval shipyard and the city of Portsmouth, and how closely the two have been entwined. The artifacts, an extensive collection of books and other naval related publications housed there make the Naval Shipyard Museum a nationally known resource for naval historians and researchers.

DID YOU KNOW?

The building which houses this museum was originally the maintenance shop for the ferries which crossed the Elizabeth River from Portsmouth's High Street to downtown Norfolk.

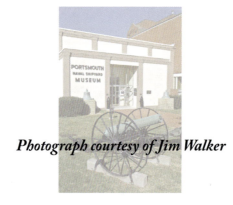

Photograph courtesy of Jim Walker

PASTA & RICE

LINGUINE WITH WHITE CLAM SAUCE

- 4 tablespoons butter
- 3 garlic cloves, minced
- 2 tablespoons chopped onions
- 1 (6½-ounce) can clams, undrained
- 3 ounces cream cheese, softened
- 2-3 tablespoons chopped fresh parsley
- ¼-⅓ cup white wine, optional
- Seafood seasoning to taste, such as Old Bay, optional
- Salt and pepper to taste
- 8 ounces linguine, cooked al dente and drained

Melt butter in a shallow pan over medium-low heat. Add garlic and onions and sauté until onions are softened. Add clams with juice and stir to blend. Whisk in cream cheese until smooth. Stir in parsley. Add wine and boil until sauce thickens. Season with seafood seasoning and salt and pepper to taste. Serve over linguine.

YIELDS 2-4 SERVINGS

CREAMY ITALIAN TOSS

- 1¼ cups mayonnaise
- 1 teaspoon prepared mustard
- 1 tablespoon red wine vinegar
- 1 garlic clove, minced
- ⅛ teaspoon dried oregano
- ⅛ teaspoon dried basil
- ⅛ teaspoon herb garlic seasoning
- Chopped fresh parsley to taste
- Cayenne pepper to taste, optional
- Salt and pepper to taste
- 1 pound thin spaghetti, broken into thirds
- 1 cup grape tomatoes, quartered
- 1 cup slivered unpeeled zucchini (see below)
- 1½ cups chopped mixed green, yellow and orange bell peppers
- ¼ cup chopped green onions
- Sliced pepperoni to taste

Mix mayonnaise and next 9 ingredients in a container; cover and refrigerate overnight. Cook pasta according to package directions; drain and cool slightly. Blend mayonnaise mixture into pasta. Refrigerate until ready to serve, or proceed. Toss pasta with tomatoes and remaining 4 ingredients. Serve immediately.

YIELDS 8-10 SERVINGS

To sliver zucchini, slice into ⅛-inch thick circles, stack and cut matchstick style.

Turn a pasta side or salad into an entrée by adding one of the following: Chicken, ham, smoked salmon, tuna or turkey.

HEART OF THE HARBOR

BELLISIMO! SPAGHETTI SAUCE

1 tablespoon butter	1 tablespoon tomato paste
1 tablespoon olive oil	1 cup dry white wine
5 garlic cloves, pressed	2 (14-ounce) cans diced Italian tomatoes, undrained
3 ounces thinly sliced bacon, finely chopped	1½ cups chicken broth
1 large carrot, finely diced	3 tablespoons chopped fresh parsley, divided
1 medium-large onion, finely diced	3 tablespoons chopped fresh basil, divided
2 stalks celery, finely diced	Salt and freshly ground black pepper
1 pound coarsely ground beef chuck	1 pound spaghetti
1 pound coarsely ground pork	¼ cup heavy cream
4 ounces sweet Italian sausage, casing removed	Freshly grated Parmesan cheese

Melt butter with oil in a large skillet. Add garlic and next 4 ingredients and cook over low heat 5-7 minutes or until onions are softened. Add beef, pork and sausage. Cook until done, crumbling into small pieces. Blend in tomato paste. Add wine and stir 3-4 minutes. Add tomatoes with juice, broth and 1 tablespoon each parsley and basil. Bring to a boil. Reduce heat to low and season with salt and pepper. Simmer, stirring occasionally, 1 hour, 30 minutes. Sauce should be very thick. Cook spaghetti according to package directions; drain and return to pot. Add cream to meat sauce along with remaining parsley and basil. Stir to blend and adjust seasoning as needed. Add 2-3 cups meat sauce to spaghetti and toss. Pour spaghetti into a large bowl. Top with remaining meat sauce and sprinkle with Parmesan cheese. Leftovers may be refrigerated several days.

YIELDS 6-8 SERVINGS

Check with your butcher regarding ground pork; some require a day or two notice as the grinder has to be cleaned each time a different meat is ground.

EASY RICE OR ORZO CASSEROLE

6 tablespoons margarine or butter	1 (6- to 7-ounce) can sliced mushrooms, drained
1 cup rice or orzo	1 (8-ounce) can sliced water chestnuts, drained
1 (10½-ounce) can condensed French onion soup	
1 cup water	

Preheat oven to 350 degrees. Melt margarine in a 1½- to 2-quart dish. Add rice and remaining 4 ingredients. Stir to mix and cover dish. Bake 1 hour.

YIELDS 6-8 SERVINGS

GREEK ORZO AND BROCCOLI

¾ cup orzo	4½ teaspoons chopped walnuts
2 cups fresh broccoli florets	1 tablespoon olive oil
¼ cup crumbled feta cheese	¼ teaspoon dried red pepper flakes
¼ cup shaved Parmesan cheese	¼ teaspoon black pepper
2 tablespoons minced fresh basil	

Cook orzo in a large saucepan in boiling water 7 minutes. Add broccoli and cook 2-3 minutes longer or until pasta is tender; drain. In a small bowl, combine feta, Parmesan and basil; set aside. Sauté walnuts in oil 1 minute in a small, nonstick skillet. Stir in pepper flakes and black pepper and cook and stir 1 minute. Pour walnuts over pasta mixture and toss well. Stir in cheese mixture and toss to coat.

YIELDS 4 SERVINGS

PORTSIDE MAC 'N CHEESE

1 (16-ounce) package penne pasta, cooked and drained	1½ tablespoons olive oil
8 ounces shredded sharp Cheddar cheese	1 cup chopped onions
½ cup shredded Parmesan cheese	1 cup milk
½ cup shredded Asiago cheese	1 cup sour cream
3 cups baby spinach leaves, chopped	¼ cup coarse ground mustard
½ cup seeded and chopped tomatoes	1 egg
1½ tablespoons butter	½ teaspoon black pepper

Preheat oven to 350 degrees. In a very large bowl, combine pasta and next 5 ingredients; set aside. Melt butter with oil over medium heat in a pan. Add onions and sauté just until softened. In a separate bowl, whisk together milk and next 3 ingredients. Blend in pepper and onions. Pour sauce over pasta mixture and blend. Spoon mixture into a 9x13-inch baking dish. Bake, uncovered, 20-25 minutes or until heated through.

YIELDS 12 SERVINGS

For a cheesier flavor, top with extra cheese of your choice and return to oven until melted.

ORANGE-CRANBERRY RICE PILAF

3	tablespoons unsalted butter		1	bay leaf
1	onion, minced		½	cup dried sweetened cranberries, finely chopped
½	teaspoon salt		6	green onions, finely chopped
1½	cups long grain rice			Freshly ground black pepper to taste
1¾	cups chicken broth		½	cup pine nuts, toasted, optional
3	wide strips orange zest			
½	cup fresh orange juice			

Melt butter in a large saucepan over medium-high heat. Add onions and salt and cook 3 minutes or until softened. Add rice and cook, stirring occasionally, 3 minutes or until rice is translucent. Stir in broth and next 3 ingredients and bring to a boil. Cover, reduce heat to low and cook 20 minutes or until liquid has been absorbed and rice is tender. Remove from heat. Sprinkle cranberries and green onions over rice, cover and let stand 10 minutes longer. Discard bay leaf and orange zest. Fluff rice with a fork. Season to taste with pepper and salt and sprinkle pine nuts on top.

YIELDS 4-6 SERVINGS

Toast pine nuts on a baking sheet at 350 degrees 3-5 minutes, checking often.

ORZO WITH CARAMELIZED ONIONS AND ASIAGO

6-7	cups chicken or vegetable stock			Kosher salt and freshly ground black pepper to taste
1	tablespoon unsalted butter		3	cups orzo
1	tablespoon extra virgin olive oil		1½	cups grated Asiago cheese
1	large sweet onion, coarsely chopped		1	cup chopped fresh cilantro or parsley

Bring stock to a boil in a saucepan. In a large skillet over medium heat, melt butter with oil. Add onions and sauté 5 minutes or until translucent. Season lightly with salt and pepper. Add orzo and cook and stir until lightly browned. Gradually ladle stock into skillet and bring to a boil. Turn off heat, cover and let stand 20 minutes; the orzo should absorb the liquid. If any liquid remains, cook over low heat until absorbed. Add cheese and cilantro, reserving a small amount of cilantro for garnish. Stir constantly until cheese is melted. Garnish with cilantro and serve hot.

YIELDS 8-10 SERVINGS

PASTA WITH CREAMY TUSCAN TOMATO SAUCE

¾-1	pound penne pasta, or pasta of choice	½	cup oil-packed sun-dried tomatoes, finely chopped
5	slices bacon, finely chopped	1	teaspoon dried basil
1	medium onion, finely chopped	½	cup sliced black olives
2	large garlic cloves, minced	½	cup finely grated Parmesan cheese
¼	teaspoon salt		
¼	teaspoon black pepper		
1	cup heavy cream		

Prepare pasta according to package directions; drain, reserving 1 cup pasta water. Cook bacon in a large skillet over medium-low heat, stirring occasionally, 8-10 minutes or until brown. Remove bacon to paper towel to drain, reserving 2 tablespoons fat in skillet. Add onions and next 3 ingredients to skillet and cook until onions are soft and light brown. Crumble bacon and add to skillet along with cream and next 3 ingredients. Simmer until cream is slightly thickened. Add pasta and Parmesan cheese, tossing to coat. Blend in enough reserved pasta water, if needed, to bring to desired consistency.

YIELDS 4-6 SERVINGS

PASTA WITH SPINACH AND TOMATOES

1	pound penne or fettuccini pasta	4	large garlic cloves, chopped
1	pound fresh spinach, washed and drained		Salt and pepper to taste
8	tomatoes, peeled and seeded		Freshly shredded or grated Parmesan cheese
½	cup olive oil		

Cook pasta according to package directions; drain. Cut spinach and tomatoes into narrow strips and set aside. Heat oil in a large skillet. Add garlic and sauté until pale golden. Add spinach and salt and pepper. Cook and stir over low heat for a few minutes. Add tomatoes, reduce heat and simmer, stirring occasionally, about 25 minutes. Toss with cooked pasta and serve with Parmesan cheese.

YIELDS 8 SERVINGS

LINGUINE AND SUN-DRIED TOMATOES

1	(6½-ounce) jar sun-dried tomatoes packed in oil	2-3	ounces fresh basil, coarsely chopped
3	carrots, peeled and diced ¼-inch		Salt to taste
4	large garlic cloves, minced	⅓	teaspoon pepper
2	medium or large shallots, finely chopped	¾	pound linguine, cooked according to package directions
¼	cup dry white wine	3-4	ounces finely shredded Parmesan cheese

Drain oil from tomatoes and pour into large skillet. Cut tomatoes in half or quarters. Cook carrots in boiling salted water until crisp tender and drain immediately, rinsing with cold water to stop cooking. Set aside. Heat oil in skillet over low heat and sauté garlic and shallots, slowly, until soft. Add wine and continue cooking on medium-low until reduced by ⅓. Reduce heat to low and add sun-dried tomatoes and basil. Stir in salt and pepper and simmer about 5 minutes. Add carrots and linguine. Toss with Parmesan cheese. Serve and pass the Parmesan cheese.

YIELDS 2-3 SERVINGS

PRIMO POLENTA

1½	cups unsalted chicken broth	½	cup and 2 tablespoons polenta, not the instant kind
1½	cups heavy cream	¼	cup freshly grated Parmesan cheese
⅛	teaspoon freshly ground nutmeg	¼	cup freshly grated fontina cheese
¼	teaspoon white pepper		

In a saucepan bring broth and cream to a boil; add seasonings and stir. While simmering, add polenta and continue to stir until polenta pulls away from sides of pan. Add grated cheeses and stir until thoroughly melted and combined.

YIELDS 6-8 SERVINGS

PASTA & RICE

RAISIN RICE WITH CURRY

¼ cup chopped onions	1 cup instant rice
3 tablespoons butter, melted	¼ cup raisins
1¼ cups water	½ teaspoon curry powder
1 cube chicken bouillon	

Sauté onions in butter in a saucepan until tender. Add water and bouillon cube and bring to a boil. Stir in rice, raisins and curry. Return to a boil. Cover, remove from heat and let stand 8-10 minutes.

YIELDS 4-6 SERVINGS

SPAGHETTI WITH PORTOBELLOS, SAGE AND WALNUTS

12 ounces spaghetti	Kosher salt and freshly ground black pepper to taste
3 large Portobello mushroom caps, gills removed	⅔ cup loosely packed fresh sage leaves
3 tablespoons extra virgin olive oil	⅓ cup coarsely chopped walnuts, toasted
½ cup unsalted butter	½ cup freshly grated Parmigiano-Reggiano cheese

Bring a large pot of salted water to a boil. Add spaghetti and cook 9 minutes or until al dente. Drain, reserving 1 cup pasta water; set pasta and reserved water aside. Thinly slice mushrooms and cut into 2-inch lengths. Heat oil and 2 tablespoons butter in a 12-inch skillet until butter melts. Add mushrooms and season with salt and pepper. Cook over medium heat, stirring occasionally, 4-5 minutes or until brown and tender. Transfer mushrooms to a bowl and set aside. In same skillet, melt remaining 6 tablespoons butter over medium heat. Add sage leaves and cook, stirring occasionally, 3-5 minutes or until dark and crisp. Return mushrooms to skillet along with walnuts, pasta and ½ cup reserved pasta water. Toss continuously 1-2 minutes until pasta is well coated and moist, adding more pasta water as needed. If skillet isn't large enough, toss in pasta pot. Season with salt and pepper and mound in bowls. Sprinkle generously with cheese and serve hot.

YIELDS 4 SERVINGS

Toast whole or chopped walnuts at 350 degrees 3-5 minutes, stirring occasionally. Check often as nuts can burn very quickly.

PESTO PASTA WITH ASPARAGUS

- 1 pound asparagus, trimmed
- 1 (20-ounce) package cheese tortellini
- 1 (8½-ounce) jar sun-dried tomatoes in oil, diced
- ¾ cup prepared pesto sauce, or to taste
- ½ cup pine nuts, toasted
- Extra virgin olive oil

Cut asparagus into bite-size pieces. Cook tortellini according to package directions, adding asparagus to cooking water for last 2 minutes of cooking. Test for desired level of doneness before removing from heat. Drain. Add tomatoes, pesto sauce and pine nuts and toss well. If needed, add a little olive oil or sun-dried tomato oil.

YIELDS 4-6 SERVINGS

To toast, spread pine nuts in a single layer on a baking sheet. Bake in center of oven at 350 degrees 3-5 minutes or until golden brown, shaking or stirring several times.

ARTICHOKE PASTA WITH ASIAGO

- 2 tablespoons olive oil
- 8 ounces mushrooms, sliced
- 2 garlic cloves, minced
- 1 teaspoon dried oregano
- 1 (9-ounce) can artichoke hearts, well drained
- 1½ cups chicken stock
- 2 teaspoons lemon juice
- 1 teaspoon lemon zest
- ¼ red bell pepper, diced
- 3 tablespoons butter
- 6 ounces pasta, cooked and drained
- 1½ tablespoons chopped fresh parsley
- ¾ cup grated Asiago cheese
- Salt and pepper to taste
- Shredded cheese of choice

Heat olive oil in a large skillet. Add mushrooms, garlic and oregano and sauté 4 minutes or until golden. Coarsely chop artichokes and add to skillet; sauté. Add stock and next 3 ingredients and cook 5 minutes or until slightly thickened. Add butter and stir until melted. Toss in pasta, parsley and Asiago cheese. Season with salt and pepper. Sprinkle with shredded cheese.

YIELDS 6 SERVINGS

A great side dish with grilled meat or fish.

PASTA & RICE

VENETIAN PASTA WITH ARTICHOKES

- ½ cup olive oil
- 5 garlic cloves, chopped
- ¼ cup chopped onions
- Pinch of dried red pepper flakes, or to taste
- ⅓ cup white wine
- 1 (28-ounce) can Italian-style tomatoes with juice
- 2 (6-ounce) jars marinated artichoke hearts, drained
- ½ cup kalamata olives
- ⅓ cup chopped fresh parsley
- Salt and pepper to taste
- Italian seasoning to taste
- 1 (16-ounce) package penne pasta, cooked

Heat oil in a large skillet. Add garlic, onions and pepper flakes and sauté. Add wine and simmer 3-5 minutes. Stir in tomatoes and simmer 20 minutes. Halve or quarter artichokes and add to sauce along with olives and parsley. Season with salt and pepper and Italian seasonings. Simmer 5 minutes. Toss sauce with pasta.

YIELDS 8 SERVINGS

CHEESY MACARONI AND CHEESE

- 1 (16-ounce) package elbow macaroni
- ½ cup finely chopped onions
- 2 cups shredded sharp Cheddar cheese
- Salt and pepper to taste
- 1 (8- to 12-ounce) block sharp Cheddar cheese
- 1 (12-ounce) can evaporated milk
- 1 cup water

Preheat oven to 375 degrees. Cook macaroni in boiling salted water 7 minutes; drain and rinse with cold water. Add onions and shredded cheese to macaroni and stir well. Season with salt and pepper and spread mixture in a greased 9x13-inch baking dish. Slice block of cheese into strips. Arrange strips over macaroni mixture to cover completely. Mix evaporated milk with water and pour over casserole. Bake 25-30 minutes or until light brown. Let stand a few minutes before serving.

YIELDS 12-15 SERVINGS

This dish transports well and is great for pot luck dinners. It's even better the next day!

KID'S FAVORITE MAC-N-CHEESE

1	pound macaroni	⅛	teaspoon black pepper
6	tablespoons butter, melted	1	pint whole milk
6	tablespoons flour	1	pound Velveeta cheese, shredded
1	teaspoon salt	1	(16-ounce) package shredded Cheddar cheese

Preheat oven to 350 degrees. Cook macaroni until tender, drain and rinse. Transfer macaroni to a 2-quart baking dish. Melt butter in a saucepan over low heat. Add flour, salt and pepper to make a roux. Whisk in milk until smooth. Add Velveeta, stirring until blended. Pour cheese sauce over macaroni and sprinkle with Cheddar cheese. Bake 30 minutes.

YIELDS 4-6 SERVINGS

GOURMET GRITS

½	cup coarsely chopped button mushrooms		Dash of salt
4	tablespoons butter	1¼	cups white grits, not instant
4½	cups unsalted chicken broth	½	cup grated fontina cheese
½	cup good dry white wine	4	tablespoons butter
1	cup half-and-half	¼	cup minced chives

In a 4-quart saucepan, sauté mushrooms in butter until they just begin to soften. Add chicken broth, wine, half-and-half and salt to pan and bring to a boil. Add grits and continue to cook on medium-high heat or simmer, stirring, until grits are cooked, about 20-25 minutes. Remove from heat and stir in cheese and chives and stir until all cheese is melted.

YIELDS 8-10 SERVINGS

For a main course add sautéed shrimp!

CHILDREN'S MUSEUM OF VIRGINIA

The Tidewater Children's Museum, founded in 1980 in the basement of the Portsmouth Public Library, was a project of the Portsmouth Service League. By 1994, it had been moved to its present High Street location and renamed the Children's Museum of Virginia, reflecting its position as the largest children's museum in the Commonwealth. A major renovation and expansion is expected to be completed in 2011.

DID YOU KNOW?

The Children's Museum of Virginia has an official mascot, Andalo (AHN do lo), who encourages children to be curious, creative, and connected to the wonder of the world around them.

Photograph courtesy of Bett Cornetta

VEGETABLES & SIDES

ASPARAGUS BUNDLES

2½ pounds thin asparagus spears, ends trimmed	2 teaspoons sugar
10 green onions, tops only	1 teaspoon dried oregano
2 red bell peppers, each cut into 10 strips	1 teaspoon dried tarragon
1 cup finely chopped onions	1 teaspoon dry mustard
1 cup red wine vinegar	1 teaspoon Worcestershire sauce
½ cup water	½ teaspoon salt
	¼ teaspoon black pepper

Cook asparagus, covered, in a small amount of boiling water 5 minutes or until tender. Drain, rinse with cold water and drain again. Place green onion tops in a bowl and add boiling water to cover. Drain immediately and rinse with cold water. Gather asparagus into 10 bundles. Add 2 bell pepper strips to each bundle. Tie each bundle with a green onion. Place bundles in a 9x13-inch baking dish. Combine chopped onions and remaining 9 ingredients in a bowl. Pour mixture over bundles, cover and chill. This may be done up to 8 hours before serving. Remove bundles from marinade before serving.

YIELDS 10 SERVINGS

"I serve this dish on Christmas Eve. Everyone enjoys the taste and how the colors reflect the holiday."

BEACH BEANS

8 slices bacon	½-¾ cup firmly packed brown sugar
2 sweet onions, sliced into rings and separated	1 teaspoon salt
2 (15-ounce) cans lima beans, undrained	1 teaspoon dry mustard
2 (15-ounce) cans baked beans, undrained	¼ cup white vinegar
1 (15-ounce) can kidney beans, undrained	¼ cup catsup

Preheat oven to 350 degrees. Cook bacon in a large Dutch oven until crispy; drain bacon, reserving drippings in pot. Crumble bacon and set aside. Add onions to drippings and sauté until tender. Stir in bacon, undrained beans, brown sugar and remaining 4 ingredients. Spoon mixture into a lightly greased shallow 2-quart baking dish. Bake 1 hour or until bubbly.

YIELDS 8 SERVINGS

VEGETABLES & SIDES

BUTTERY BAKED MASHED POTATOES

5	pounds Yukon Gold potatoes, peeled
4	tablespoons butter, softened
8	ounces cream cheese, softened
8	ounces sour cream

Milk as needed
Salt and pepper to taste
½ cup butter, melted

Preheat oven to 350 degrees. Cook potatoes in boiling water until soft; drain. Mash potatoes with 4 tablespoons softened butter. Mix in cream cheese and sour cream. Add milk if potatoes seem dry and season with salt and pepper. Spoon mashed potatoes into a greased 9x13-inch casserole dish. Top with melted butter. Potatoes may be prepared a day ahead up to this point, covered and refrigerated; bring to room temperature before proceeding. Bake, uncovered, 20-30 minutes.

YIELDS 10-12 SERVINGS

Variation: Sprinkle crumbled bacon and grated Cheddar cheese over top, if desired.

MASHING POTATOES

To mash potatoes, use a food mill or potato ricer. A food processor will make them gummy.

BEST KEPT SECRET SPUDS

4	medium baking potatoes, sliced as steak fries
2	garlic cloves, chopped
2	teaspoons olive oil

Kosher salt to taste
Chopped fresh parsley
Grated Parmesan cheese to taste

Preheat oven to 450 degrees. Place sliced potatoes in a large bowl. Brown garlic in oil. Remove garlic with a slotted spoon and drain on paper towel, reserving oil in pan. Pour garlic-seasoned oil over potatoes, stirring to coat. Spread potatoes in a single layer on a baking sheet. Season with salt and browned garlic. Bake 45 minutes, turning once. Garnish with parsley and Parmesan cheese.

YIELDS 4-6 SERVINGS

VEGETABLES & SIDES

BROCCOLI BUDS

- 3 heads broccoli
- 1 cup vinegar
- 1 tablespoon granulated sugar
- 1 tablespoon dried dill
- 1 teaspoon salt
- 1 tablespoon finely chopped red bell pepper
- 1 teaspoon garlic salt
- 1½ cups vegetable oil
- 1 lemon, thinly sliced

Separate large buds from each head of broccoli and place in a zip-top bag. Combine vinegar and next 6 ingredients and pour over broccoli. Seal and refrigerate 24 hours, turning occasionally. Drain and serve garnished with lemon slices.

YIELDS 10 SERVINGS

"If you prefer small florets, cut these after buds have been drained."

BUTTERNUT SQUASH CASSEROLE

- 2 cups cooked, thoroughly drained and mashed butternut squash (1 medium squash)
- 3 eggs, beaten
- ½-¾ cup granulated sugar
- ½ cup milk
- 5 tablespoons butter, melted
- 1 teaspoon ground ginger
- 1 teaspoon coconut flavoring
- 3 tablespoons flaked coconut

Preheat oven to 350 degrees. Combine all ingredients and place in a lightly greased 8-inch square baking dish. Bake 55-60 minutes.

YIELDS 6 SERVINGS

CORN PUDDING

- 2 (12-ounce) cans niblet corn, drained
- ¼ cup granulated sugar
- 1 cup milk
- 4 eggs
- 6 tablespoons all-purpose flour
- 6 tablespoons butter, melted
- 1½ teaspoons vanilla
- Cinnamon or nutmeg to taste

Preheat oven to 425 degrees. Combine all ingredients except cinnamon in a blender and process 15-20 seconds. Pour mixture into a lightly greased 8-inch square baking dish and sprinkle with cinnamon. Bake 30 minutes or until top is browned and firm. To double, use a 9x13-inch baking dish.

YIELDS 4-6 SERVINGS

CHEESE PUFF

10 slices bread, crusts removed, cubed	1 teaspoon salt
8 ounces sharp cheese, shredded	Dash of cayenne pepper
3 eggs, beaten	4 tablespoons butter
2 cups milk	

Layer bread cubes and cheese in a greased 2-quart shallow casserole dish; repeat layers at least once. Combine eggs and next 3 ingredients and pour over layers. Dot with butter. Cover and let stand 1-2 hours, or refrigerate overnight, to allow bread to absorb liquid. When ready to bake, preheat oven to 300 degrees. Bake, uncovered, about 1 hour. Mixture puffs up as it bakes and makes a delicious side dish.

YIELDS 6-8 SERVINGS

GOAT CHEESE SOUFFLÉ

2 (4-ounce) logs goat cheese, softened	2 teaspoons chopped fresh thyme, or ½ teaspoon dried
⅔ cup whole milk	
2 tablespoons butter	2 teaspoons chopped fresh rosemary, or ½ teaspoon dried
3 tablespoons all-purpose flour	
¼ cup freshly grated Parmesan cheese	¼ teaspoon black pepper
4 large egg yolks	6 large egg whites
2 tablespoons chopped fresh chives	¼ teaspoon salt

Preheat oven to 350 degrees. Cut one cheese log into 6 equal rounds. Place 1 round in each of 6 greased (¾-cup) soufflé dishes or custard cups. Crumble remaining cheese log into a large bowl; set aside. Bring milk to a simmer over low heat in a small saucepan. Remove from heat. Melt butter in a heavy medium saucepan over medium-high heat. Blend in flour and stir 2 minutes. Gradually whisk in hot milk. Continue to cook, whisking constantly, 2 minutes or until mixture is smooth and resembles thick paste. Pour mixture over crumbled cheese in large bowl. Whisk in Parmesan cheese and next 5 ingredients. Cool mixture to lukewarm. In a separate bowl, beat egg whites with an electric mixer until stiff but not dry, gradually adding salt. Gently fold one-fourth of egg whites into cheese mixture to lighten. Fold in remaining whites and gently blend. Divide mixture among soufflé dishes. Place dishes on a baking sheet. Bake 22 minutes or until soufflés are puffed and golden brown on top.

YIELDS 6 SERVINGS

FIRE AND ICE TOMATOES

6 large ripe tomatoes, peeled and cut into wedges	1½ teaspoons mustard seed
1 large green bell pepper, sliced into strips	½ teaspoon salt
1 red onion, cut into rings	4½ teaspoons granulated sugar
¾ cup cider vinegar	⅛ teaspoon cayenne pepper
½ teaspoon celery salt	½ teaspoon black pepper
	½ cup cold water

Place tomatoes, bell peppers and onions in a shallow container. Combine vinegar and remaining 7 ingredients and pour over vegetables. Refrigerate 24 hours, turning tomatoes 2-3 times.

YIELDS 8-10 SERVINGS

A great summer side dish with a kick!

GOOD FORTUNE BLACK-EYED PEAS

2 tablespoons olive oil	½ teaspoon dried basil
½ medium onion, chopped	¼ teaspoon dried red pepper flakes
2 garlic cloves, chopped	2 tablespoons catsup
2 (15-ounce) cans ranch style black-eyed peas seasoned with bacon	1 tablespoon Worcestershire sauce
1 (14½-ounce) can diced tomatoes with Italian herbs	½ teaspoon cumin
1 bay leaf	½ teaspoon cinnamon
½ teaspoon dried oregano	½ teaspoon sugar
	Salt and pepper to taste

Heat oil in a medium saucepan. Add onions and sauté 3 minutes. Add garlic and sauté 2-3 minutes. Add black-eyed peas and next 10 ingredients; gently stir. Season with salt and pepper. Simmer on low 12-15 minutes. Turn off heat and let stand 20 minutes. Remove bay leaf before serving. Best when made several hours to a day ahead, allowing flavors to marry.

YIELDS 4-6 SERVINGS

"My mom created this tasty New Year's Eve dish and serves it every year for good luck."

GREEK GREEN BEANS

2	pounds fresh green beans	1	bottle balsamic vinaigrette
½	red onion, thinly sliced	1	teaspoon dried oregano
1	pound cherry tomatoes, halved	½	teaspoon garlic powder
8	ounces crumbled feta cheese, divided		

Steam green beans 7-10 minutes or until crisp-tender. When done, immediately immerse in cold water until cool; drain. Place beans in a large bowl. Add onions, tomatoes and 6 ounces feta cheese. In a separate bowl, mix 1 cup vinaigrette, oregano and garlic powder. Pour dressing mixture over vegetables and toss. Chill 4 hours or overnight. Before serving, add more vinaigrette, if needed, and sprinkle remaining cheese on top.

YIELDS 8 SERVINGS

Canned green beans can be substituted; omit steaming.

GRILLED GARLIC TOMATOES

6	large ripe tomatoes	3	tablespoons olive oil
	Salt and pepper to taste	2	ounces grated Parmesan cheese
6	garlic cloves, minced	2	tablespoons chopped fresh thyme

Preheat grill to medium-high. Cut tomatoes in half and sprinkle each half with salt and pepper; set aside. In a small skillet, sauté garlic in oil over medium heat 1-2 minutes; remove from heat and set aside. Using a barbeque rack, arrange tomatoes, cut-side down, on grill and cook 3-5 minutes or until light brown. Turn tomatoes using tongs and drizzle 1½ teaspoons reserved garlic oil over each tomato half. Grill 3-5 minutes longer or until bottoms are brown. Remove tomatoes to a platter and sprinkle with cheese and thyme.

YIELDS 12 SERVINGS

HONEY-MUSTARD VIDALIA ONIONS

6	sweet onions, Vidalia recommended because of shape	2	tablespoons spicy mustard
		2	tablespoons honey
3	tablespoons red wine or red wine vinegar	½	teaspoon salt
4	tablespoons butter, melted	¼	teaspoon ground cloves

Preheat oven to 350 degrees. Peel onions and slice one-fourth off the top of each. Place onions in a baking dish, cut-side up. Mix vinegar and remaining 5 ingredients and spoon over onions. Bake 30 minutes or until tender. Serve warm.

YIELDS 6 SERVINGS

HOME FRIES WITH CARAMELIZED ONIONS

2 teaspoons granulated sugar	3 tablespoons butter
¼ cup water	3 tablespoons vegetable oil
1 medium yellow onion, coarsely chopped	4 medium white potatoes, peeled and coarsely chopped
2 teaspoons salt	¼ cup warm water
1 teaspoon black pepper	

Combine sugar, ¼ cup water and onions in a small saucepan over medium heat. Cook until onion mixture reduces and onions turn golden brown; set aside. Place a 10-inch cast-iron skillet over medium heat. Add salt and pepper and cook about 2 minutes to season skillet. Add butter and oil. Increase heat and add potatoes. When potatoes brown around the edges, turn. Add ¼ cup warm water, cover and cook 15 minutes or until liquid evaporates and potatoes are tender. Fold in caramelized onions. Serve for breakfast, lunch or dinner!

YIELDS 4 SERVINGS

"Behind every good, enjoyable, scrumptious, mouth-watering recipe, there is a story. Coming from a family of 12, we used a lot of potatoes. My mama could buy 10-pound sacks for little or nothing, but during those times, little or nothing was something. We'd eat potatoes in every way imaginable. Hot, cold and any way in between. My favorite was and still is Home Fries!"

HERBED GREEN BEANS

1½ pounds fresh green beans, trimmed	1½ teaspoons chopped fresh parsley
1 lemon	½ teaspoon sea salt
3 tablespoons butter	½ teaspoon black pepper
1 tablespoon finely sliced fresh sage leaves (about 6 large leaves)	

Cook green beans in a large pot of boiling salted water 5 minutes or until crisp-tender; drain. Using a vegetable peeler, cut off lemon peel in strips. Thinly slice lemon strips. Melt butter in a large skillet over medium-high heat. Add sage and lemon peel, reserving some peel for garnish. Sauté 2 minutes or until fragrant. Add beans and toss until heated through. Sprinkle with parsley. Season with salt and pepper and toss to combine flavors. Garnish with reserved lemon peel.

YIELDS 4 SERVINGS

ITALIAN GREEN BEAN MEDLEY

- ¼ cup extra virgin olive oil
- 2 tablespoons white or dark balsamic vinegar
- 1 teaspoon minced garlic
- 1 teaspoon granulated sugar
- 14 ounces fresh green beans
- 6 ounces Portobello mushrooms, cut into chunks
- 10 grape tomatoes, cut in halves or thirds
- 4 ounces pine nuts, toasted (about ¾ cup)
- ¼ cup balsamic basil vinaigrette, optional

Heat oil in a 12-inch skillet. Add vinegar and garlic and cook 2 minutes. Stir in sugar. Add beans and mushrooms and sauté 5-7 minutes. Add grape tomatoes and cook 1-2 minutes longer. Add pine nuts and gently toss. Adjust flavor by adding vinegar, oil or vinaigrette, if needed.

YIELDS 6 SERVINGS

To toast pine nuts, place in a 350 degree oven on a shallow baking sheet 3-5 minutes, checking often.

Portobello mushrooms have very dark gills. Most recipe do not call for the removal of these as they are completely edible but they are apt to cause a dish to turn dark and unappealing. Remove stem and scrape off gills with the edge of a teaspoon. A grapefruit spoon is the perfect tool for this job.

MANDARIN SQUASH

- 2 pounds yellow squash, unpeeled and diced small
- Salt to taste
- 2 tablespoons butter
- 1 (11-ounce) can Mandarin oranges
- 2 tablespoons firmly packed brown sugar
- ¼ teaspoon nutmeg
- Slivered almonds, toasted

Cook squash in a saucepan of boiling salted water until just tender; drain. Add salt and butter to squash and stir until butter melts. Place squash in a serving dish. Pour juice from oranges into same saucepan. Add brown sugar and bring to a boil. Boil 5 minutes. Stir in nutmeg and remove from heat. Add oranges. Pour mixture over squash and sprinkle almonds on top.

YIELDS 4-6 SERVINGS

Toast almonds in a single layer on a baking sheet in center of oven. Bake at 350 degrees for 3-5 minutes or until golden brown, shaking or stirring several times.

NOODLE PUDDING (KUGEL)

8 ounces broad noodles	2 apples, sliced
2 tablespoons butter	¼ cup raisins
3 eggs, beaten	½ cup chopped nuts
1 cup granulated sugar	1 cup sour cream
1½ teaspoons cinnamon	1 (16-ounce) container cottage cheese

Preheat oven to 350 degrees. Cook noodles in boiling water; drain. Heat butter in a skillet. Add noodles and cook just until noodles absorb butter. Add eggs and remaining 7 ingredients in order listed. Spoon mixture into a well-greased baking dish. Bake 30 minutes.

YIELDS 10-12 SERVINGS

PICKLED BEETS

½ cup granulated sugar	2 teaspoons pumpkin pie spice
½ cup vinegar	1 pound beets, peeled, cooked and sliced
8-10 whole cloves, or to taste	

Dissolve sugar in vinegar in a small saucepan and bring to a slight boil. Add cloves and pumpkin pie spice and simmer a few minutes. Pour mixture over sliced beets. If using canned beets, add a little beet juice for color.

YIELDS 4-6 SERVINGS

Resist buying canned beets; try this simple recipe and you will see the difference.

MARINATED BRUSSELS SPROUTS

1 (16-ounce) package frozen Brussels sprouts	½ teaspoon dried dill
½ cup Italian salad dressing, Wishbone recommended	2 tablespoons chopped green onions
	2 tablespoons chopped pimentos or roasted red peppers

Cook Brussels sprouts according to package directions. Combine dressing and remaining 3 ingredients and pour over sprouts. Refrigerate overnight.

YIELDS 4 SERVINGS

"A neighbor brought this dish to our annual neighborhood holiday party. It received many compliments and to this day, they are the only Brussels sprouts I truly enjoy!"

VEGETABLES & SIDES

ROASTED VIDALIA ONIONS WITH BALSAMIC VINEGAR

- 2 large Vidalia onions
- 2½ tablespoons balsamic vinegar
- 2½ tablespoons water
- 2½ tablespoons extra virgin olive oil
- ½ teaspoon salt
- Black pepper to taste
- 4 sprigs fresh thyme

Cut off top of onions and remove skins, keeping root end intact. Slice each onion into 6 equal wedges. Place wedges, rounded-side down, in a terra cotta onion roaster. Combine vinegar, water and oil and pour over onions. Sprinkle with salt and pepper. Tuck thyme sprigs in among onion wedges. Cover roaster and place in a cold oven. Roast at 400 degrees for 45 minutes, basting occasionally until tender.

YIELDS 4 SERVINGS

If you do not have an onion roaster, use a covered ovenproof baking dish or any baking dish and cover with foil.

"Roasted onions are the perfect complement to any feast. Roasting tempers the pungency of onions and brings out the fragrant sweetness. This wonderful dish is easy and fool proof."

SPINACH AND ARTICHOKE CASSEROLE

- ½ cup chopped onions
- ½ cup butter
- 2 (10-ounce) packages frozen chopped spinach, thawed
- 1 (15-ounce) can artichoke hearts, drained and quartered, liquid reserved
- 1 cup sour cream
- ½ cup Parmesan cheese, plus extra for topping
- 1 teaspoon salt

Preheat oven to 350 degrees. Sauté onions in butter in a small saucepan over medium heat until translucent; set aside. Drain and press most of the liquid out of spinach, but do not make too dry. Mix spinach with artichokes and ¼ cup reserved artichoke liquid in a mixing bowl. Add sour cream, Parmesan cheese and salt. Spoon mixture into a 2-quart casserole dish and sprinkle with extra Parmesan cheese. Bake 20-25 minutes.

YIELDS 6 SERVINGS

SHERRIED CARROTS WITH APRICOTS

1	pound carrots, sliced	¼	cup chopped fresh parsley, plus extra for garnish
4	tablespoons butter		
1	medium onion, thinly sliced	2	tablespoons sherry
6	ounces dried apricots, cut into thin strips		Salt and pepper to taste

Cook carrots in water until tender; drain. Melt butter in a large saucepan. Add onions and sauté until lightly browned. Add carrots, apricots, parsley and sherry and blend well. Season with salt and pepper and garnish with extra parsley.

YIELDS 4-6 SERVINGS

SQUASH CAKES

- 1 large yellow squash, shredded (about 2 cups)
- 2 large green onions, finely chopped
- 1 clove garlic, pressed
- ¼-½ cup all-purpose flour
- 2 teaspoons granulated sugar
- ½ cup shredded mild Cheddar cheese
- 2 tablespoons chopped fresh dill
- 1 egg
- 1 teaspoon salt
- ¼ teaspoon black pepper
- Butter or bacon fat for frying
- Lemon wedges

Place squash in a clean dish towel and twist to remove excess moisture. Mix squash with next 9 ingredients until there are no lumps, adjusting amount of flour needed to reach a batter consistency. Grease a skillet with butter or bacon fat over medium heat. Drop batter by spoonful into hot pan. Fry until golden brown on both sides, turning once. Adjust heat if butter starts to burn. Drain cakes on paper towels. Serve with lemon wedges.

YIELDS 6-8 SERVINGS

"A great accompaniment for any meat entrée."

VEGETABLES & SIDES

SUMMER TOMATO PIE

1	(9-inch) pie crust, unbaked	¼	teaspoon lemon pepper
2	cups peeled, seeded and chopped tomatoes	4-6	ounces shredded Cheddar cheese
¼	teaspoon salt	½	cup mayonnaise
1	teaspoon dried basil	1-2	ounces grated Parmesan cheese

Preheat oven to 350 degrees. Bake pie crust 5-6 minutes or until very lightly browned; cool. Combine tomatoes and next 3 ingredients and place in cooled crust. Mix together Cheddar cheese and mayonnaise and spoon over tomatoes. Sprinkle Parmesan cheese on top. Bake 30 minutes.

YIELDS 6-8 SERVINGS

GRANNY SMITH'S SWEET POTATOES

3	pounds sweet potatoes, peeled	¼	cup cornstarch
2	cups firmly packed brown sugar, divided	2	Granny Smith apples, unpeeled
½	teaspoon vanilla	1	cup self-rising flour
½	teaspoon cinnamon	1	cup chopped pecans
½	teaspoon nutmeg	½	cup butter
½	teaspoon allspice		

Preheat oven to 350 degrees. Cut potatoes into small chunks and place in a saucepan with enough water to almost cover. Add 1 cup brown sugar and next 4 ingredients. Cook until potatoes are tender. Mix cornstarch with a small amount of cold water and add to potatoes. Continue to cook until thickened; do not mash as mixture should be somewhat chunky. Slice apples and arrange in a 9x13-inch baking dish. Spoon potato mixture over apples. Mix remaining 1 cup brown sugar, flour and pecans. Blend in butter to form large crumbs. Spread mixture over potatoes. Bake 30-40 minutes or until topping is cooked.

YIELDS 10-12 SERVINGS

TOMATOES BABICHE

6 medium tomatoes	½ cup mayonnaise
Salt and pepper to taste	⅓ cup sour cream
1 (6-ounce) jar marinated artichoke hearts, drained	1 teaspoon curry powder
	1 teaspoon lemon juice
1 (4½-ounce) jar marinated mushrooms, drained	1 tablespoon dried minced onions
	Finely chopped parsley for garnish

Peel tomatoes and scoop out center. Sprinkle inside and out generously with salt and pepper. Chop artichokes and mushrooms in a food processor. Fill each tomato cavity with artichoke mixture. Mix mayonnaise and next 4 ingredients. Filled tomatoes and sauce may be prepared to this point, covered and refrigerated up to a day ahead. When ready to serve, top filled tomatoes with sauce and sprinkle with parsley.

YIELDS 6 SERVINGS

Peeling tomatoes and peaches is made simpler using the following method: Score slightly with a knife at top or bottom. Place in boiling water to cover for 15-20 seconds. Remove and test; if peel doesn't come off easily, return to water for a few seconds more. Ripeness and size effect time. Plunge immediately into ice cold water to cool, then peel.

SWEET POTATO-ORANGE CASSEROLE

2 (16-ounce) cans vacuum-packed sweet potatoes	½ teaspoon salt
	2 tablespoons rum
¼ cup firmly packed brown sugar	1 (11-ounce) can Mandarin oranges, drained
2 tablespoons butter, melted	

TOPPING

¼ cup chopped pecans	2 tablespoons butter, melted
1½ tablespoons firmly packed brown sugar	

Preheat oven to 375 degrees. Mash sweet potatoes in a mixing bowl. Beat in brown sugar and next 3 ingredients. Fold in oranges. Spoon mixture into a greased 2-quart casserole dish. Combine all topping ingredients and sprinkle over casserole. Bake 30 minutes.

YIELDS 8-9 SERVINGS

VEGETABLE TOWER

- 1 medium eggplant, peeled
- 1-2 tomatoes, sliced
- ½ teaspoon dried basil, or to taste
- 1 onion, thinly sliced
- ½ cup butter, melted, divided
- ½ teaspoon kosher salt
- ½ teaspoon Italian seasoning, or to taste
- Black pepper to taste
- 6 ounces mozzarella cheese, shredded
- ½ cup dry bread crumbs
- 2 tablespoons freshly grated Parmesan cheese

Preheat oven to 400 degrees. Slice eggplant into ½-inch rounds (about 6) and arrange in a single layer in a 9x13-inch baking dish. Top each slice with 1 tomato slice, basil and 1 slice onion. Drizzle 4 tablespoons melted butter evenly over towers. Season with salt, Italian seasoning and pepper. Bake, covered, 20-25 minutes. Remove from oven and uncover. Sprinkle with mozzarella cheese. Combine bread crumbs, Parmesan cheese and remaining 4 tablespoons melted butter and sprinkle over each tower. Bake, uncovered, 10-15 minutes or until light brown. Serve immediately.

YIELDS 6 SERVINGS

SOUTHERN YELLOW SQUASH

- 6 cups sliced yellow squash (2 pounds)
- 4-6 green onions, chopped
- 4 tablespoons butter
- Salt and pepper to taste
- 1 egg, beaten
- ½ cup sour cream
- 6 slices bacon, cooked and crumbled, divided
- ½ cup shredded Swiss or mozzarella cheese
- 1 cup shredded Cheddar cheese

Preheat oven to 350 degrees. Sauté squash and green onions in butter in a large skillet until tender. Remove from heat and season lightly with salt and pepper. Combine egg, sour cream and half the bacon and blend with squash mixture. Spoon half of mixture into a greased 2-quart baking dish. Sprinkle Swiss cheese on top. Spoon remaining squash mixture over cheese. Sprinkle with Cheddar cheese and top with remaining bacon. Bake 20 minutes or until bubbly.

YIELDS 6-8 SERVINGS

ZIPPY ZUCCHINI

1 cup sliced onions	1 medium tomato, peeled and chopped
3 tablespoons butter	1 (0.7-ounce) envelope dry Italian salad dressing mix
2 pounds zucchini, unpeeled and sliced	

Sauté onions in butter until lightly browned. Add zucchini and tomatoes. Stir in dressing mix. Bring to a boil. Reduce heat, cover and simmer 10 minutes or until zucchini is tender.

YIELDS 10 SERVINGS

MOCK HOLLANDAISE

½ cup mayonnaise	1½ teaspoons fresh lemon juice, or to taste
2 teaspoons prepared mustard	Salt to taste

Mix all ingredients together in a saucepan. Cook over low heat; do not boil. Serve warm over vegetables.

YIELDS 2-4 SERVINGS

ROASTED ASPARAGUS

8 ounces fresh asparagus, trimmed	½ teaspoon sugar
1 tablespoon olive oil	⅛ teaspoon salt

Preheat oven to 400 degrees. Place asparagus in a 10x15-inch baking dish. Mix oil, sugar and salt and drizzle over asparagus. Bake 8-12 minutes or to desired doneness, turning once halfway through.

YIELDS 3-4 SERVINGS

If asparagus are thick, use a vegetable peeler to peel stems for a more attractive presentation and easier cutting.

VEGETABLES & SIDES

SUMMER TOMATO TREAT

- 1 large tomato, sliced
- ¼ cup chopped red onions
- ¼ cup crumbled blue cheese, or to taste
- Catalina salad dressing to taste

Place sliced tomatoes on a plate. Top with onions and blue cheese. Drizzle with salad dressing to taste. May be prepared up to 30 minutes ahead.

YIELDS 4 SERVINGS

BAKED PINEAPPLE

- 8 eggs
- ½ cup butter, softened
- 1¾ cups granulated sugar
- 2 (15½-ounce) cans crushed pineapple, drained
- 10 slices bread, cubed (easier when frozen)

Preheat oven to 350 degrees. Beat together eggs, butter and sugar. Fold in pineapple and bread cubes. Spoon mixture into a greased 8-inch square baking dish. Bake 45 minutes or until top begins to brown. Serve hot, warm or cold.

YIELDS 8-10 SERVINGS

A delicious dish, especially with ham.

To select a good pineapple, grasp one of the inner leaves of the crown of the fruit and give a light tug straight up from the top of the fruit. Do not pull it sideways at all. If the leaf comes out easily, your pineapple is ripe and ready to go.

Desserts

FRESNEL LENS

This rare first-order Fresnel lens was installed in the Hog Island lighthouse on Virginia's Eastern Shore in 1895. The second largest lens of its type in the United States, it shines as a landmark on the Portsmouth waterfront near High Street Landing. Housed in a pavilion designed to resemble the lantern room of a lighthouse, this valuable artifact is on loan to the city from the United States Coast Guard.

DID YOU KNOW?

Light from this lens is visible for at least 18 miles at sea when it is lit by only a 24 watt light bulb.

Photograph courtesy of Jim Walker

COCOA APPLE CAKE

BATTER

- 2½ cups all-purpose flour
- 2 cups granulated sugar
- 2 tablespoons unsweetened cocoa
- 1 teaspoon baking soda
- 1 teaspoon cinnamon
- 3 eggs
- 1 cup margarine
- ½ cup coffee-flavored liqueur, such as Kahlúa, or water
- 1 tablespoon vanilla
- 1 (12-ounce) package chocolate chips
- 1 cup finely chopped nuts of choice
- 2 green apples, chopped

FROSTING

- ½ cup butter, softened
- 8 ounces cream cheese, softened
- Confectioners' sugar as needed
- Coffee-flavored liqueur to taste, such as Kahlúa
- Vanilla to taste

Preheat oven to 325 degrees. Combine flour and next 4 ingredients in a large bowl. In a separate bowl, mix eggs and next 3 ingredients. Add liquid mixture to dry ingredients and mix until blended. Fold in chocolate chips, nuts, and apples. Pour batter into a greased and floured 12-cup Bundt or tube pan. Bake 55-60 minutes. Cool completely before removing from pan.

To make frosting, cream butter and cream cheese together with an electric mixer. Sift in confectioners' sugar until desired consistency is reached. Add liqueur and vanilla to taste. Drizzle frosting over cooled cake.

YIELDS 8-10 SERVINGS

KIDDIE KONES

- 1 (18¼-ounce) package cake mix of choice
- 24 flat-bottom ice cream cones
- Frosting of choice
- Sprinkles and/or gumballs for topping

Prepare cake batter according to package directions. Place cones in muffin tins for easier transfer to oven. Fill each cone three-fourths full with cake batter. Bake according to package directions; cool. Spread frosting over cooled cupcakes and decorate with sprinkles and/or gumballs.

YIELDS 24 SERVINGS

A children's party favorite! Let them decorate their own cupcake.

CREAM CHEESE POUND CAKE

1½ cups butter, softened	3 cups all-purpose flour
8 ounces cream cheese, softened	Vanilla extract to taste
3 cups granulated sugar	Whipped cream and sliced strawberries for garnish, optional
6 eggs, room temperature	

Blend butter and cream cheese with an electric mixer in a very large bowl. Gradually beat in sugar. Add eggs and mix well. Add flour and vanilla and mix well; do not overmix. Fold batter into a lightly greased large tube pan. Place in cold oven and bake at 300 degrees for 1 hour, 45 minutes or until lightly browned. Garnish with whipped topping and strawberry slices.

YIELDS 8-10 SERVINGS

To easily split cake layers, insert about 4 to 5 toothpicks into the layer's circumference where you want to split the layer. Take thread or dental floss around the edge of the layer, weaving under and over the toothpicks. Cross the ends of the floss and pull in the opposite direction and it will easily slice through the cake.

SOUR CREAM POUND CAKE

1 cup butter, softened	2 teaspoons vanilla extract
3 cups granulated sugar	2-3 teaspoons almond extract
6 eggs	3 cups all-purpose flour
¼ teaspoon baking soda	Confectioners' sugar, optional
1 (8-ounce) container sour cream	

Preheat oven to 325 degrees. Cream butter and granulated sugar together in a mixing bowl. Add eggs one at a time, beating well after each addition. In a separate bowl, mix baking soda and next 3 ingredients. Add mixture alternately with flour to creamed mixture and blend well. Pour batter into a greased and floured tube pan. Bake 1 hour, 15 minutes or until cake tests done. Cool in pan for 15 minutes before removing to a rack. Sprinkle with confectioners sugar before serving.

YIELDS 16 SERVINGS

AMARETTI POUND CAKE (ALMOND WEDDING CAKE)

1	cup unsalted butter, softened	¾	teaspoon almond extract
2	cups granulated sugar	1¾	cups sifted cake flour
5	eggs	¼	cup canola oil
1	tablespoon amontillado sherry	⅓	cup amaretti cookies, crushed

Preheat oven to 325 degrees. Cream butter with sugar. Beat in eggs. Add sherry and remaining 4 ingredients and mix well. Pour into a greased and floured tube pan. Bake 1 hour, 5 minutes or until done. Cool in pan before serving.

YIELDS 10 SERVINGS

> There is a difference when an adverb is placed before or after an ingredient. For example: 1 cup flour, sifted means to sift flour after it is measured. 1 cup sifted flour means to sift flour before it is measured. This can make a big difference in the quality of your finished product.

CHOCOLATE CHIP BUNDT CAKE

1	(18¼-ounce) package yellow cake mix with pudding	4	large eggs
1	(3.9-ounce) package instant chocolate pudding mix	8	ounces sour cream
		¾	cup water
½	cup granulated sugar	1	(6-ounce) package semisweet chocolate chips
¾	cup vegetable oil		Sifted confectioners' sugar for dusting

Preheat oven to 350 degrees. Combine cake mix, pudding mix and sugar in a mixing bowl. Add oil and next 3 ingredients and mix well. Stir in chocolate chips. Pour batter into a greased and floured Bundt pan. Bake 1 hour or until a toothpick inserted in the center comes out clean. Cool 10 minutes. Remove from pan and cool completely. Dust with confectioners' sugar.

YIELDS 10-12 SERVINGS

Delicious served warm with vanilla ice cream and chocolate syrup. Or drizzle with a red berry sauce.

"This recipe was introduced to many of us by a dear friend and neighbor. She greeted all newcomers with this wonderful cake and it has become a symbol of friendship."

DOUBLE CHOCOLATE MINIATURE CAKES

1¼ cups granulated sugar, divided	½ teaspoon salt
3 ounces cream cheese, softened	¾ cup water
1 egg, unbeaten	⅓ cup vegetable oil
1 egg yolk, unbeaten	1 egg white
Dash of salt	1 tablespoon vinegar
½ cup semisweet chocolate chips	1 teaspoon vanilla
1½ cups sifted all-purpose flour	¾ cup slivered almonds, toasted and chopped
¼ cup unsweetened cocoa	
¾ teaspoon baking soda	

Preheat oven to 350 degrees. In a small bowl with a mixer on medium speed, beat ¼ cup sugar and next 4 ingredients until smooth. Stir in chocolate chips; set aside. In a separate bowl, sift together flour and next 3 ingredients. Combine water and next 4 ingredients in another bowl and beat well with a fork. Add water mixture all at once to dry ingredients and stir with a spoon until well combined. Fill each of 12 paper-lined (3-inch) muffin cups about half full with cocoa batter. Into center of batter, spoon 1 tablespoon cream cheese mixture. Generously sprinkle each top with about 1 tablespoon sugar and then with almonds. Bake 25-30 minutes or until a toothpick inserted in the center comes out clean and cupcakes are golden. Cool in pan 10 minutes, then remove to a rack to finish cooling. Remove paper liners and arrange on a plate with fresh fruit for a beautiful dessert.

YIELDS 12 SERVINGS

"In 1965, we moved into our new home and began attending a church nearby. One morning, I was visited by a member of the church to welcome me. She came bearing a lovely basket of fruit and these wonderful cupcakes. Some things you never forget."

Store well wrapped chocolate in a cool dry place to prevent "bloom". This is a grayish discoloration caused by rapid changes in temperature, humidity or storing in too warm a temperature. It can still be used and the color disappears when melted.

SUNSHINE ANGEL CAKE

1 (16-ounce) package angel food cake mix	1 cup granulated sugar
1 (0.25-ounce) envelope unflavored gelatin	Dash of salt
¼ cup cold water	1 cup heavy cream, whipped, plus extra for topping
1 cup boiling water	
1 cup orange juice	1 (7-ounce) package coconut, toasted
Juice of 1 lemon	

Prepare cake mix according to package directions; cool. Dissolve gelatin in ¼ cup cold water. Add 1 cup boiling water and next 4 ingredients and mix well. Refrigerate until gelatin starts to thicken. Fold in whipped cream. Break cooled cake into pieces. Using a tube pan or 9x13-inch baking dish, layer half of cake followed by half of gelatin. Repeat layers, ending with gelatin. Refrigerate 8 hours or overnight. Serve topped with whipped cream and toasted coconut.

YIELDS 10 SERVINGS

A 16-ounce cake mix is needed for gelatin to set properly.

To toast coconut, spread on a baking sheet and toast at 350 degrees until golden, tossing frequently.

COOKING GREAT FOOD IS GREAT LEARNING

Dry ingredients change as they are mixed with wet ingredients. What happens when we add whipped egg whites or yeast or food coloring? Cooking is chemistry in action. What a wonderful...and tasty... way to learn.

AWESOME CARROT CAKE

BATTER

- 2 cups all-purpose flour
- 2 teaspoons baking soda
- ½ teaspoon salt
- 2 teaspoons cinnamon
- 3 eggs, beaten
- ¾ cup vegetable oil or corn oil
- ¾ cup buttermilk
- 2 cups granulated sugar
- 2 teaspoons vanilla
- 3 ounces crushed pineapple, well drained
- 2½ cups shredded carrots
- 3½ ounces canned or frozen coconut
- 1 cup chopped black walnuts
- 1 cup golden raisins

BUTTERMILK GLAZE

- 1 cup granulated sugar
- ½ cup buttermilk
- ½ teaspoon baking soda
- ½ cup butter
- 1 tablespoon light corn syrup
- 1 teaspoon vanilla

CREAM CHEESE FROSTING

- ½ cup butter, softened
- 8 ounces cream cheese, softened
- 1 teaspoon vanilla
- 2-2½ cups confectioners' sugar

Preheat oven to 350 degrees. Combine flour and next 3 ingredients; set aside. In a separate bowl, beat eggs. Blend in oil and next 3 ingredients until smooth. Blend in dry ingredients. Stir in pineapple and remaining 4 batter ingredients. Divide batter among three 9-inch greased and floured cake pans. Bake 35-40 minutes or until done. Combine all glaze ingredients except vanilla in a heavy saucepan. Boil 4 minutes, stirring often. Remove from heat and stir in vanilla. Spread glaze over each cake layer immediately after baking. Cool cake in pans at least 15 minutes. Remove from pans to cool completely before frosting. To make frosting, cream butter and cream cheese together. Mix in vanilla and confectioners' sugar until smooth. Spread over top of cooled cake layers. Stack layers and spread frosting on sides of cake.

YIELDS 12-14 SERVINGS

Always store flours and sugars in airtight containers. Humidity is not a friend to these pantry items.

BETE NOIRE (BLACK BEAST)

- 8 ounces unsweetened chocolate, chopped
- 4 ounces semisweet or bittersweet chocolate, chopped
- 1⅓ cups granulated sugar
- ½ cup water
- 5 extra large eggs, room temperature
- 1 cup unsalted butter, cut into small pieces, softened

GANACHE

- 5 ounces bittersweet chocolate, cut into tiny pieces
- ½ cup heavy cream
- Fresh berries or whipped cream for garnish

Preheat oven to 350 degrees. Grease a deep 9-inch cake pan (not a springform pan). Place a circle of wax or parchment paper on bottom, covering completely. Grease the paper. Place both chocolates in a food processor and process until in tiny pieces. Bring sugar and water to a rolling boil in a small saucepan. Crack eggs into a small bowl; set aside. With processor on, add boiling sugar syrup to chocolate. Add butter, piece by piece. Add eggs, one at a time. Process until mixture is very smooth. Pour batter into prepared pan. Place pan in a slightly larger pan with sides at least 2 inches high. Place pans in center of oven and pour hot water into larger pan to a 1-inch depth. Bake 25-30 minutes; do not overbake. Cool in pan 10 minutes. Run a sharp knife around the sides to release cake. Cover with plastic wrap and unmold onto a baking sheet. Remove parchment. For ganache, place chocolate in a small metal or heatproof bowl. Scald cream and pour over chocolate. Let stand a couple minutes. Stir gently until smooth. Cool 15-20 minutes and pour over cake. Be careful, if too warm, ganache will run down onto the plate. Garnish with fresh berries or whipped cream.

YIELDS 14-16 SERVINGS

CHOCOLATE CHIP KAHLÚA CAKE

- 1 (18¼-ounce) package devil's food cake mix
- 1 (3.4-ounce) package instant French vanilla pudding mix
- 2 eggs
- ¼ cup vegetable oil
- 16 ounces sour cream
- ½ cup coffee-flavored liqueur, such as Kahlúa
- 1 (12-ounce) package semisweet chocolate chips

Preheat oven to 350 degrees. Using an electric mixer, blend all ingredients, except chocolate chips, 3 minutes at medium speed. Gently stir in chocolate chips. Pour batter into a greased Bundt pan. Bake 45-60 minutes or until cake pulls away from sides of pan and springs back to the touch; a toothpick test will not work on this cake.

YIELDS 10-12 SERVINGS

CHOCOLATE LAVA CAKES

5	ounces bittersweet or semisweet chocolate, chopped	3	large egg yolks
10	tablespoons unsalted butter	1½	cups confectioners' sugar
3	large eggs	½	cup all-purpose flour
			Vanilla or peppermint ice cream

MINT FUDGE SAUCE, OPTIONAL

4½	ounces bittersweet or semisweet chocolate, chopped	⅓	cup hot water
2	ounces unsweetened chocolate, chopped	¼	cup light corn syrup
		¾	teaspoon peppermint extract

Preheat oven to 425 degrees. Melt chocolate and butter together over low heat; cool slightly. Whisk eggs with egg yolks in a large bowl. Whisk in sugar, then cooled chocolate and flour. Pour batter evenly into six greased (6-ounce) soufflé dishes or custard cups. Recipe may be made a day ahead to this point, covered and chilled until ready to bake. Bake 12 minutes or until sides are set but center remains soft and runny, or up to 15 minutes for chilled batter. Run a small knife around cakes to loosen and immediately turn onto plates. Serve with ice cream and Mint Fudge Sauce. To make sauce, melt both chocolates in the top of a double boiler over barely simmering water. Add hot water, corn syrup and mint extract and whisk until smooth. Cool slightly. Sauce may be made up to 2 days ahead, covered and chilled. To serve, warm sauce over low heat, stirring constantly.

YIELDS 6 SERVINGS

After greasing, dust chocolate cake pans with cocoa instead of flour for better flavor and no chalky appearance. For cake mixes, dust with a little of the dry mix.

SUPERB CHOCOLATE CAKE

2	cups all-purpose flour	¼	teaspoon salt
2	cups granulated sugar	½	cup margarine or butter
1	teaspoon cinnamon	2	eggs
1	cup water	1	teaspoon baking soda
½	cup solid vegetable shortening	½	cup buttermilk
¼	cup unsweetened cocoa	1	tablespoon vanilla

SUPERB CHOCOLATE FROSTING

½	cup butter or margarine	1	teaspoon vanilla
¼	cup unsweetened cocoa	¼	cup milk
1	(1-pound) package confectioners' sugar, sifted		

Preheat oven to 350 degrees. Sift together flour, sugar and cinnamon in a bowl; set aside. In a saucepan, combine water and next 4 ingredients. Bring to a boil. Add hot mixture to dry ingredients and blend well. Add eggs and next 3 ingredients and beat well. Pour batter into a greased and lightly floured 9x13-inch cake pan or two 8-inch cake pans. Bake 40-45 minutes or until a toothpick inserted in center comes out clean. Cool on a rack. For frosting, melt butter with cocoa in a medium saucepan. Remove from heat and add confectioners' sugar and vanilla, beating well. Slowly blend in milk. Spread frosting over cooled cake.

YIELDS 8-10 SERVINGS

HOW OLD IS YOUR BAKING POWDER?

Mix 1 teaspoon with ⅓ cup warm water. If it fizzes, use it. If not, it is no longer effective.

WHITE CHOCOLATE ICE BOX CAKE

- 1 (20- to 22-ounce) package fudge brownie mix
- 1 (6-ounce) package white baking chocolate or chips
- 1½ cups heavy cream, divided
- 2 tablespoons coffee-flavored liqueur, such as Kahlúa, optional
- 2 ounces bittersweet chocolate, grated

FUDGE SAUCE
- ½ cup unsweetened cocoa
- ⅓ cup granulated sugar
- ¼ cup firmly packed brown sugar
- ½ cup heavy cream
- 1 tablespoon coffee-flavored liqueur, such as Kahlúa
- 1 tablespoon strong coffee
- 4 tablespoons butter

Preheat oven to temperature indicated on brownie package. With one piece of foil, line bottom of a 10-inch springform pan, letting foil extend about 1 inch up sides of pan. Grease foil. Prepare brownie mix according to directions on package. Pour 1½ cups batter into prepared pan. Bake 25 minutes or until a toothpick inserted in center comes out with moist crumbs attached. (Bake remaining batter in a separate pan for future use.) Cool in pan 15 minutes, then lift foil with brownie from pan to a rack. Cool completely. Remove foil and return brownie to pan. In a heavy saucepan, melt white chocolate with ¼ cup cream over low heat, stirring until smooth. Remove from heat and stir in liqueur. Cool 20 minutes or to room temperature. Using an electric mixer on high speed, beat remaining 1¼ cups cream until soft peaks form. Stir a large spoonful of whipped cream into chocolate mixture, then fold this mixture into whipped cream. Spread half of mousse mixture over brownie in pan. Sprinkle with grated chocolate and spoon on remaining mousse. Refrigerate at least 8 hours. Drizzle with warm or room temperature fudge sauce. To make sauce, combine cocoa and both sugars in a heavy saucepan. Stir in cream and remaining 3 ingredients and bring to a boil over medium heat. Boil 1 minute, stirring constantly. Remove from heat and cool.

YIELDS 8-10 SERVINGS

The addition of a bit of salt in a cake or cookie recipe is to enhance sweetness.

PRALINE LAYER CAKE

½ cup butter	1 (18¼-ounce) package devil's food cake mix
¼ cup heavy cream	1¼ cups water
1 cup firmly packed brown sugar	⅓ cup vegetable oil
¾ cup chopped pecans	3 eggs

TOPPING

1¾ cups heavy cream
¼ cup confectioners' sugar
¼ teaspoon vanilla

Preheat oven to 325 degrees. Combine butter, cream and brown sugar in a small saucepan. Cook over low heat, stirring occasionally, until butter is melted. Pour evenly into two greased 9-inch round cake pans. Sprinkle evenly with pecans. Combine cake mix and next 3 ingredients in a large bowl. Beat with an electric mixer on low speed until moistened, then increase to high speed and beat 2 minutes. Carefully spoon batter over praline mixture in pans. Bake 35 minutes or until cake springs back when lightly touched. Cool in pans on wire racks 5-7 minutes, no longer or praline layer will stick to pan. Run a knife around edge and slightly raise to loosen cake and praline layer. Cover each pan with a cake plate and quickly invert; remove pans. Cool completely or refrigerate. Using an electric mixer, prepare topping. Beat cream until soft peaks form. Add confectioners' sugar and vanilla and beat on high speed until stiff peaks form. Spread half the topping on one cake layer. Top with second layer, praline-side up and spread with remaining topping. Refrigerate until ready to serve.

YIELDS 8-10 SERVINGS

IN A HURRY PECAN CAKE

1 (18¼-ounce) package butter pecan cake mix	¾ cup vegetable oil
1 cup water	4 eggs
	1 can coconut pecan frosting

TOPPING

½ cup firmly packed brown sugar	¼ cup milk
2 tablespoons butter	½ pound confectioners' sugar

Preheat oven to 350 degrees. Mix together cake mix and next 4 ingredients. Pour batter into a greased and floured Bundt pan. Bake 45-50 minutes; cool. Combine brown sugar, butter and milk in a saucepan over low heat. Bring to a boil, stirring until well blended. Add confectioners' sugar and mix well. Pour mixture over cooled cake.

YIELDS 8-10 SERVINGS

DESSERTS

LIGHT AND EASY NO BAKE CAKE

1½ cups graham cracker crumbs	1 cup plus 3 tablespoons superfine sugar, divided
5 tablespoons butter or margarine, melted	3 eggs, separated
2 squares semisweet chocolate	1 teaspoon vanilla
1 square unsweetened chocolate	Whipped cream or chocolate curls for garnish
1 cup butter, softened	

In a medium bowl, mix cracker crumbs and melted butter until well blended. Press crumbs into a greased shallow 2-quart baking dish or 9-inch springform pan. Refrigerate until ready to use. Melt all chocolate together. Using an electric mixer, cream together softened butter and 1 cup superfine sugar in a large bowl. Add egg yolks, one at a time, beating well for 2-3 minutes after each addition. Blend in melted chocolate and vanilla; set aside. In a separate bowl, beat egg whites with remaining 3 tablespoons superfine sugar until soft peaks form. Fold whites into chocolate mixture and spoon over chilled crust. Freeze 24 hours before serving. Top with whipped cream or chocolate curls for garnish.

YIELDS 8-10 SERVINGS

Make your own superfine sugar by placing granulated sugar in a food processor or blender and processing until powdery.

MELTING CHOCOLATE

When melting chocolate, be sure no water or steam droplets get into the chocolate. It will "seize" (clump and harden) and will not melt again. To remedy this, add clarified butter or vegetable oil, a little at a time, and stir until smooth. If melting in microwave, be sure it is perfectly dry inside or you will have the same results. Chocolate will scorch or burn if melted over direct heat.

OLD FASHIONED COCONUT CAKE

BATTER

- 1 (18¼-ounce) package golden butter cake mix
- 3 large eggs
- ½ cup unsalted butter, softened
- ⅓ cup sweetened cream of coconut
- ⅓ cup water
- 1½ tablespoons dark rum

FROSTING

- 16 ounces cream cheese, softened
- ½ cup unsalted butter, softened
- ½ cup sweetened cream of coconut
- ¾ cup sifted confectioners' sugar
- 1 teaspoon vanilla
- 10 ounces sweetened flaked coconut (about 3 cups)

Preheat oven to 375 degrees. Combine all batter ingredients and beat with an electric mixer on low speed until smooth. Increase to medium speed and beat 4 minutes. Divide batter between two greased and floured 9-inch cake pans. Bake 25 minutes or until a toothpick inserted in center comes out clean. Cool in pans 10 minutes. Cut around cake edges to loosen and turn out onto racks to cool completely. To make frosting, beat cream cheese, butter and cream of coconut with an electric mixer in a large bowl until smooth. Beat in confectioners' sugar and vanilla. Place a cooled cake layer, flat-side up, on a platter. Spread layer with ¾ cup frosting and sprinkle with ¾ cup coconut. Top with second cake layer, flat-side down. Cover top and sides of cake with remaining frosting. Press remaining coconut over top and sides of cake. Chill cake 1 hour or until frosting is firm. Cake can be made a day ahead, covered loosely and kept chilled until 1 hour before serving.

YIELDS 12-14 SERVINGS

BANANA-PINEAPPLE CAKE

- 3 cups all-purpose flour
- 2 cups granulated sugar
- 1 teaspoon salt
- 1 teaspoon baking soda
- 3 eggs, slightly beaten
- 2 cup mashed banana (3-4 bananas)
- 1 cup vegetable oil
- 1 (15½-ounce) can crushed pineapple, undrained
- 1½ teaspoons vanilla
- Confectioners' sugar for dusting

Preheat oven to 350 degrees. In a large bowl, thoroughly combine flour and next 3 ingredients. Make a well in the center of dry ingredients. In a separate bowl, combine eggs and next 4 ingredients. Add mixture to dry ingredients and stir until well moistened. Pour batter into a greased and floured 10-inch tube pan. Bake 60-65 minutes or until a toothpick inserted in the center comes out clean. Cool in pan 15 minutes. Remove from pan and cool on a wire rack. Sprinkle with confectioners' sugar.

YIELDS 10 SERVINGS

RUM CREAM CAKE

3 eggs	1 teaspoon baking powder
1 cup granulated sugar	2 tablespoons cold water
1 cup all-purpose flour	2 tablespoons rum
Pinch of salt	

RUM CREAM

2 (¼-ounce) envelopes unflavored gelatin	2 ounces Jamaican rum
¼ cup cold water	1 cup heavy cream, whipped
2 cups scalded milk	3 tablespoons sliced almonds, toasted, optional
¾ cup granulated sugar	
4 egg yolks, beaten	

Preheat oven to 350 degrees. Beat eggs until light. Gradually beat in sugar until thick and pale in color. Sift together flour, salt and baking powder 3 times. Stir water and dry ingredients into egg mixture. Add rum. Pour batter into a 9-inch springform pan. Bake 25 minutes. Cool cake in pan. To make cream, soak gelatin in cold water 5 minutes in a saucepan. Pour scalded milk over softened gelatin and blend well. Stir in sugar. Heat mixture; do not boil. Pour heated mixture over egg yolks, stirring constantly. Gradually stir in rum; set aside to cool. When mixture begins to set, blend in whipped cream and pour over cake in pan. Top with almonds and refrigerate until set. Unmold when ready to serve. Cake may be made a day or two ahead.

YIELDS 12-14 SERVINGS

To toast, spread almonds in a single layer on a baking sheet. Toast at 350 degrees 3-5 minutes or until golden, shaking pan occasionally and watching closely.

DELICIOUS DATE NUT TORTE

¼ cup all-purpose flour	2 eggs, separated
½ teaspoon baking powder	¾ cup granulated sugar
1½ cups dates, cut into small pieces	½ teaspoon vanilla
1½ cups chopped pecans	

Preheat oven to 275 degrees. Sift together flour and baking powder. Add dates and pecans. In a large bowl, beat egg yolks with sugar and vanilla. In a small bowl, beat egg whites until peaks form but are not dry. Pour flour mixture into beaten yolks and mix well. Fold in egg whites until well blended. Spoon mixture into a greased 8-inch round cake pan. Bake 50 minutes or until light brown.

YIELDS 8 SERVINGS

VODKA-KAHLÚA CAKE

- ½ cup chopped pecans
- 1 (18¼-ounce) package butter cake mix
- 1 (3.4- to 3.9-ounce) package instant vanilla or chocolate pudding mix
- ½ cup coffee-flavored liqueur, such as Kahlúa
- ½ cup vodka
- ½ cup water
- ½ cup vegetable oil
- 4 eggs

GLAZE

- ¼ cup water
- 1 cup granulated sugar
- ½ cup butter
- ¼ cup vodka
- ¼ cup coffee-flavored liqueur, such as Kahlúa

Preheat oven to 350 degrees. Scatter chopped pecans in the bottom of a greased and floured 10-inch tube or Bundt pan. In a large bowl, using an electric mixer on medium speed, combine cake mix and next 6 ingredients and beat 2 minutes. Pour batter over pecans in pan. Bake 50-60 minutes, checking for doneness after 50 minutes; do not overbake. Prepare glaze while cake bakes. In a small saucepan, bring water, sugar and butter to a boil over medium-high heat. Remove from heat and stir in vodka and liqueur. Let glaze cool while cake bakes and reheat before pouring over cake. When finished baking, remove cake from oven and poke holes in top with a wooden pick. Immediately pour warm glaze over cake while still in pan. Cool cake before removing from pan.

YIELDS 8-10 SERVINGS

YORKTOWN GINGERBREAD

- 2 cups all-purpose flour
- 1 cup firmly packed light brown sugar
- 1 teaspoon cinnamon
- 1 teaspoon ground ginger
- ¼ teaspoon salt
- ½ cup butter
- 1 teaspoon baking soda
- 1 cup buttermilk
- 1 egg
- ¼ cup molasses
- 1 cup sliced almonds, divided

Preheat oven to 350 degrees. Sift together flour and next 4 ingredients. Cut in butter until mixture resembles coarse crumbs. Set aside 1 cup of mixture. Combine baking soda and buttermilk and add to remaining crumb mixture. Stir in egg and molasses, mixing with a spoon until well blended. Add ½ cup almonds. Spread batter in a greased 9-inch square baking pan. Sprinkle reserved crumb mixture and remaining ½ cup almonds on top. Gently swirl some of topping into batter. Bake until almonds are light golden brown.

YIELDS 10-12 SERVINGS

OUIE GOOIE TART

CRUST

- ⅓ cup granulated sugar
- 10½ tablespoons butter
- 2 cups flour
- ½-1 ounce coffee beans, optional, chopped in a coffee grinder

FILLING

- 3 eggs
- 2 egg yolks
- ¾ cup granulated sugar
- 8 ounces 64% dark chocolate, chopped
- 1½ cups heavy cream, preferably 40%
- 1-1½ ounces prepared espresso
- Coffee beans, ground into powder

SAUCE

- 6 ounces 55% chocolate or semisweet chocolate
- 2 ounces milk chocolate
- 2 ounces white chocolate
- 7 ounces heavy cream, preferably 40%
- Cocoa powder for topping, optional

Cream together sugar and butter with an electric mixer. With mixer on lowest speed, add flour and blend until dough pulls together into a ball. If needed, add water, a little at a time. Pat dough into a 10-inch pie pan. Press chopped coffee beans into dough. Refrigerate crust until chilled. When cooled, preheat oven to 350 degrees. Bake crust 12 minutes. Remove and set aside; retain oven temperature.

For filling, beat eggs and egg yolks together in a saucepan. Add sugar and beat until well blended. Add chopped chocolate and cream and heat, stirring well, 1½-2 minutes or until melted. Blend in espresso. Allow filling to cool, then pour into baked crust. Place coffee bean powder in a shaker and dust over top of tart. After dusting, bake tart 25 minutes or until center is slightly set and wiggles when touched. Cool.

Melt all sauce ingredients together in a glass bowl in a microwave. Stir sauce until smooth and pour over top of cooled tart. Allow to cool to room temperature. Dust top with cocoa powder before serving.

YIELDS 6 SERVINGS

Most brands of cream list the percentage of milk fat on the container. Forty percent is not necessary to this recipe, but it will result in a richer, denser and creamier finished product.

Fresh egg whites will keep refrigerated 2-4 days. Yolks (unbroken and covered with water) will keep 2-4 days.

CHOCOLATE TART

8 ounces semisweet chocolate	4 eggs, beaten
1 cup granulated sugar	1 cup heavy cream
1 cup butter	¼ cup confectioners' sugar
½ cup brewed coffee, or ¼ cup espresso	½ teaspoon vanilla

Preheat oven to 350 degrees. Butter an 8½-inch springform pan and line with foil. Melt together chocolate, sugar and butter in a saucepan over low to medium heat until sugar is dissolved. Remove from heat and whisk in coffee and eggs until well blended. Pour mixture into prepared pan. Bake 30 minutes or until crust forms on top with a 2-inch raised ridge. Cool in refrigerator. Tart can be refrigerated 3-4 days, or frozen, until ready for topping. To prepare topping, beat cream until peaks form. Slowly beat in confectioners' sugar and vanilla. Spread topping over cooled tart. Refrigerate until ready to serve. Serve with ice cream or fresh berries.

YIELDS 6-8 SERVINGS

COCONUT CHESS PIE

½ cup butter, softened	½ cup 40% heavy cream
2 cups granulated or firmly packed light brown sugar	Juice and zest of 1 lemon
1 tablespoon all-purpose flour	¾ cup coconut milk
3 eggs	1 cup grated fresh coconut, or unsweetened flaked coconut
2 egg yolks	

SAUCE

Juice and zest of 1 lemon	1 cup coconut milk
1½ teaspoons all-purpose flour	1 cup granulated sugar

Preheat oven to 325 degrees. Beat butter and sugar with an electric mixer on high speed until creamed. Beat in flour quickly. Beat eggs and egg yolks, one at a time, into mixture. Blend in cream. Add lemon juice and zest and coconut milk. Stir in grated coconut. Pour mixture into a pie pan. Bake 25 minutes; check for doneness. For sauce, combine lemon juice and zest in a small saucepan. Blend in flour. Whisk in coconut milk. Cook over low heat for 2-3 minutes. Stir in sugar and cook 2-3 minutes longer. To serve, place a piece of pie on an individual plate and pour 1 ounce of sauce on top.

YIELDS 8 SERVINGS

CRANBERRY PIE

½ cup butter, softened	1 (12-ounce) package cranberries, slightly crushed
1½ cups granulated sugar	1 cup chopped pecans
3 eggs, separated	1 (9-inch) pie crust, unbaked

Preheat oven to 375 degrees. Cream butter and sugar with an electric mixer. Blend in egg yolks. Stir in cranberries and pecans. Beat egg whites until stiff and fold into cranberry filling. Spoon filling into pie crust. Bake 40 minutes.

YIELDS 8 SERVINGS

PERFECT CRUST

½ cup margarine, softened	1½ cups all-purpose flour
8 ounces cream cheese, softened	

Mix all ingredients together, blending thoroughly. Form into a ball and refrigerate, covered, for 30 minutes before using.

YIELDS 1 (9-INCH) PIE CRUST, COBBLER, OR POT PIE TOPPING

CHOCOLATE MERINGUE PIE

1½ cups granulated sugar	6 tablespoons margarine, melted
3 tablespoons plus 1 teaspoon unsweetened cocoa	5 eggs, separated
	1½ teaspoons vanilla
¼ teaspoon salt	1 (9-inch) pie crust
1 (12-ounce) can evaporated milk	Sugar to taste

Preheat oven to 350 degrees. Mix sugar, cocoa and salt with a fork in a saucepan. Stir in milk. Add margarine and blend over low heat; do not boil. Beat egg yolks slightly in a bowl. Add some of hot mixture to egg yolks, stirring well. Blend egg mixture into hot milk mixture and stir well. Mix in vanilla. Pour filling into pie crust. Bake 20 minutes. In a separate bowl, beat egg whites until stiff, adding sugar to taste. Spread meringue over baked pie, sealing edges all around. Return to oven and bake until meringue is light golden brown.

YIELDS 8-10 SERVINGS

DESSERTS

CHOCOLATE BOURBON PIE

4	tablespoons butter or margarine, melted and cooled	1	(6-ounce) can evaporated milk
3½	tablespoons unsweetened cocoa	2	eggs, beaten
1½	cups granulated sugar	2	tablespoons bourbon
	Pinch of salt	1	(9-inch) pie crust, unbaked
		¼	cup chopped pecans, optional

Preheat oven to 350 degrees. Mix butter and next 5 ingredients in a medium bowl. Stir in bourbon. Pour mixture into pie crust. Top with pecans. Bake 45 minutes.

YIELDS 6-8 SERVINGS

CHART HOUSE MUD PIE

- ½ (3- to 4-ounce) package chocolate wafers, crushed
- 4 tablespoons butter, melted
- 1 quart coffee ice cream, softened
- ½ cup chocolate fudge sauce, well chilled
- Whipped cream and slivered almonds for garnish

Mix wafer crumbs with butter and press into a 9-inch pie pan. Spoon ice cream over cookie crust and freeze until ice cream is firm. Top with cold fudge sauce. Store, covered, in freezer for about 10 hours before serving. Serve on chilled dessert plates and garnish with whipped cream and almonds.

YIELDS 8 SERVINGS

WHIPPING WHIPPED CREAM

Make sure bowl and beaters are clean and well chilled. Use heavy cream. Do not overbeat or it will become watery. Whipped cream is ready when stiff peaks form when lifted with a spoon.

GREAT PECAN PIE

- 1 (1-pound) package light brown sugar
- ½ cup butter, softened
- 4 eggs
- 2 tablespoons plain cornmeal
- 2 tablespoons water
- 2 tablespoons vanilla
- Pinch of salt
- 2 cups broken pecans
- 2 (9-inch) pie crusts, unbaked

Preheat oven to 350 degrees. Cream sugar and butter. Add eggs and next 5 ingredients and mix well. Pour filling into pie crusts. Bake 30-35 minutes or until a toothpick comes out clean.

YIELDS 16 SERVINGS

For a crisper crust, bake crust slightly before pouring in filling.

NO CRUST APPLE PIE

- ½ cup butter, softened
- Pinch of salt
- 1 tablespoon granulated sugar
- 2 tablespoons milk
- 1 egg yolk, beaten
- 1¼ cups all-purpose flour
- 1 teaspoon baking powder
- 4-5 apples, peeled and sliced

TOPPING

- ¾ cup granulated sugar
- 1½ tablespoons all-purpose flour
- ¼ teaspoon cinnamon
- 3 tablespoons butter, softened

Preheat oven to 350 degrees. Blend butter and next 6 ingredients with a hand mixer in a large bowl. Gently mix in apples. Spoon mixture into a 9- to 10-inch pie pan. Mix all topping ingredients together in a small bowl and spread over apple mixture. Place in oven with foil or baking sheet underneath. Bake 50 minutes or until apples are soft. Serve warm with vanilla ice cream.

YIELDS 8-10 SERVINGS

"A new twist on an old favorite."

DESSERTS

HARVEST APPLE PIE

2 (9- to 10-inch) pie crusts	3 tablespoons granulated sugar
5-6 Red Delicious apples, peeled and sliced	1 teaspoon salt
3 tablespoons butter or margarine	1 teaspoon cinnamon
⅓ cup corn syrup	1 tablespoon cornstarch

TOPPING

1 tablespoon butter or margarine	1 tablespoon all-purpose flour
1½ tablespoons corn syrup	¼ cup chopped walnuts or pecans
¼ cup firmly packed brown sugar	

Preheat oven to 400 degrees. Lay a single layer pie crust in a pie pan. Layer apple slices on crust. Mix butter and next 5 ingredients and pour mixture over apples; not all of mixture may be needed. Top pie with second pie crust and pinch edges together to seal. Make several slits near center for steam vents. Bake on center rack of oven for 1 hour. For topping, heat butter and next 3 ingredients in a saucepan. Drizzle topping over pie for last 5 minutes of baking time. Sprinkle with chopped nuts and bake 3-5 minutes longer.

YIELDS 6-8 SERVINGS

"My girlfriend and I use to spend every Black Friday baking pies instead of shopping. We would spend the day sharing stories, laughter and wine. Then we would split the number of pies, put them in our freezers and give them away for Christmas gifts. I now do this with my 2 daughters…a great tradition that creates wonderful memories."

KRISPY ICE CREAM PIE

½ cup butter	2 quarts vanilla ice cream, softened
1 cup semisweet chocolate chips	Chocolate curls or shavings for garnish, optional
1 tablespoon water	
3 cups crisp rice cereal, such as Rice Krispies	

Melt together butter, chocolate and water. Mix in cereal. Divide and press mixture into two 9-inch pie pans and freeze. Spread ice cream into frozen shells and freeze until ready to serve. Garnish as desired.

YIELDS 16 SERVINGS

"Try mint chocolate chip or peppermint ice cream at holiday time."

GOOBER PIE

- 4 ounces cream cheese, softened
- 1 cup confectioners' sugar
- ⅓ cup chunky peanut butter
- ½ cup milk
- 9 ounces frozen nondairy whipped topping, thawed
- 1 (9-inch) graham cracker pie crust, baked
- Chopped peanuts for garnish, optional

Whip cream cheese with an electric mixer. Gradually beat in confectioners' sugar and peanut butter until smooth and fluffy. Slowly add milk and blend thoroughly. Fold in whipped topping. Pour filling into baked pie crust. Garnish with peanuts. Freeze until ready to serve.

YIELDS 8 SERVINGS

"When the Portsmouth Service League sponsored the Ladies Professional Golf Tournament, Jan Stephenson, a professional golfer, stayed in our home. A couple of months before her arrival each year, she would request that I serve this pie each evening during her stay."

VERMONT MAPLE CREAM PIE

- 2 extra large eggs
- 2 extra large egg yolks
- 1 cup firmly packed brown sugar
- 1 cup heavy cream
- ½ cup dark maple syrup
- ½ teaspoon vanilla
- 1 (9-inch) pie crust, unbaked
- 1 cup heavy cream
- ¼ cup chopped pecans or walnuts, toasted, optional

Preheat oven to 350 degrees. Whisk eggs and egg yolks together. Add brown sugar and next 3 ingredients. Stir until sugar dissolves. Pour mixture into pie crust. Bake 30 minutes. Carefully remove from oven and cover with tented foil. Return to oven and bake 25-30 minutes longer or until almost firm. Cool thoroughly. Beat cream until peaks form and spread over pie. Sprinkle with nuts and refrigerate until ready to serve.

YIELDS 8 SERVINGS

Toast nuts at 325 degrees 4-5 minutes, watching carefully to prevent burning.

PEACH ICE CREAM PIE

1¼ cups plus 2 tablespoons granulated sugar, divided	45 vanilla wafers, divided
½ teaspoon cinnamon	4 tablespoons butter, melted
1 teaspoon vanilla	1-1½ quarts vanilla ice cream
4 cups peeled and diced peaches, divided	1 cup heavy cream

Combine ½ cup sugar, cinnamon and vanilla in a saucepan. Melt mixture together over medium heat. Add 2 cups peaches and cook 5 minutes longer or until sugar is dissolved and mixture is bubbly. Remove from heat and cool 1 hour at room temperature. In a food processor, combine 35 vanilla wafers with ½ cup sugar and process until fine. Add melted butter and process until well combined. Press mixture into the bottom and up the sides of a 9- or 10-inch pie pan. Freeze crust 30 minutes. Remove ice cream from freezer until slightly softened. Coarsely crush remaining 10 vanilla wafers. Place softened ice cream in a large bowl. Add cooled peach mixture and crushed wafer crumbs. Stir lightly, forming swirls, and pour into crust. Freeze 3 hours. For sauce, blend remaining 2 cups peaches with ¼ cup sugar in a food processor until puréed; refrigerate. In a bowl, whip cream with remaining 2 tablespoons sugar until stiff peaks form; refrigerate. To serve, drizzle peach sauce on individual plates. Add a slice of pie and top with whipped cream.

YIELDS 8-10 SERVINGS

Other fresh fruit in season can be substituted for peaches.

PEELING PEACHES

Peeling peaches is quick and easy by this method: Place a peach in boiling water and blanch about 20 seconds, then quickly cool in cold water to stop cooking. For stubborn skins, return to boiling water for a few more seconds. This works for a number of vegetables, fruits and nuts.

EASY BUTTERSCOTCH PIE

- 1 (9-inch) deep dish pie shell (graham or pastry), baked
- 1 quart coffee ice cream, softened
- 1 quart vanilla ice cream, softened

BUTTERSCOTCH SAUCE
- 1 egg yolk
- 4 tablespoons butter
- ⅓ cup light corn syrup
- ⅔ cup brown sugar
- ¼ cup water

Fill pie shell halfway with coffee ice cream. Freeze until fairly firm. Repeat with vanilla ice cream, filling to top of pie crust. Freeze. When pie is frozen solid, remove from freezer and, using a very sharp knife (it may have to sit out a few minutes) cut pie into desired number of servings. Return cut pie to freezer until ready to serve.

For sauce, beat egg yolk lightly in a saucepan. Mix in butter and remaining 3 ingredients. Cook over low heat until thick. Cool and refrigerate.

To serve, warm sauce in microwave and drizzle over pie slices.

YIELDS 6-8 SERVINGS

This may also be made in a 2-quart baking dish using a graham cracker crust.

BEST EVER RUGALACH

- 2 cups all-purpose flour
- 1 cup butter or margarine
- ¾ cup sour cream
- 1 egg yolk
- 1 cup granulated sugar
- 1 heaping teaspoon cinnamon
- ¾ cup chopped pecans
- ¾ cup raisins

Blend together flour and next 3 ingredients. Divide dough into 6-7 balls. Wrap each in flour-coated wax paper. Refrigerate until firm. When ready to bake, preheat oven to 375 degrees. Mix sugar and remaining 3 ingredients to make a filling. Working with one ball at a time, roll out each ball into a thin circle and sprinkle with some filling. Cut into wedges and roll up each wedge, starting with outer edge of circle. Bake on an ungreased baking sheet 20 minutes or until lightly browned.

YIELDS ABOUT 5 DOZEN

DESSERTS

ALMOND-APRICOT SOFT BISCOTTI

- 2¾ cups sifted all-purpose flour
- 1½ cups granulated sugar
- ½ cup butter, cut into pieces
- 2½ teaspoons baking powder
- 1 teaspoon salt
- 1 teaspoon ground ginger
- 3½ ounces white chocolate
- 1⅔ cups slivered almonds, toasted
- 2 large eggs
- 5 tablespoons apricot-flavored brandy
- 2 teaspoons almond extract
- 1 (6-ounce) package dried apricots, coarsely chopped

Combine flour and next 5 ingredients in a food processor and process until a coarse meal forms. Add white chocolate and process until finely chopped. Add toasted almonds and pulse 5 times. In a small bowl, beat together eggs, brandy and almond extract. Pour mixture into processor. Add apricots and process to blend. Transfer dough to a parchment paper-covered baking sheet. Shape dough into 3 logs, each about 12x2-inches. Refrigerate dough 30 minutes or until firm. When ready to bake, preheat oven to 350 degrees. Bake 30 minutes or until golden; cool completely. Reduce heat to 300 degrees. Using a serrated knife, cut logs into ½-inch thick slices and place slices, cut-side up, on baking sheet. Bake 10 minutes. Turn slices and bake 10 minutes longer. Transfer slices to racks to cool. Store in an air-tight container, or freeze for up to 6 months.

YIELDS 72 BISCOTTI

Toast almonds at 350 degrees for 3-5 minutes, stirring every few minutes. Watch closely as almonds can burn quickly. Cool completely before adding to recipe.

APPLE SQUARES

- 1¾ cups granulated sugar
- 2 eggs
- 1 cup butter, softened
- 2 cups all-purpose flour
- 1 teaspoon salt
- 1 teaspoon baking soda
- 1 teaspoon baking powder
- 1 teaspoon cinnamon
- 1 teaspoon vanilla
- 3 cups peeled and coarsely chopped apples
- 1 cup chopped nuts, optional

Preheat oven to 350 degrees. In a large bowl, mix sugar, eggs and butter. Blend in flour and next 4 ingredients. Mix in vanilla. Stir in apples and nuts. Pour mixture into a lightly greased 9x13-inch glass baking dish. Bake 45-60 minutes. Cool and cut into squares.

YIELDS 16-20 SERVINGS

HEART OF THE HARBOR

APRICOT BARS

- ⅔ cup dried apricots, rinsed
- ½ cup butter, softened
- ¼ cup granulated sugar
- 1⅓ cups all-purpose flour, sifted, divided
- ½ teaspoon baking powder
- ¼ teaspoon salt
- 1 cup firmly packed brown sugar
- 2 eggs, well beaten
- ½ teaspoon vanilla
- ½ cup chopped pecans
- Confectioners' sugar for dusting

Preheat oven to 350 degrees. Place apricots in a saucepan and cover with water. Bring to a boil and cook 10 minutes. Drain, cool and chop; set aside. Mix butter, granulated sugar and 1 cup flour until crumbly. Press mixture into a greased 8-inch square baking dish. Bake 20-25 minutes. Sift together remaining ⅓ cup flour, baking powder and salt. In a separate bowl, gradually blend brown sugar into well beaten eggs with an electric mixer. Blend in dry ingredients and vanilla. Stir in pecans and apricots and spread over baked crust. Bake 25-30 minutes. Cool in pan before cutting into bars. Dust with confectioners' sugar.

YIELDS 9-12 SERVINGS

BROWN SUGAR BROWNIES

- 1 (1-pound) package light brown sugar
- ¾ cup butter or margarine, melted
- 3 eggs, beaten
- 2⅔ cups all-purpose flour
- 2 teaspoons baking powder
- 1 teaspoon salt
- 1 teaspoon vanilla
- 1 cup coarsely chopped pecans
- 1 (12-ounce) package semisweet chocolate chips

Preheat oven to 350 degrees. Stir sugar into melted butter. Blend in eggs. Sift together flour, baking powder and salt. Gradually add dry ingredients to butter mixture, stirring by hand until just moistened; do not overmix. Gently blend in vanilla, pecans and chocolate chips. Spread mixture into a lightly greased 9x13-inch baking dish. Bake 30-35 minutes or until a toothpick inserted in the center comes out clean.

YIELDS 12-16 SERVINGS

COCONUT KEY LIME BARS

CRUST
- 5 ounces ginger thins
- Pinch of salt
- 3 tablespoons firmly packed light brown sugar
- 4 tablespoons unsalted butter

FILLING
- 2 ounces cream cheese, softened
- 1 tablespoon fresh Key lime zest
- 1 (14-ounce) can sweetened condensed milk
- 1 egg yolk
- ½ cup fresh Key lime juice
- ¾ cup sweetened shredded coconut, toasted, for topping

Preheat oven to 325 degrees. Place rack in center of oven. Line bottom and sides of an 8-inch square pan with foil and spray with cooking spray. To prepare crust, pulse ginger thins in a food processor about 10 seconds. Add salt and brown sugar and pulse in 1-second intervals, 10-12 times. Melt butter, cool slightly and drizzle over crumbs in food processor. Pulse until crumbs are uniformly moistened. Press crumb mixture evenly and firmly into the bottom of prepared pan. Bake 18-20 minutes or until deep golden brown; cool on a wire rack. For filling, stir cream cheese with lime zest using a rubber spatula in a medium bowl until creamy and thoroughly combined. Whisk in milk until smooth. Whisk in egg yolk. Gently blend in lime juice; mixture will thicken slightly. Pour filling into cooled crust and smooth surface with spatula. Bake 15-20 minutes or until set and edges begin to pull away from side of pan. Cool on wire rack 1-1½ hours or to room temperature. When cool, cover and refrigerate 2 hours or until completely chilled. Sprinkle toasted coconut on top. Let stand at room temperature about 15 minutes before cutting into 2-inch squares.

YIELDS 16 SERVINGS

To toast coconut, spread on a baking sheet in a thin layer. Bake in center of oven at 325 degrees 7-10 minutes, shaking or stirring often. Check often after 5 minutes to prevent burning.

EASY PECAN BARS

- 1 cup butter, melted
- 1½ cups all-purpose flour
- 1 (1-pound) package granulated sugar
- 1 teaspoon baking powder
- 2 eggs
- 2 teaspoons vanilla
- 1 heaping cup chopped pecans
- Confectioners' sugar for dusting

Preheat oven to 350 degrees. Combine butter and next 5 ingredients and blend well. Stir in pecans. Pour mixture into a greased 9x13-inch pan. Bake 35-40 minutes. Cool completely. Sprinkle confectioners' sugar on top and cut into bars. Best when served the day they are baked.

YIELDS 12-16 SERVINGS

FRENCH VANILLA MACAROON BARS

5 tablespoons butter or margarine, softened	1 teaspoon vanilla
1 (18¼-ounce) package moist French vanilla cake mix	2 tablespoons water
	1½ cups coconut
1 egg	½ cup semisweet chocolate chips

Preheat oven to 350 degrees. Cut butter into cake mix with a fork until it resembles coarse crumbs. Mix in egg and next 3 ingredients. Pour batter into a greased 9x13-inch baking pan. Bake 16-22 minutes. Cool in pan 15 minutes. Cut into bars, leaving in pan to finish cooling. In a small saucepan, melt chocolate over low heat, stirring constantly. Drizzle chocolate over bars. Cool 1 hour, 30 minutes before serving.

YIELDS 15 SERVINGS

INITIAL COOKIES

2¼ cups all-purpose flour	1 cup granulated sugar
2 teaspoons baking powder	1 large egg, beaten
½ teaspoon salt	½ teaspoon vanilla
½ cup butter, softened	¼ cup milk

Combine flour, baking powder and salt; set aside. Cream butter. Gradually beat in sugar. Blend in egg and vanilla and mix well. Add dry ingredients alternately with milk to creamed mixture. Chill dough at least 1 hour. When ready to bake, preheat oven to 375 degrees. Remove about ¼ cup dough at a time from refrigerator. Form each ¼-cup dough into 3-4 desired letters on a greased baking sheet. Be sure to keep letters plump and large. Bake 6-8 minutes.

YIELDS 12-16 INITIALS

This recipe may also be used to make rolled cookies.

To adhere sprinkles to cookies while baking, lightly brush tops with a bit of water before adding sprinkles then bake.

TUFFIES

2	cups firmly packed light brown sugar	⅛	teaspoon salt
¾	cup margarine, melted	1	teaspoon vanilla
2	eggs, lightly beaten	1	cup chopped pecans
1	cup all-purpose flour		Sifted confectioners' sugar for dusting

Preheat oven to 300 degrees. Combine all ingredients except confectioners' sugar in order listed. Grease bottom and sides of an 8-inch square baking pan and line bottom with wax paper. Spoon dough into pan. Bake 1 hour or until a toothpick inserted comes out clean. Turn out onto wax paper that has been sprinkled with confectioners' sugar. Remove wax paper lining and dust with more confectioners' sugar. Cut into squares while warm.

YIELDS 36 SERVINGS

"This recipe was given to me by a student in my Home Economics class. I was teaching at Jefferson High School in Roanoke, Virginia. I usually get many compliments on the Tuffies, which taste like Chess Pie if cooked correctly. The secret is in the time cooked."

PEANUT BUTTER COOKIES

1	cup peanut butter, creamy or chunky	1	large egg
1	cup granulated sugar	½	cup chopped nuts, optional

Preheat oven to 350 degrees. Mix all ingredients together in a large bowl. Drop dough by teaspoonfuls onto baking sheets. Bake 10-12 minutes.

YIELDS 3 DOZEN

This is a great and easy recipe — they disappeared!

Make sure baking pans cool between cookie batches.

ORANGE BARS

1½ cups sifted all-purpose flour	1½ teaspoons baking powder
⅓ cup instant powdered milk	½ cup butter, softened
½ cup granulated sugar	1 egg
¼ teaspoon salt	2 teaspoons vanilla
½ cup orange juice	6 ounces chocolate chips
1 tablespoon orange zest	

GLAZE

2 cups confectioners' sugar	1 teaspoon orange zest
3 tablespoons orange juice	

Preheat oven to 350 degrees. Beat together flour and next 9 ingredients. Fold in chocolate chips. Spread batter in a greased 12x7-inch baking pan. Bake 20-25 minutes or until cake pulls away from sides of pan. Combine all glaze ingredients and blend well. Spread glaze over cake immediately after removing from oven. Cool and cut into squares.

YIELDS 12-16 SERVINGS

ZESTY OATMEAL-CHOCOLATE CHIP COOKIES

½ cup unsalted butter, softened	½ teaspoon ground cinnamon
¾ cup granulated sugar	¼ teaspoon ground nutmeg
1 cup firmly packed light brown sugar	⅛ teaspoon ground cloves
1 teaspoon salt	1 cup quick-cooking oats
1 teaspoon vanilla extract	2 cups chopped pecans
2 large eggs	1½-2 teaspoons freshly grated orange zest
1½ cups flour	1 (12-ounce) package semisweet chocolate chips
1 teaspoon baking soda	

Preheat oven to 350 degrees. Using an electric mixer, beat butter until light and fluffy. Add both sugars, salt and vanilla and beat 3 minutes or until well mixed. Stir in eggs, one at a time. In a separate bowl, sift together flour and next 4 ingredients. Gradually add half of flour mixture to creamed mixture with mixer on low speed. When incorporated, add second half. Stir in oats and remaining 3 ingredients. Drop by tablespoons onto a large parchment-lined baking sheet. Bake 10-12 minutes or until golden. Remove from oven and cool cookies on a rack. Store at room temperature in a cookie jar or other airtight container.

YIELDS ABOUT 3 DOZEN

CHOCOLATE-SALTINE BITES

- 1 sleeve saltine crackers
- 1 cup granulated sugar
- 1 cup butter
- 1 (12-ounce) package semisweet chocolate chips

Preheat oven to 350 degrees. Line a 10x15-inch jelly roll pan with foil, letting it ride up the sides of pan. Cover bottom of pan with saltines, cutting crackers in half to fill the last row, if necessary. Combine sugar and butter in a small saucepan and bring to a boil. Cook 3 minutes. Pour mixture over crackers, spreading evenly to cover. Bake 12-15 minutes or until bubbly and edges begin to brown. Sprinkle evenly with chocolate chips and return to oven until chips are soft enough to spread, checking often. Remove from oven and spread chips evenly to completely cover crackers. Refrigerate until firm. Lift foil by one corner and peel off crackers. Break into pieces or cut into irregular shapes using a very sharp chef's knife. Store indefinitely in an airtight container.

DIRT

- 1 (1-pound) package cream-filled chocolate sandwich cookies, frozen
- 4 tablespoons margarine or butter
- 8 ounces cream cheese, softened
- 1 cup confectioners' sugar
- 2 (6-ounce) boxes instant vanilla pudding mix
- 3½ cups milk
- 1 (12-ounce) container nondairy whipped topping, thawed

Using a food processor or a plastic bag and a rolling pin, process or crush cookies until about the consistency of potting soil; set aside. Cream margarine, cream cheese and confectioners' sugar together. Blend pudding mix with milk 2 minutes or until thick. Mix in cream cheese mixture. Fold in whipped topping. In new 6-inch plastic flower pots or a trifle bowl, layer pudding and cookie crumbs, repeating layers and ending with cookies. Refrigerate until ready to serve.

YIELDS 4-6 SERVINGS

For special effect, put silk flowers in the "soil" with gummy worms and serve with a gardening trowel. Consider individual cups with lids for easy transport.

BROWNIE TRIFLE

- 1 (19.8-ounce) package fudge brownie mix
- ¼ cup coffee-flavored liqueur, such as Kahlua
- 1 (3.9-ounce) package instant chocolate fudge pudding mix
- 8 (1.4-ounce) English toffee candy bars, broken into small pieces
- 1 (12-ounce) container frozen non-dairy whipped topping, thawed

Prepare and bake brownie mix according to package directions. Remove from oven and pierce top with holes while still in pan. Brush liqueur over top. Cool completely, then crumble brownie into pieces. Prepare pudding mix according to package directions; do not chill. Place half of crumbled brownie in the bottom of a 3-quart trifle bowl or large glass bowl. Layer half of pudding on top. Sprinkle with half of candy pieces. Top with half of whipped topping. Repeat layers. Cover and chill 8 hours.

YIELDS 16-18 SERVINGS

BREAD PUDDING WITH WHISKEY SAUCE

BREAD PUDDING

- 1½ loaves French or Italian bread, broken up and allowed to dry out
- 2 tablespoons butter, melted
- 1 egg, beaten
- ½ teaspoon vanilla
- 1½ cups firmly packed brown sugar
- 4 cups granulated sugar
- 1 quart milk

WHISKEY SAUCE

- 1 cup unsalted butter
- 1 pound confectioners' sugar
- 2 ounces whiskey
- ½ cup heavy cream

Combine all bread pudding ingredients in a bowl. Transfer mixture to a 9x13-inch baking pan. Allow to rest at least 1 hour. When ready to bake, preheat oven to 350 degrees. Bake 1 hour, 30 minutes. To make sauce, melt butter in a heavy saucepan. Slowly whisk in sugar. Add whiskey. Slowly whisk in cream. Pour sauce over pudding while warm.

YIELDS 12 SERVINGS

FABULOUS CARAMEL FLAN

1½	cups granulated sugar, divided	2	(12-ounce) cans evaporated milk
4	eggs, beaten	1	tablespoon vanilla

Preheat oven to 350 degrees. Pour 1 cup sugar into a warm pan over medium heat. Gently stir until sugar browns and becomes caramel. Quickly pour 2-3 teaspoons caramel into each of six (6-ounce) ramekins, tilting to swirl caramel around the sides. Reheat caramel if it starts to harden. In a blender, combine eggs, milk, vanilla and remaining ½ cup sugar and process until mixed. Pour mixture into ramekins. Pour boiling water into a 9x13-inch baking pan. Place ramekins in baking pan. Bake 1 hour or until a knife inserted just off center comes out clean. Cool and refrigerate. When ready to serve, use a knife to cut around edge to loosen flan. Invert each flan onto an individual plate.

YIELDS 6 SERVINGS

"My grandmother received this authentic easy flan recipe from a Mexican nurse she worked with 34 years ago. She passed it on to me."

LIME SOUFFLÉ

½	cup granulated sugar, divided		Juice of 1 lime
3	egg yolks		Zest of 2 limes
⅓	cup flour	5	egg whites
¾	cup milk		Confectioners' sugar for dusting
3	tablespoons heavy cream		

Preheat oven to 425 degrees. Mix ¼ cup sugar and egg yolks together. Sift in flour. Combine milk and cream in a saucepan and heat to a gentle boil. Beat hot liquid into sugar mixture. Return mixture to saucepan and cook over medium heat until thickened. Beat in lime juice and zest; cool. Beat egg whites until stiff peaks form. Beat in remaining ¼ cup sugar, 1 teaspoon at a time, until thick and glossy. Fold 1 teaspoon beaten egg whites into cooled batter to loosen, then fold in remaining beaten whites. Spoon batter into 4 greased and sugared ramekins. Place ramekins on a baking sheet. Bake 10-12 minutes or until tops are browned and centers wobble slightly. Dust with confectioners' sugar. Lemons may be used instead of limes.

YIELDS 4 SERVINGS

When zesting fruit, make sure to remove only the colored part of the skin. The white part, pith, is very bitter.

CAFÉ LITE

- 2 (3-ounce) packages ladyfingers, split
- 1 cup strong fresh coffee, room temperature, divided
- 8 ounces low fat cream cheese, softened
- 2 cups skim milk
- 2 (1.4-ounce) packages fat-free, sugar-free instant vanilla pudding mix
- 1 (8-ounce) container fat-free whipped topping, thawed, divided
- Crushed cookie crumbs of choice, optional

Brush cut side of ladyfingers with ¼ cup coffee and place, cut-side up, on bottom and up sides of a 2-quart serving bowl. Beat cream cheese. Slowly blend in remaining ¾ cup coffee, then milk. Add pudding mix and stir until blended. Gently fold in half the whipped topping. Spoon mixture over ladyfingers in bowl. Cover and refrigerate overnight. When ready to serve, top with remaining whipped topping and sprinkle with cookie crumbs.

YIELDS 8 SERVINGS

DOUBLE CHOCOLATE CHEESECAKE WITH GANACHE TOPPING

- 1½ cups cream-filled chocolate sandwich cookie crumbs (about 18)
- 24 ounces cream cheese, softened
- 1 (14-ounce) can sweetened condensed milk
- 2 teaspoons vanilla
- 4 eggs
- 1 (12-ounce) package semisweet chocolate chips, melted

GANACHE

- ¾ cup heavy cream
- 1 (6-ounce) package semisweet chocolate chips
- 1 (6-ounce) package milk chocolate chips

Preheat oven to 300 degrees. Press cookie crumbs into bottom and halfway up the sides of a 9-inch springform pan. Using an electric mixer on medium speed, beat cream cheese until smooth. Add condensed milk and vanilla and beat on low speed until combined. Add eggs, one at a time, beating on low speed. Add melted chocolate and beat until just combined. Pour batter into crust. Bake 1 hour, 5 minutes or until set. Turn off heat and leave cake in oven 30 minutes longer with door closed. Remove from oven and run a sharp knife around the outer edge of cake. Cool in pan on a wire rack. Cover and chill 8 hours in pan. For ganache, bring cream to a boil over medium heat. Quickly remove from heat and stir in all chocolate chips until melted and smooth. Cool 30 minutes. Remove sides of pan and place cake on a large plate. Pour ganache over cake. Chill 1 hour before serving.

YIELDS 8-10 SERVINGS

CHOCOLATE MOUSSE

- 1 (12-ounce) package semisweet chocolate chips
- 2 eggs
- 1 tablespoon coffee-flavored liqueur, such as Kahlúa or Tia Maria
- Pinch of cinnamon
- 1½ cups half-and-half
- Whipped cream, optional

Blend chocolate chips and next 3 ingredients in a blender for 1 minute or until almost liquefied; hold in blender. Warm half-and-half in a saucepan over medium-high heat until bubbles form on top. Remove from heat and slowly add to chocolate mixture with blender on low speed. Blend 1 minute longer or until smooth. Pour mixture into 6 sherbet glasses, cover and refrigerate 2 hours or until firm. Top with whipped cream.

YIELDS 6 SERVINGS

BAKED PEARS

- 6 medium Bosc pears
- 1½ cups port wine
- ½ cup granulated sugar

Preheat oven to 350 degrees. Cut off bottom of pears so they will stand upright in a baking dish. Cover with wine and sugar. Bake about 1 hour, basting frequently. May be served drizzled with crème fraîche or chocolate sauce.

YIELDS 6 SERVINGS

HOMEMADE PEPPERMINT ICE CREAM

- 12 ounces peppermint stick candy
- 10 cups half-and-half, divided
- 2 cups sugar
- 2 tablespoons vanilla
- ⅛ teaspoon salt
- 6 ounces peppermint stick candy, crushed, optional

Break up 12 ounces candy in a 1-quart container. Add 2 cups half-and-half and refrigerate overnight to dissolve. The next day, combine remaining 8 cups half-and-half with sugar until dissolved. Stir in vanilla, salt and 6 ounces crushed candy. Add dissolved candy mixture and blend well. Pour mixture into a 1-gallon ice cream freezer container and churn according to machine instructions.

FOOL PROOF FUDGE

2½ cups chocolate chips	2 teaspoons vanilla
1 (12-ounce) can evaporated milk	

Melt chocolate with milk over low heat in a saucepan, stirring until smooth. Remove from heat and blend in vanilla. Pour into a greased 8-inch square pan and let stand until set.

YIELDS 12-16 PIECES

For chocolate kisses, place mixture into a pastry bag and squeeze small amounts of mixture onto a lightly greased or wax paper-lined baking sheet.

PUPPY CHOW

1 (6-ounce) package chocolate chips	1 (14-ounce) package wheat cereal squares (6 cups), such as Wheat Chex
¼ cup creamy peanut butter	1 cup confectioners' sugar

Melt chocolate chips in a large bowl in a microwave. Stir in peanut butter until well blended. Add cereal and stir to coat thoroughly. Sift confectioners' sugar into a large zip-top bag. Spoon cereal into bag, seal and shake until all pieces are coated with sugar.

YIELDS 12 SERVINGS

"Grandchildren (and their parents) cannot keep their hands out of this!"

THOMAS JEFFERSON BRANDY

1 quart vanilla ice cream	5 ounces brandy

Combine both ingredients in a blender. Spoon into individual Jefferson cups. Store in freezer, covered, until ready to serve. Remove from freezer and let stand at room temperature about 10 minutes before serving.

YIELDS 6 SERVINGS

Index

SEABOARD BUILDING

One of America's oldest railroads, the Portsmouth and Roanoke Railroad Company, erected its distinctive station and office building on the Portsmouth waterfront in 1894. It became the municipal building for several years after the Seaboard headquarters moved to Richmond in 1958. A restaurant, art gallery, offices and apartments now occupy the building.

DID YOU KNOW?

Acquisition of the Seaboard property by the city after 1958, opened the way for the waterfront development now seen from the Seaboard Building north to the Tidewater Yacht Marina.

We gratefully acknowledge those who so willingly contributed their time and effort to the success of Heart of the Harbor. To the contributors, we are so thankful for your enthusiasm in sharing your favorite recipes. To the testers, we are very appreciative of your hard work, creativity and dedication to the quality of this cookbook. All were invaluable to the completion of this project.

Christopher Academy
Elsie Ackerman
Betty Adams
Iole Aguero
Virginia Allman
Joan Anderson
Dana Andrews
Grace Armistead
Marie B. Armstrong
Alice Pettus Ash
Betty Atkinson
Cinda Axley
Carolyn Ayers
Barbara Baker
Shelby Balderson
Stafford Balderson
Maxine S. Barney
Peggy Bartlett
John Benbow
Beth Blasdell
Debbie Bohan
Cindy Bolling
Ethel Bouwam
Ginny Brandriff
Robin Breslauer
L. Ashley Brooks
Cheryle Brown
Sarah Brown
Betsy Browne
Beverley Burchette
Lesley Burgess

Sandy Burgess
Laurie Burnham
Jennifer Byers
Dena Cain
Laura Lou Campbell
Micki Campbell
Ruth M. Carkeek
Claire Carmen
Bonnie Carmines
Charlene Carney
Evelyn Carr
B. Cherry
JoAnn Cherry
Julianne Cherry
Kathel Cherry
Lilian M. Collier
Susan Comer
Judy Condra
M. Copeland
Anna Cornetta
Bett Cornetta
Christie Cornetta
Jim Cornetta
Victoria Cornetta
Gloria Creecy
Mary Curro
Joan Damsey
Horace L. Deans
Julie Deans
Karen DiVita
Valerie Dobson

Alice Dodson
Vanessa A. Dodson
Nancy Donahue
Esther Duffen
Connie Dunn
Barbara J. Early
Katherine Eason
Kathy B. Eberwine
Anne H. Edwards
Judith Facenda
Erin P. Farrow
Malcolm Fortson
Martha F. Fortson
Christine Fowler
Randy Fuller
Patty Gallagher
Sarah Gallagher
Ruth Ellen Gans
Frances J. Gill
Lisa Goldberg
Judy Goldman
Denise Goode
Joan Goodstein
Beverly Graubics
Carol Greene
Geraldine J. Gregg
Donna Grier
Stephen Grunnet
Betty Jo Gwaltney
Trish Halstead
Laurina Hamlet

Mary Haneman
Tracey Hardee
Monette Harrell
Pearl Harrell
Robert Harrell
Carolyn Harshaw
Dorthy M. Hill
Elaine Hinton
Kristine Hoff
Suzie Hogan
Joan Hoggard
Kathy Holbrook
Maureen Hook
Sue Hornof
Lida R. Hudson
Norma Hurley
Karen Ittel
John Jackson
Joan Jacobson
Suzanne Jacobson
Bettie Ann Johnson
Carol Johnson
Chris Justice
Nancy K. Kanter
Betsy Karotkin
Beverly Karr
Nancy Kay
Pat Kearney
Kathleen Keil
Anne W. Kenny
M. Jane Kilduff

Brenda Kincaid	Linda Mitchell	Sharon Quinn	Avery St. George
Pam Kloeppel	Michael Moreland	Jennifer Ramsdell	Betty St.George
Jean Knapp	Shannon Moreland	Judy Rauch	Deborah St.George
Lisa Knight	Stephanie Moreland	Susan Reddecliff	Katie St. George
Jessica Kovalcik	Linda Morgan	Anne Resolute	Linda S. St.George
Alice Koziol	Cindy Morris	Mary Ann Resolute	Marissa St. George
Maria Lambert	Suzanne Morrison	Kendall Rhodes	E.Ann Stokes
Lee Lamer	Carol Morse	Shirley A. Richards	Carolyn Sturgis
Earlene Lampman	Beverly Murray	Zelma Rivin	Shelly Swanson
Jeanne Larcombe	Dave Muscarella	Mary Lou Rose	Ilene Swartz
Rebecca Larys	Betty Neumann	Christy Rudisill	Phyllis D. Sykes
Mary Ainslie Latimer	Boo Niblo	Jean Rush	Pat Tayloe
Julia Lauer	Denyse H. O'Connor	Wanda Russo	Patty Thomas
Mary Lauer	Pat J. Orgain	Jean Rutherford	Eileen Thomason
Elizabeth Lawson	Bob Ossman	Terry Sanchez	Barbara Tilley
June Leckrone	Fran Ossman	Karina Sanved	Debbie Todd
Dottie Lindley	Frances Padden	Tara Saunders	Jack Trant
Jeanne K. Livesay	MaryJo Palmer	Elizabeth Schleck	Josephine J. Trant
Mary Logwood	Elizabeth Pappas	Ruth Schnabel	Jeanne Twine
Wendy Long	Nancy Peck	Alvin C. Schweizer II	Rita J Tyroler
Renee Luciano	Lidie Peery	Violet Scutero	Olga Valdivieso
Diane Lynch	Judy Perry	Danette Seward	Jennifer Vierrether
Dora Majer	Nancy Perry	Dottie Seward	Cornelia Wachsmann
Julie MacKinlay	Steve Perry	Jean H. Shackelford	Judy Walker
Katie Mansoor	Ellen Person	Tammy Shaia	Mary Jo Watkins
Christine McArtor	Jeryl-Rose Phillips	Joe Sharl	Mildred Watkins
Linda McGraw	Jim Pierce	Eileen Sher	Verle Weiss
Linda McKone	Patricia Fresco-Poirrier	Sandra Sher	Richard Welton
Martha McLean	Linda Polenzani	Susan Shiembob	Richard H. Wentz
Betty Jean McMurran	Lou Pollard	Kathy Sonny	Julia Wheeler
Julie Mendelson	Nancy Pontier	Pam Spence	Patricia Whitehurst
Carol Meyers	DeLane W. Porter	Ann Spivey	Lynn M. Wiggins
Carole Michaels	Eleanor Porter	Dee Stegall	Florence Witt
Nancy F. Midgette	Langhorne Porter	Jean Steingold	Henriann Woleben
Mary Miklos	Pam Pruden	Kathleen Stenicka	Tammy Woods
Charlotte Minor	Blanche Queen	Debbie Stephens	Nancy Wren
			Lu Zazanis

A

APPETIZERS *(see also Dips & Spreads)*
- Anchovies Marinated in Herbs and Pimentos 16
- Artichoke Appetizer 17
- Baked Cheese Olives 35
- Beach Shrimp Appetizers 15
- Best Pickled Shrimp 26
- Black Bean and Goat Cheese Quesadillas 25
- Cheese Wafers Extraordinaire 23
- Country Ham Roll 13
- Crispy Prosciutto Cheese Balls with Peaches and Hazelnut-Mint Vinaigrette 29
- Cucumber-Salmon Canapés 33
- East Coast Oysters 22
- Gourmet Cashews 31
- Jalapeño-Pimento Squares 10
- Layered Crab Wheel 13
- Lightship Puffed Shrimp 26
- Marinated Shrimp 10
- Nutty Blue Cheese Grapes 9
- Nutty Grapes 9
- Pita Pizza 23
- Portobello Bruschetta 21
- Potent Meatballs 25
- Reggie's Wedges 20
- Sausage Hors D'oeuvres 12
- Seasoned Pretzels 34
- Sesame-Ginger Shrimp 19
- Shrimp Supreme 27
- Smoked Salmon Roll-Ups 20
- Smoked Turkey with Peanut Sauce 24
- So Good Almonds 33
- Spicy Roasted Pecans 32
- Tipsy Eye of Round 22
- White Cheddar with Apples 18
- Zippy Mushrooms 31

APPLES
- Apple and Chicken Pâté 18
- Apple Harvest Salad 98
- Apple Pancake Grande 52
- Apple Squares 215
- Cocoa Apple Cake 191
- Granny Smith's Sweet Potatoes 184
- Harvest Apple Pie 211
- Morning Glory Muffins 56
- No Crust Apple Pie 210
- Seared Scallops on Bacon and Spinach Salad 103
- Slumber Party Casserole 48
- Tropical Salad with Curried Chicken 104
- White Cheddar with Apples 18

APRICOTS *(Fruit & Preserves)*
- Almond-Apricot Soft Biscotti 215
- Apricot Bars 216
- Apricot-Cream Cheese Delight 19
- Sherried Carrots with Apricots 183
- Sweet and Savory Pork Roast 115

ARTICHOKES
- Artichoke Appetizer 17
- Artichoke Dip 17
- Artichoke Pasta with Asiago 168
- Artichoke-Rice Salad 99
- Garden Club Chicken Salad 93
- Garlic Chicken with Artichokes and Sun-Dried Tomatoes 147
- Orzo Salad with Black Beans and Artichokes 97
- Overnight Pasta Salad with Creamy Basil Dressing 101
- Prepaing an Artichoke for Cooking 17
- Spinach and Artichoke Casserole 182
- Tomatoes Babiche 185
- Venetian Pasta with Artichokes 169

ASPARAGUS
- Asparagus Bundles 173
- Asparagus Salad 99
- Creamy Asparagus Soup 63
- Pesto Pasta with Asparagus 168
- Portobello Salad with Roasted Red Peppers 105
- Roasted Asparagus 187
- Top O' the Morning Bake 52

AVOCADOS
- Avocado and Crab Salad 81
- Best Shredded Chicken Salad 82
- European Salad 91
- Kaleidoscope Salad 105

B

BANANAS
- Banana-Pineapple Cake 203
- Simple Banana Bread 57

BEANS & PEAS
- Beach Beans 173
- Black Bean and Chicken Quesadilla 152
- Black Bean and Goat Cheese Quesadillas 25
- Black Bean Salad or Salsa 83

INDEX

Chuck Full of Chili Dip 34
Crockpot Lemon Chicken Tagine 155
Easy Minestrone 77
Faki (Greek Lentil Soup) 67
Family Favorite Marinated Bean Salad 95
Garlic Soup with Spinach and White Beans 76
Good Fortune Black-Eyed Peas 177
Greek Green Beans 178
Hearty Winter Soup 67
Herbed Green Beans 179
Italian Green Bean Medley 180
Italian Meatball Soup 66
Kickin' Chicken Curry 150
Orzo Salad with Black Beans and Artichokes 97
Pork Chalupas 117
Seawall Shrimp and Pea Salad 103
Texas Caviar 28

BEEF
Bellisimo! Spaghetti Sauce 162
Chuck Full of Chili Dip 34
Italian Meatball Soup 66
London Broil 120
One Pot Spaghetti Sauce 118
Perfect Beef Tenderloin 118
Potent Meatballs 25
Reubenesque Dip 10
Texas Brisket 111
Tipsy Eye of Round 22
Wildly Delicious Steak Salad 89

BEETS
Beet Aspic 81
Beet Salad 82
Borscht (Cold Beet Soup) 63
Lobster with Tarragon Sauce 134
Pickled Beets 181

BEVERAGES
Amaretto Slush 39
Blushing Bride's Punch 41
Bourbon Slush 40
Butterball 40
Cable Car Martini 40
Chilled Strawberry Smoothie 41
Chocolate Martini 38
Coffee Punch 39
Deckside Summer Tea 37
French Kiss 36
Half-and-Half 42
Hot Buttered Rum Cider 38
Mojitos 37
Olde Towne Cosmopolitan 39
Red Sangría 42
Sundowner 37
Tidal Wave 36
Vodka Slush 36
White Sangría 42

BREADS & MUFFINS
Colonel Crawford's Coffee Cake 59
Cranberry Bread 57
Cream Cheese Braid 50
Dried Cherry Scones 58
Focaccia Bread 60
Mexican Corn Bread 54
Monterey Topper for Bread 59
Morning Glory Muffins 56
Orange Date Mini Muffins 56
Orange Glazed Cranberry Pumpkin Bread 55
Peach Coffee Cake 58
Pumpkin Bread 55
Simple Banana Bread 57
Zucchini Loaf 54

BREAKFAST & BRUNCH
Apple Pancake Grande 52
Bacon and Onion Quiche 53
Best Ever Brunch Eggs 51
Cheesy-Tomato Ham Bake 51
Chesapeake Bay Crab Pie 49
Colonel Crawford's Coffee Cake 59
Cream Cheese Braid 50
Delicious Spinach Bake 49
Elegant Grand Marnier™ Toast 53
Mini Bacon and Egg Pastries 47
Museum's Lunch Bunch Quiche 47
Mushroom Crust Deep Dish 46
Peach Coffee Cake 58
Serbian Egg Casserole 46
Slumber Party Casserole 48
Stuffed French Toast Feast 48
Tomato Quiche 45
Top O' the Morning Bake 52
Yummy Tummy French Toast 45

BROCCOLI
Broccoli Buds 175
Greek Orzo and Broccoli 163
Shrimp and Broccoli Sauté 125
Tortellini Salad with Shrimp 100

INDEX

BRUSSELS SPROUTS, Marinated 181

C

CABBAGE
    Napa Cabbage Salad 96
    Potato-Cabbage Soup 69
    Waldorf Cole Slaw. 98

CAKES *(see Desserts)*

CANDY *(see Desserts)*

CARROTS
    Awesome Carrot Cake 196
    Baked Salmon with Spinach and Carrots 135
    Morning Glory Muffins 56
    Oregon Crab Stew. 68
    Sherried Carrots with Apricots 183
    Swordfish en Papillote 137

CASSEROLES
    Baked Pineapple 188
    Beach Beans. 173
    Butternut Squash Casserole. 175
    Buttery Baked Mashed Potatoes 174
    Cheese Puff 176
    Cheesy Macaroni and Cheese 169
    Cheesy-Tomato Ham Bake 51
    Corn Pudding 175
    Easy Rice or Orzo Casserole 162
    Goat Cheese Soufflé 176
    Granny Smith's Sweet Potatoes 184
    Kid's Favorite Mac-n-Cheese. 170
    Noodle Pudding (Kugel) 181
    Portside Mac 'N Cheese 163
    Serbian Egg Casserole. 46
    Slumber Party Casserole 48
    Southern Yellow Squash. 186
    Spinach and Artichoke Casserole 182
    Summer Tomato Pie 184
    Sweet Potato-Orange Casserole. 185
    Top O' the Morning Bake. 52

CAVIAR Pie 30

CEREALS & GRAINS *(see also Rice)*
    Cheese Wafers Extraordinaire. 23
    Gourmet Grits 170
    Primo Polenta 166
    Puppy Chow. 226
    Zesty Oatmeal-Chocolate Chip Cookies 220

CHEESE
    Almond-Raspberry Brie. 30
    Artichoke Pasta with Asiago 168
    Baked Cheese and Bacon Dip 15
    Baked Cheese Olives. 35
    Black Bean and Goat Cheese Quesadillas 25
    Blue Cheese Dressing 84
    Caprese Salad Surprise 84
    Cheese Puff 176
    Cheese Wafers Extraordinaire. 23
    Cheesy Macaroni and Cheese 169
    Cheesy-Tomato Ham Bake 51
    Chicken Boursin with Spinach and Prosciutto. . . 157
    Chuck Full of Chili Dip 34
    Crispy Prosciutto Cheese Balls with
        Peaches and Hazelnut-Mint Vinaigrette 29
    Goat Cheese Soufflé 176
    Hot Fiesta Spinach Dip. 11
    It's a Breeze Brie. 16
    Jalapeño-Pimento Squares 10
    Kid's Favorite Mac-n-Cheese. 170
    Mushroom Crust Deep Dish 46
    Nutty Blue Cheese Grapes 9
    Orzo with Caramelized Onions and Asiago 164
    Portside Mac 'N Cheese 163
    Savory Blue Cheese Tart. 21
    Serbian Egg Casserole 46
    Shrimp and Feta Cheese with Pasta 124
    Tangy Pimento Cheese 24
    White Cheddar with Apples 18

CHERRY Scones, Dried 58

CHILI, Chicken 64

CHOCOLATE *(see Desserts)*

CLAMS *(see Seafood)*

COCONUT
    Awesome Carrot Cake 196
    Coconut Chess Pie 207
    Coconut Key Lime Bars 217
    Curryer than Ives Spread 14
    Five Cup Salad 93
    French Vanilla Macaroon Bars 218
    Old Fashioned Coconut Cake 203
    Sunshine Angel Cake 195

CONDIMENTS & SAUCES
    Bellisimo! Spaghetti Sauce. 162
    Cucumber-Dill Sauce 127
    Dipping Sauce for Chicken or Pork 156
    Horseradish Sauce. 22
    Hot Sauce 153
    Jezebel Sauce for Pork. 121

INDEX

Marinade for Pork, Lamb or Pheasant 121
Mixed Berry Salsa for Fish 133
Mock Hollandaise 187
Mustard Horseradish Sauce
    for Beef Tenderloin 118
One Pot Spaghetti Sauce 118
Peanut Sauce 24
Peppercorn Sauce for Beef Tenderloin or Steak ... 117
Pickled Beets 181
Pineapple Salsa 145
Spicy Peach Chutney 158
Stir-Fry Sauce 153
Sugared Pecans 107
Tartar Sauce 122

COOKIES & BARS (see Desserts)
CORN
Black Bean Salad or Salsa 83
Boiled Seafood Pot 144
Chunky Potato-Crab Chowder 65
Corn Pudding 175
Crab and Corn Bisque 66
Deluxe Corn Salad 85
Kaleidoscope Salad 105
Mexican Corn Bread 54
Southwestern Pizza 155
Summer Harvest Corn Soup 72
Taco Soup for a Crowd 72
Texas Caviar 28

CRAB (see Seafood)
CRANBERRY (Fruit & Sauce)
Cranberry Bread 57
Cranberry-Nut Cheese Spread 33
Cranberry-Orange Salad 86
Cranberry Pie 208
Orange-Cranberry Rice Pilaf 164
Orange Glazed Cranberry Pumpkin Bread 55
Poppy Seed Salad 106
Sweet and Savory Pork Roast 115

CUCUMBERS
Cucumber-Dill Sauce 127
Cucumber-Salmon Canapés 33
Orange-Cucumber Salad 96

D
DATES
Delicious Date Nut Torte 204
Orange Date Mini Muffins 56

DESSERTS
Cakes
  Amaretti Pound Cake
    (Almond Wedding Cake) 193
  Awesome Carrot Cake 196
  Banana-Pineapple Cake 203
  Bete Noire (Black Beast) 197
  Chocolate Chip Bundt Cake 193
  Chocolate Chip Kahlúa Cake 197
  Chocolate Lava Cakes 198
  Cocoa Apple Cake 191
  Cream Cheese Pound Cake 192
  Delicious Date Nut Torte 204
  Double Chocolate Miniature Cakes 194
  In A Hurry Pecan Cake 201
  Kiddie Kones 191
  Light and Easy No Bake Cake 202
  Old Fashioned Coconut Cake 203
  Praline Layer Cake 201
  Rum Cream Cake 204
  Sour Cream Pound Cake 192
  Sunshine Angel Cake 195
  Superb Chocolate Cake 199
  Vodka-Kahlúa Cake 205
  White Chocolate Ice Box Cake 200
  Yorktown Gingerbread 205

Candy
  Chocolate-Saltine Bites 221
  Fool Proof Fudge 226

Cookies & Bars
  Almond-Apricot Soft Biscotti 215
  Apple Squares 215
  Apricot Bars 216
  Best Ever Rugalach 214
  Brown Sugar Brownies 216
  Coconut Key Lime Bars 217
  Easy Pecan Bars 217
  French Vanilla Macaroon Bars 218
  Initial Cookies 218
  Orange Bars 220
  Peanut Butter Cookies 219
  Tuffies 219
  Zesty Oatmeal-Chocolate Chip Cookies 220

Frostings, Glazes & Icings
  Buttermilk Glaze 196
  Cream Cheese Frosting 196
  Ganache 197

INDEX

    Lemon or Orange Glaze 50
    Superb Chocolate Frosting 199
Frozen Desserts
    Chart House Mud Pie 209
    Easy Butterscotch Pie 214
    Goober Pie 212
    Homemade Peppermint Ice Cream 225
    Krispy Ice Cream Pie 211
    Peach Ice Cream Pie 213
    Thomas Jefferson Brandy 226
Miscellaneous
    Baked Pears 225
    Bread Pudding with Whiskey Sauce 222
    Brownie Trifle 222
    Café Lite 224
    Chocolate Mousse 225
    Dirt 221
    Double Chocolate Cheesecake
      with Ganache Topping 224
    Fabulous Caramel Flan 223
    Lime Soufflé 223
    Puppy Chow 226
    Rum Cream 204
    Whipping Whipped Cream 209
Pies & Tarts
    Chart House Mud Pie 209
    Chocolate Bourbon Pie 209
    Chocolate Meringue Pie 208
    Chocolate Tart 207
    Coconut Chess Pie 207
    Cranberry Pie 208
    Easy Butterscotch Pie 214
    Goober Pie 212
    Great Pecan Pie 210
    Harvest Apple Pie 211
    No Crust Apple Pie 210
    Ouie Gooie Tart 206
    Peach Ice Cream Pie 213
    Perfect Crust 208
    Vermont Maple Cream Pie 212
Sauces
    Butterscotch Sauce 214
    Fudge Sauce 200
    Mint Fudge Sauce 198
DIPS & SPREADS
    Almond-Raspberry Brie 30
    Amaretto Fruit Dip 12
    Apple and Chicken Pâté 18
    Apricot-Cream Cheese Delight 19
    Artichoke Dip 17
    Baked Cheese and Bacon Dip 15
    Black Bean Salad or Salsa 83
    Black Olive Dip 31
    Caviar Pie 30
    Chuck Full of Chili Dip 34
    Cranberry-Nut Cheese Spread 33
    Curried Cheese Ball 28
    Curryer than Ives Spread 14
    Delicious Crabmeat Dip 15
    Dipping Sauce for Chicken or Pork 156
    Green with Envy Spread 14
    Hot Fiesta Spinach Dip 11
    Hot Vidalia Onion Dip 11
    It's a Breeze Brie 16
    Kahlúa Fruit Dip 12
    Mom's Lobster Mold 32
    Pineapple Salsa 145
    Port O' Call Clam Dip 28
    Pretzel Dip 34
    Quick and Easy Southwestern Dip 20
    Reubenesque Dip 10
    Savory Blue Cheese Tart 21
    S'hroom Spread 9
    Spicy Buffalo Chicken Dip 19
    Tangy Pimento Cheese 24
    Texas Caviar 28
    Will Make You Dance Salsa 14

E

EGGPLANT
    Portobello Bruschetta 21
    Vegetable Tower 186
EGGS *(see also Breakfast & Brunch)*
    Best Ever Brunch Eggs 51
    Caviar Pie 30
    Cheesy-Tomato Ham Bake 51
    Egg White Tips 48
    Elegant Grand Marnier™ Toast 53
    Mini Bacon and Egg Pastries 47
    Museum's Lunch Bunch Quiche 47
    Mushroom Crust Deep Dish 46
    Serbian Egg Casserole 46
    Slumber Party Casserole 48
ENCHILADAS, Creamy Chicken 150

F

FISH *(see Seafood)*
FROSTINGS *(see Desserts)*
FROZEN DESSERTS *(see Desserts)*
FRUITS *(see also individual listings)*

    Almond-Apricot Soft Biscotti 215
    Apple and Chicken Pâté 18
    Apple Harvest Salad 98
    Apple Pancake Grande 52
    Apple Squares 215
    Apricot Bars 216
    Apricot-Cream Cheese Delight 19
    Awesome Carrot Cake 196
    Baked Pears 225
    Baked Pineapple 188
    Banana-Pineapple Cake 203
    Beautiful Holiday Salad 94
    Best Ever Rugalach 214
    Chilled Strawberry Smoothie 41
    Chilled Watermelon Soup 65
    Cocoa Apple Cake 191
    Coconut Key Lime Bars 217
    Cranberry-Orange Salad 86
    Cranberry Pie 208
    Crispy Prosciutto Cheese Balls with
        Peaches and Hazelnut-Mint Vinaigrette 29
    Curried Chicken and Peach Salad 88
    Delicious Date Nut Torte 204
    Dried Cherry Scones 58
    Dry Rub Chicken with Spicy Peach Chutney 158
    European Salad 91
    Five Cup Salad 93
    French Vanilla Macaroon Bars 218
    Great Grape Salad 91
    Harvest Apple Pie 211
    Lime Soufflé 223
    Linguine with Tuna, Capers and Raisins 139
    Luscious Lemon Salad 95
    Mandarin Squash 180
    Mango Chicken Salad 92
    Mixed Berry Salsa for Fish 133
    Morning Glory Muffins 56
    No Crust Apple Pie 210
    Nutty Blue Cheese Grapes 9
    Nutty Grapes 9
    Old Fashioned Coconut Cake 203
    Orange Bars 220

    Orange-Cranberry Rice Pilaf 164
    Orange-Cucumber Salad 96
    Orange Date Mini Muffins 56
    Orange Glazed Cranberry Pumpkin Bread 55
    Peach Coffee Cake 58
    Peach Ice Cream Pie 213
    Polynesian Chicken 154
    Poolside Strawberry and Spinach Salad 102
    Poppy Seed Salad 106
    Raisin and Brown Rice-Ginger Salad 83
    Raisin Rice with Curry 167
    Red Sangría 42
    Refreshing Pear Salad 97
    Sherried Carrots with Apricots 183
    Simple Banana Bread 57
    Slow Cooker Moroccan Chicken 146
    Stuffed French Toast Feast 48
    Summer Peach Soup 77
    Sunshine Snapper with Pineapple Salsa 145
    Sweet Potato-Orange Casserole 185
    Tropical Crab Cakes 136
    Tropical Salad with Curried Chicken 104
    Waldorf Cole Slaw 98
    White Cheddar with Apples 18

G

GARLIC
    Chicken Satay 151
    Garlic Chicken with
        Artichokes and Sun-Dried Tomatoes 147
    Garlic Soup with Spinach and White Beans 76
    Grilled Garlic Tomatoes 178

GLAZES *(see Desserts)*

GRAPES
    Great Grape Salad 91
    Island Chicken Salad with Curry 88
    Nutty Blue Cheese Grapes 9
    Nutty Grapes 9
    Pecan Chicken Salad 108

GRILLING RECIPES
    Carolina-Style Ribs 120
    Citrus Zest for Fish 143
    Dry Rub Chicken with Spicy Peach Chutney 158
    Grilled Chicken with
        Rosemary Mustard Cream 157
    Grilled Garlic Tomatoes 178
    Grilled Marinated Leg of Lamb 112
    Grilled Romaine 93

INDEX

    Lamb Kabobs with
        Green Olive and Mint Sauce 111
    Mixed Berry Salsa for Fish. 133
    Perfectly Grilled Lamb Chops. 112
    Sunshine Snapper with Pineapple Salsa. 145
    Super Grilled Chicken for Two 158
    Wildly Delicious Steak Salad. 89

K
KID FRIENDLY RECIPES
    Cranberry Bread 57
    Dirt 221
    Five Cup Salad 93
    Fool Proof Fudge. 226
    Great Grape Salad 91
    Initial Cookies 218
    Kiddie Kones 191
    Kid's Favorite Mac-n-Cheese. 170
    Krispy Ice Cream Pie 211
    Peanut Butter Cookies 219
    Pita Pizza 23
    Pumpkin Bread 55
    Seasoned Pretzels 34
    Slumber Party Casserole 48
    Sunshine Angel Cake 195
    Yummy Tummy French Toast. 45
KUGEL, Noodle Pudding. 181

L
LAMB
    Grilled Marinated Leg of Lamb. 112
    Lamb Kabobs with
        Green Olive and Mint Sauce 111
    Perfectly Grilled Lamb Chops. 112
LEEKS
    Lobster with Tarragon Sauce. 134
    Potato, Leek and Onion Soup 69
    Three Onion Soup. 73
LEMON
    Lemon Dressing 98
    Lemon or Orange Glaze. 50
    Luscious Lemon Salad 95
    Salmon with Lemon-Mustard Sauce 127
    Zesty Lemon Chicken. 148
LIME
    Coconut Key Lime Bars 217
    Lime Soufflé. 223

LOBSTER *(see Seafood)*

M
MANGOES
    Calypso Fish Fillets 142
    Mango Chicken Salad. 92
MUSHROOMS
    Mushroom Crust Deep Dish. 46
    Portobello Bruschetta. 21
    Portobello Salad with Roasted Red Peppers 105
    S'hroom Spread. 9
    Spaghetti with Portobellos, Sage and Walnuts 167
    Zippy Mushrooms. 31

MUSSELS *(see Seafood)*

N
NUTS
    Almond-Apricot Soft Biscotti 215
    Almond-Raspberry Brie. 30
    Awesome Carrot Cake 196
    Brown Sugar Brownies. 216
    Country Ham Roll 13
    Cranberry-Nut Cheese Spread 33
    Delicious Date Nut Torte 204
    Easy Pecan Bars. 217
    Gourmet Cashews. 31
    Great Grape Salad 91
    Great Pecan Pie 210
    In A Hurry Pecan Cake 201
    Island Chicken Salad with Curry 88
    Napa Cabbage Salad 96
    Nutty Blue Cheese Grapes 9
    Nutty Grapes 9
    Pecan Chicken Salad. 108
    Poppy Seed Salad. 106
    Praline Layer Cake 201
    Raisin and Brown Rice-Ginger Salad. 83
    So Good Almonds. 33
    Spaghetti with Portobellos,
        Sage and Walnuts. 167
    Spicy Roasted Pecans 32
    Spinach Tortellini Salad with Sugared Pecans. . . . 107
    Sugared Pecans 107
    Tuffies. 219
    Yorktown Gingerbread 205
    Zesty Oatmeal-Chocolate Chip Cookies 220

O

OLIVES
Anchovies Marinated in Herbs and Pimentos 16
Baked Cheese Olives 35
Black Olive Dip 31
Garden Club Chicken Salad 93
Greek Quesadillas 149
Green with Envy Spread 14
Kaleidoscope Salad 105
Orange Roasted Tilapia 130
Polynesian Chicken 154
Reggie's Wedges 20
Tangy Greek Salad 102
Texas Caviar 28
Tomato Quiche 45

ONIONS
Bacon and Onion Quiche 53
Best Pickled Shrimp 26
Chicken Chili 64
Home Fries with Caramelized Onions 179
Honey-Mustard Vidalia Onions 178
Hot Vidalia Onion Dip 11
Oregon Crab Stew 68
Orzo with Caramelized Onions and Asiago 164
Pork Chops with Sweet Onion and Capers 116
Potato, Leek and Onion Soup 69
Roasted Vidalia Onions with Balsamic Vinegar 182
Three Onion Soup 73

ORANGE *(Fruit & Juice)*
Cranberry-Orange Salad 86
Do Ahead Company Salad 90
Five Cup Salad 93
Lemon or Orange Glaze 50
Mandarin Squash 180
Orange Balsamic Broiled Salmon 131
Orange Bars 220
Orange-Cranberry Rice Pilaf 164
Orange-Cucumber Salad 96
Orange Roasted Tilapia 130
Sunshine Angel Cake 195
Sweet Potato-Orange Casserole 185

OYSTERS *(see Seafood)*

P

PASTA
Artichoke Pasta with Asiago 168
Athenian Orzo Salad 100
Bellisimo! Spaghetti Sauce 162
Cajun Shrimp Pasta 144
Cheesy Macaroni and Cheese 169
Creamy Italian Toss 161
Easy Minestrone 77
Easy Rice or Orzo Casserole 162
Greek Orzo and Broccoli 163
Kid's Favorite Mac-n-Cheese 170
Linguine and Sun-Dried Tomatoes 166
Linguine with Shrimp Scampi 139
Linguine with Tuna, Capers and Raisins 139
Linguine with White Clam Sauce 161
Lobster with Tarragon Sauce 134
Mediterranean Shrimp Over Pasta 133
Napa Cabbage Salad 96
Noodle Pudding (Kugel) 181
Orzo Salad with Black Beans and Artichokes 97
Orzo with Caramelized Onions and Asiago 164
Overnight Pasta Salad with Creamy Basil Dressing 101
Pasta with Creamy Tuscan Tomato Sauce 165
Pasta with Spinach and Tomatoes 165
Penne Pasta with Chicken and Tomatoes 154
Pesto Pasta with Asparagus 168
Portside Mac 'N Cheese 163
Savory Spaghetti Sauce with Italian Sausages 115
Shrimp and Feta Cheese with Pasta 124
Spaghetti with Portobellos, Sage and Walnuts 167
Spinach Tortellini Salad with Sugared Pecans 107
Tortellini Salad with Shrimp 100
Venetian Pasta with Artichokes 169

PEACHES
Crispy Prosciutto Cheese Balls with Peaches and Hazelnut-Mint Vinaigrette 29
Curried Chicken and Peach Salad 88
Peach Coffee Cake 58
Peach Ice Cream Pie 213
Red Sangría 42
Spicy Peach Chutney 158
Summer Peach Soup 77

PEAS *(see Beans & Peas)*

PEANUT BUTTER
Goober Pie 212
Peanut Butter Cookies 219
Peanut Sauce 24
Puppy Chow 226

PEARS
Baked Pears 225
Refreshing Pear Salad 97

INDEX

PEPPERS
- Chicken Chili. 64
- Chuck Full of Chili Dip 34
- Creamy Italian Toss. 161
- Fast and Easy Chicken with Peppers 156
- Jalapeño-Pimento Squares. 10
- Pineapple Salsa 145
- Portobello Bruschetta. 21
- Portobello Salad with Roasted Red Peppers 105
- Roasted Red Pepper Soup 70
- Roasting Bell Peppers. 70
- Southwestern Pizza. 155
- Swordfish with Browned Butter
  and Roasted Red Pepper-Caper Sauce 138
- Texas Caviar. 28
- Will Make You Dance Salsa 14

PIES & TARTS *(see Desserts)*

PINEAPPLE
- Baked Pineapple 188
- Banana-Pineapple Cake 203
- Five Cup Salad 93
- Island Chicken Salad with Curry 88
- Luscious Lemon Salad 95
- Pineapple Salsa 145
- Polynesian Chicken. 154

PIZZA, Southwestern 155

POLENTA, Primo 166

PORK
- Bacon and Onion Quiche 53
- Baked Cheese and Bacon Dip 15
- Bellisimo! Spaghetti Sauce. 162
- Boiled Seafood Pot 144
- Carolina-Style Ribs. 120
- Cheesy-Tomato Ham Bake 51
- Chicken Boursin with Spinach and Prosciutto. . . . 157
- Country Ham Roll 13
- Crab Eileen. 143
- Crispy Prosciutto Cheese Balls with
  Peaches and Hazelnut-Mint Vinaigrette 29
- Crockpot North Carolina Style BBQ 113
- Crustacean Sensation 71
- Flemish Pork Chops 113
- Hearty Winter Soup 67
- Italian Meatball Soup 66
- Jumpin' Jambalaya. 68
- Mini Bacon and Egg Pastries. 47
- Museum's Lunch Bunch Quiche 47
- Pork Chalupas 117
- Pork Chops with Sweet Onion and Capers 116
- Sausage Hors D'oeuvres 12
- Savory Spaghetti Sauce with Italian Sausages 115
- Sweet and Savory Pork Roast. 115
- Top O' the Morning Bake. 52

POTATOES
- Best Kept Secret Spuds. 174
- Boiled Seafood Pot 144
- Buttery Baked Mashed Potatoes 174
- Chunky Potato-Crab Chowder 65
- Crowd Pleasing Potato Salad. 87
- Home Fries with Caramelized Onions. 179
- Mashing Potatoes 174
- Potato-Cabbage Soup 69
- Potato, Leek and Onion Soup 69

POT STICKERS, Spinach Soup with 74

POULTRY
Chicken
- Apple and Chicken Pâté 18
- Best Shredded Chicken Salad. 82
- Black Bean and Chicken Quesadilla. 152
- Chicken Boursin with
  Spinach and Prosciutto 157
- Chicken Chili 64
- Chicken in Sherry Cream Sauce. 152
- Chicken Lettuce Wraps. 153
- Chicken Satay. 151
- Creamy Chicken Enchiladas. 150
- Crockpot Lemon Chicken Tagine. 155
- Curried Chicken and Peach Salad. 88
- Dry Rub Chicken with
  Spicy Peach Chutney 158
- Fast and Easy Chicken with Peppers 156
- Flavor for Chicken 64
- Garden Club Chicken Salad 93
- Garlic Chicken with
  Artichokes and Sun-Dried Tomatoes 147
- Greek Quesadillas. 149
- Grilled Chicken with
  Rosemary Mustard Cream 157
- Herbed Cornish Hens 147
- Island Chicken Salad with Curry 88
- Italian Chicken 145
- Kickin' Chicken Curry 150
- Mango Chicken Salad. 92
- Mexicano Chicken 149

INDEX

Paella 129
Pecan Chicken Salad 108
Penne Pasta with Chicken and Tomatoes 154
Polynesian Chicken 154
Portuguese Chicken and Rice Soup
   (Sopa de Galinha) 78
Sherry-Honey Glazed Chicken 148
Slow Cooker Moroccan Chicken 146
Southwestern Pizza 155
Spicy Buffalo Chicken Dip 19
Super Grilled Chicken for Two 158
Taco Soup for a Crowd 72
Tropical Salad with Curried Chicken 104
Zesty Lemon Chicken 148

Turkey
   Smoked Turkey Breast
      with Herb Barbecue Sauce 146
   Smoked Turkey with Peanut Sauce 24

PUMPKIN
Orange Glazed Cranberry Pumpkin Bread 55
Pumpkin Bread 55

Q

QUESADILLAS
Black Bean and Chicken Quesadilla 152
Black Bean and Goat Cheese Quesadillas 25
Greek Quesadillas 149

QUICHE
Bacon and Onion Quiche 53
Museum's Lunch Bunch Quiche 47
Tomato Quiche 45

R

RAISINS
Awesome Carrot Cake 196
Linguine with Tuna, Capers and Raisins 139
Raisin and Brown Rice-Ginger Salad 83
Raisin Rice with Curry 167

RICE
Artichoke-Rice Salad 99
Easy Rice or Orzo Casserole 162
Jumpin' Jambalaya 68
Orange-Cranberry Rice Pilaf 164
Paella 129
Portuguese Chicken and Rice Soup
   (Sopa de Galinha) 78
Raisin and Brown Rice-Ginger Salad 83

Raisin Rice with Curry 167
Risotto Fit for a Prince 128

S

SALAD DRESSINGS
Balsamic Vinaigrette 108
Blue Cheese Dressing 84
Creamy Basil Dressing 101
European Salad Dressing 91
Herbed Pasta Salad Dressing 100
Lemon Dressing 98
Lettuce Dress for Dinner 90
Mother's Slaw Dressing 108
Pasta Salad Dressing 107
Poppy Seed Dressing 106
Simple Spinach Salad Dressing 107
Spinach Salad Dressing 102
Vinaigrette 99

SALADS
Apple Harvest Salad 98
Artichoke-Rice Salad 99
Asparagus Salad 99
Athenian Orzo Salad 100
Avocado and Crab Salad 81
Beautiful Holiday Salad 94
Beet Aspic 81
Beet Salad 82
Best Shredded Chicken Salad 82
Black Bean Salad or Salsa 83
Caprese Salad Surprise 84
Chilled Marinated Squash 85
Crabmeat Mousse 86
Cranberry-Orange Salad 86
Crowd Pleasing Potato Salad 87
Crunchy Spinach Salad 87
Curried Chicken and Peach Salad 88
Deluxe Corn Salad 85
Do Ahead Company Salad 90
Easy Faux Crabmeat Salad 92
European Salad 91
Family Favorite Marinated Bean Salad 95
Five Cup Salad 93
Garden Club Chicken Salad 93
Great Grape Salad 91
Grilled Romaine 93
Hot Spinach Salad 94
Island Chicken Salad with Curry 88
Kaleidoscope Salad 105

INDEX

Luscious Lemon Salad 95
Mango Chicken Salad 92
Napa Cabbage Salad 96
Orange-Cucumber Salad 96
Orzo Salad with Black Beans and Artichokes 97
Overnight Pasta Salad with
   Creamy Basil Dressing 101
Pecan Chicken Salad 108
Poolside Strawberry and Spinach Salad 102
Poppy Seed Salad 106
Portobello Salad with Roasted Red Peppers 105
Preparing Green Salad Ahead 107
Raisin and Brown Rice-Ginger Salad 83
Refreshing Pear Salad 97
Salad in a Pocket 104
Seared Scallops on Bacon and Spinach Salad 103
Seawall Shrimp and Pea Salad 103
Spinach Tortellini Salad with Sugared Pecans 107
Stewed Tomato Aspic 106
Sweet and Sauerkraut Salad 101
Tangy Greek Salad 102
Tortellini Salad with Shrimp 100
Tropical Salad with Curried Chicken 104
Waldorf Cole Slaw 98
Wildly Delicious Steak Salad 89

SAUCES *(see Condiments & Sauces)*

SAUERKRAUT
Reubenesque Dip 10
Sweet and Sauerkraut Salad 101

SEAFOOD
Clams
   Linguine with White Clam Sauce 161
   Paella 129
   Port O' Call Clam Dip 28
   Tidewater Clam Chowder 73
Crab
   Avocado and Crab Salad 81
   Baked Crabmeat 136
   Chesapeake Bay Crab Pie 49
   Chunky Potato-Crab Chowder 65
   Crab and Corn Bisque 66
   Crab Eileen 143
   Crabmeat Mousse 86
   Crabmeat Prep 123
   Crustacean Sensation 71
   Delicious Crabmeat Dip 15
   Easy Faux Crabmeat Salad 92
   Gosport Jumbo Crab Cakes 140

   Layered Crab Wheel 13
   Oregon Crab Stew 68
   Simple Crab Cakes 123
   Tropical Crab Cakes 136
Fish
   Anchovies Marinated
      in Herbs and Pimentos 16
   Baked Salmon with Spinach and Carrots 135
   Bourbon Basted Salmon 135
   Calypso Fish Fillets 142
   Citrus Zest for Fish 143
   Cucumber-Salmon Canapés 33
   Easy Foil Baked Salmon 142
   Flounder Italiano 141
   Linguine with Tuna, Capers and Raisins 139
   Mixed Berry Salsa for Fish 133
   Mustard Rubbed Tuna w
      ith Tomato Mint Relish 131
   Orange Balsamic Broiled Salmon 131
   Orange Roasted Tilapia 130
   Oven Baked Catfish 130
   Rock N' Rockfish (Striped Bass) 122
   Salad in a Pocket 104
   Salmon in White Wine with Tarragon 125
   Salmon with Lemon-Mustard Sauce 127
   Savory Seafood Sailboat 126
   Smoked Salmon Roll-Ups 20
   Sunshine Snapper with Pineapple Salsa 145
   Swordfish en Papillote 137
   Swordfish with Browned Butter
      and Roasted Red Pepper-Caper Sauce 138
   Tuna with Asian Searing Sauce 137
Lobster
   Crustacean Sensation 71
   Lobster with Tarragon Sauce 134
   Mom's Lobster Mold 32
Mussels
   Mussels Mariners' Style 132
   Paella 129
   Preparing Mussels 132
Oysters
   East Coast Oysters 22
Scallops
   Crustacean Sensation 71
   Irish Shellfish Delight 141
   Savory Seafood Sailboat 126
   Scallops and Shrimp in Herbed Cream Sauce ... 124

INDEX

Seared Scallops on
    Bacon and Spinach Salad 103

Shrimp
A Shrimp Caper 140
Beach Shrimp Appetizers 15
Best Pickled Shrimp 26
Boiled Seafood Pot 144
Cajun Shrimp Pasta 144
Crustacean Sensation 71
Fix Ahead Company Shrimp 123
Irish Shellfish Delight 141
Jumpin' Jambalaya 68
Key West Sauté 132
Lightship Puffed Shrimp 26
Linguine with Shrimp Scampi 139
Marinated Shrimp 10
Mediterranean Shrimp Over Pasta 133
Paella 129
Risotto Fit for a Prince 128
Rock N' Rockfish (Striped Bass) 122
Savory Seafood Sailboat 126
Scallops and Shrimp in
    Herbed Cream Sauce 124
Seawall Shrimp and Pea Salad 103
Sesame-Ginger Shrimp 19
Shrimp and Broccoli Sauté 125
Shrimp and Feta Cheese with Pasta 124
Shrimp Supreme 27
Tortellini Salad with Shrimp 100

SOUPS & STEWS
Bistro Tomato-Basil Soup 74
Borscht (Cold Beet Soup) 63
Chicken Chili 64
Chilled Watermelon Soup 65
Chunky Potato-Crab Chowder 65
Crab and Corn Bisque 66
Creamy Asparagus Soup 63
Crustacean Sensation 71
Easy Minestrone 77
Faki (Greek Lentil Soup) 67
Garlic Soup with Spinach and White Beans 76
Hearty Winter Soup 67
Italian Meatball Soup 66
Jumpin' Jambalaya 68
Oregon Crab Stew 68
Portuguese Chicken and Rice Soup
    (Sopa de Galinha) 78

Potato-Cabbage Soup 69
Potato, Leek and Onion Soup 69
Roasted Red Pepper Soup 70
Spinach Soup with Pot Stickers 74
Summer Harvest Corn Soup 72
Summer Peach Soup 77
Taco Soup for a Crowd 72
Three Onion Soup 73
Tidewater Clam Chowder 73
Watercress Soup 75

SPINACH
Baked Salmon with Spinach and Carrots 135
Chicken Boursin with Spinach and Prosciutto 157
Creamy Chicken Enchiladas 150
Crunchy Spinach Salad 87
Delicious Spinach Bake 49
Garlic Soup with Spinach and White Beans 76
Hearty Winter Soup 67
Hot Fiesta Spinach Dip 11
Hot Spinach Salad 94
Italian Meatball Soup 66
Pasta with Spinach and Tomatoes 165
Poolside Strawberry and Spinach Salad 102
Refreshing Pear Salad 97
Seared Scallops on Bacon and Spinach Salad 103
Spinach and Artichoke Casserole 182
Spinach Soup with Pot Stickers 74
Spinach Tortellini Salad with Sugared Pecans 107
Tropical Salad with Curried Chicken 104

SQUASH & ZUCCHINI
Butternut Squash Casserole 175
Chilled Marinated Squash 85
Creamy Italian Toss 161
Crockpot Lemon Chicken Tagine 155
Mandarin Squash 180
Savory Spaghetti Sauce with Italian Sausages 115
Southern Yellow Squash 186
Squash Cakes 183
Storing zucchini 54
Tropical Crab Cakes 136
Zippy Zucchini 187
Zucchini Loaf 54

STRAWBERRIES
Chilled Strawberry Smoothie 41
Chilled Watermelon Soup 65
Mixed Berry Salsa for Fish 133
Poolside Strawberry and Spinach Salad 102

SWEET POTATOES

Crab Eileen	143
Granny Smith's Sweet Potatoes	184
Sweet Potato-Orange Casserole	185

T

TOMATOES

Bellisimo! Spaghetti Sauce	162
Bistro Tomato-Basil Soup	74
Cheesy-Tomato Ham Bake	51
Chicken Chili	64
Fire and Ice Tomatoes	177
Garlic Chicken with Artichokes and Sun-Dried Tomatoes	147
Greek Green Beans	178
Grilled Garlic Tomatoes	178
Linguine and Sun-Dried Tomatoes	166
Mediterranean Shrimp Over Pasta	133
Mustard Rubbed Tuna with Tomato Mint Relish	131
One Pot Spaghetti Sauce	118
Oregon Crab Stew	68
Pasta with Creamy Tuscan Tomato Sauce	165
Pasta with Spinach and Tomatoes	165
Penne Pasta with Chicken and Tomatoes	154
Savory Spaghetti Sauce with Italian Sausages	115
Stewed Tomato Aspic	106
Summer Tomato Pie	184
Summer Tomato Treat	188
Taco Soup for a Crowd	72
Tomatoes Babiche	185
Tomato Quiche	45
Will Make You Dance Salsa	14

V

VEAL

Company Veal Shanks	114
Osso Buco	119

VEGETABLES *(see also individual listings)*

Easy Minestrone	77
Vegetable Tower	186

METRIC CONVERSIONS

WEIGHT EQUIVALENTS

These are not exact weight equivalents, but have been rounded up or down slightly to make measuring easier.

AMERICAN	METRIC	AMERICAN	METRIC	AMERICAN	METRIC
¼ ounce	7 grams	8 ounces (½ pound)	225 grams	16 ounces (1 pound)	455 grams
½ ounce	15 grams	9 ounces	250 grams	1 pound 2 ounces	500 grams
1 ounce	30 grams	10 ounces	300 grams	1½ pounds	750 grams
2 ounces	60 grams	11 ounces	325 grams	2 pounds	900 grams
3 ounces	90 grams	12 ounces	350 grams	2¼ pounds	1 kilogram
4 ounces	110 grams	13 ounces	375 grams	3 pounds	1.4 kilograms
5 ounces	150 grams	14 ounces	400 grams	4 pounds	1.8 kilograms
6 ounces	175 grams	15 ounces	425 grams	4½ pounds	2 kilograms
7 ounces	200 grams				

VOLUME EQUIVALENTS

These are not exact volume equivalents, but have been rounded up or down slightly to make measuring easier.

AMERICAN	METRIC	IMPERIAL
¼ teaspoon	1.25 milliliters	
½ teaspoon	2.5 milliliters	
1 teaspoon	5 milliliters	
½ tablespoon (1½ teaspoons)	7.5 milliliters	
1 tablespoon (3 teaspoons)	15 milliliters	
¼ cup (4 tablespoons)	60 milliliters	2 fluid ounces
⅓ cup (5 tablespoons)	75 milliliters	2½ fluid ounces
½ cup (8 tablespoons)	125 milliliters	4 fluid ounces
⅔ cup (10 tablespoons)	150 milliliters	5 fluid ounces (¼ pint)
¾ cup (12 tablespoons)	175 milliliters	6 fluid ounces (⅓ pint)
1 cup (16 tablespoons)	250 milliliters	8 fluid ounces
1¼ cups	300 milliliters	10 fluid ounces (½ pint)
1½ cups	350 milliliters	12 fluid ounces
1 pint (2 cups)	500 milliliters	16 fluid ounces
2½ cups	625 milliliters	20 fluid ounces (1 pint)
1 quart (4 cups)	1 liter	1¾ pints

VOLUME EQUIVALENTS

OVEN	°FAHRENHEIT	°CELSIUS	GAS MARK
very cool	250-275	130-140	½-1
cool	300	150	2
warm	325	170	3
moderate	350	180	4
moderately hot	375	190	5
moderately hot	400	200	6
hot	425	220	7
very hot	450	230	8
very hot	475	250	9

AMERICAN ABBREVIATIONS

ounce	oz.
pound	lb.
teaspoon	t.
tablespoon	T.
cup	c.
pint	pt.
quart	qt.
gallon	gal.

MEASUREMENTS AND EQUIVALENTS

60 drops	less than ⅛ teaspoon
3 teaspoons	1 tablespoon
2 tablespoons	1 fluid ounce
1 jigger	1½ fluid ounces
½ cup	8 tablespoons
½ cup	4 fluid ounces
⅝ cup	½ cup + 2 tablespoons
⅝ cup	10 tablespoons
⅓ cup	5 tablespoons + 1 teaspoon
⅔ cup	10 tablespoons + 2 teaspoons
⅔ cup	5⅓ fluid ounces
¾ cup	12 tablespoons
¾ cup	6 fluid ounces
⅞ cup	¾ cup + 2 tablespoons
⅞ cup	14 tablespoons
1 cup	16 tablespoons
1 cup	8 fluid ounces
1 cup	½ pint
1¼ cups	10 fluid ounces
1⅓ cups	10⅔ fluid ounces
1½ cups	12 fluid ounces
1⅔ cups	13⅓ fluid ounces
1¾ cups	14 fluid ounces
2 cups	16 fluid ounces
2 cups	1 pint
2½ cups	20 fluid ounces
3 cups	24 fluid ounces
3 cups	¾ quart
3½ cups	28 fluid ounces
3½ cups	⅞ quart
4 cups	1 quart
1/16 pint	2 tablespoons
⅛ pint	¼ cup
¼ pint	½ cup
⅓ pint	⅔ cup
⅜ pint	¾ cup
½ pint	1 cup
⅔ pint	1⅓ cups
⅝ pint	1¼ cups
¾ pint	1½ cups
⅞ pint	1¾ cups
1 pint	2 cups
1/16 quart	¼ cup
⅛ quart	½ cup
¼ quart	1 cup
⅓ quart	1⅓ cups
⅜ quart	1½ cups
½ quart	2 cups
⅝ quart	2½ cups
¾ quart	3 cups
⅞ quart	3½ cups
1 quart	4 cups
1 quart	2 pints
1 quart	¼ gallon
1 quart	32 fluid ounces
1 quart	.946 liters
1 liter	1.06 quarts
1 liter	4 cups + 3⅓ tablespoons
5 cups	40 fluid ounces
6 cups	1½ quarts
6 cups	48 fluid ounces
10 cups	2½ quarts
10 cups	80 fluid ounces
12 cups	3 quarts
12 cups	96 fluid ounces
3 quarts	12 cups
3 quarts	¾ gallon
4 quarts	1 gallon
4 quarts	128 fluid ounces
1/16 gallon	¼ cup

⅛ gallon	½ quart	

⅛ gallon . . . . ½ quart
¼ gallon . . . . 1 quart
⅓ gallon . . . . 1⅓ quarts
⅜ gallon . . . . 1½ quarts
½ gallon . . . . 2 quarts
⅝ gallon . . . . 2½ quarts
⅔ gallon . . . . 2⅔ quarts
¾ gallon . . . . 3 quarts
⅞ gallon . . . . 3½ quarts

1 gallon . . . . 4 quarts
1 gallon . . . . 8 pints
1 gallon . . . . 16 cups

DRY WEIGHTS

2 gallons . . . . 1 peck
8 quarts . . . . 1 peck

1 peck . . . . 8 quarts
1 peck . . . . 2 gallons
4 pecks . . . . 1 bushel

1 bushel . . . . 4 pecks
1 bushel . . . . 8 gallons
1 bushel . . . . 32 quarts
1 bushel . . . . 64 pints
1 bushel . . . . 128 cups

¼ pound . . . . 4 ounces
½ pound . . . . 8 ounces
1 pound . . . . 16 ounces

2.2 pounds . . . . 1 kilo

TOTAL VOLUME OF COMMON BAKING PANS

Pan Type	Size	Volume
Ring Molds	8½ x 2¼ inch mold	4½ cups
	9¼ x 2¾ inch mold	8 cups
Springform Pans	8 x 3 inch pan	12 cups
	9 x 3 inch pan	16 cups
Pie Plates	9 inch plate	4 cups
	10 inch plate	6 cups
Cake Pans	8 x 1¼ inch layer pan	4 cups
	8 or 9 inch layer pan	6 cups
Loaf Pans	7⅜ x 3⅝ x 2¼ inch pan	4 cups
	8½ x 3⅝ x 2⅝ inch pan	6 cups
	9 x 5 x 3 inch pan	8 cups
Square Pans	8 x 8 x 2 inch pan	8 cups
	9 x 9 x 2 inch pan	10 cups
Baking Pans and Dishes	11 x 7 x 1½ inch dish	8 cups
	11¾ x 7½ x 1¾ inch pan	10 cups
	13½ x 8½ x 2 inch glass dish	12 cups
	13 x 9 x 2 inch metal pan	15 cups
Jelly-Roll Pan	15 x 10 x 1 inch pan	10 cups

HEART OF THE HARBOR

Portsmouth Museums Foundation
420 High Street
Portsmouth, VA 23704
757-393-8939
www.portsmouthmuseumsfoundation.org

Sold to: Name _____ Phone number _____

Address _____

City _____ State _____ Zip _____

Ship to: Name _____ Phone number _____

Address _____

City _____ State _____ Zip _____

Method of Payment:

_____ Check (made payable to Portsmouth Museums Foundation)

_____ VISA _____ MasterCard

Name as it appears on card _____

Card Number _____ Expiration Date _____

Signature _____

Please send me:

_____ copies of *Heart of the Harbor*	@ $27.95 each $	_____
Virginia residents add $1.40 sales tax for each book	$	_____
Shipping and handling for 1-3 cookbooks	@ $ 5.00 $	_____
Shipping and handling for 4 or more additional cookbooks	@ $ 2.00 each $	_____
	Total enclosed $	_____

Thank you for your order.

Proceeds from the sale of our publication support the Portsmouth Museums Foundation, Inc.,
a non-profit 501(c)3 corporation.

Please copy or complete this form and mail to the above address.

HEART OF THE HARBOR

Portsmouth Museums Foundation
420 High Street
Portsmouth, VA 23704
757-393-8939
www.portsmouthmuseumsfoundation.org

Sold to: Name _____ Phone number _____

Address _____

City _____ State _____ Zip _____

Ship to: Name _____ Phone number _____

Address _____

City _____ State _____ Zip _____

Method of Payment:

_____ Check (made payable to Portsmouth Museums Foundation)

_____ VISA _____ MasterCard

Name as it appears on card _____

Card Number _____ Expiration Date _____

Signature _____

Please send me:

_____ copies of *Heart of the Harbor* @ $27.95 each $ _____

Virginia residents add $1.40 sales tax for each book $ _____

Shipping and handling for 1-3 cookbooks   @ $ 5.00 $ _____

Shipping and handling for 4 or more additional cookbooks   @ $ 2.00 each $ _____

Total enclosed $ _____

Thank you for your order.

Proceeds from the sale of our publication support the Portsmouth Museums Foundation, Inc.,
a non-profit 501(c)3 corporation.

Please copy or complete this form and mail to the above address.